T0214253

Communications
in Computer and Information Science 1124

Commenced Publication in 2007
Founding and Former Series Editors:
Phoebe Chen, Alfredo Cuzzocrea, Xiaoyong Du, Orhun Kara, Ting Liu,
Krishna M. Sivalingam, Dominik Ślęzak, Takashi Washio, Xiaokang Yang,
and Junsong Yuan

More information about this series at http://www.springer.com/series/7899

Rafael Valencia-García ·
Gema Alcaraz-Mármol ·
Javier Del Cioppo-Morstadt ·
Néstor Vera-Lucio · Martha Bucaram-Leverone (Eds.)

Technologies and Innovation

5th International Conference, CITI 2019
Guayaquil, Ecuador, December 2–5, 2019
Proceedings

Springer

Editors
Rafael Valencia-García
Universidad de Murcia
Murcia, Spain

Gema Alcaraz-Mármol
Universidad de Castilla la Mancha
Toledo, Spain

Javier Del Cioppo-Morstadt
Universidad Agraria del Ecuador
Guayaquil, Ecuador

Néstor Vera-Lucio
Universidad Agraria del Ecuador
Guayaquil, Ecuador

Martha Bucaram-Leverone
Universidad Agraria del Ecuador
Guayaquil, Ecuador

ISSN 1865-0929 ISSN 1865-0937 (electronic)
Communications in Computer and Information Science
ISBN 978-3-030-34988-2 ISBN 978-3-030-34989-9 (eBook)
https://doi.org/10.1007/978-3-030-34989-9

This Springer imprint is published by the registered company Springer Nature Switzerland AG
The registered company address is: Gewerbestrasse 11, 6330 Cham, Switzerland

CITI 2019 – Preface

The 5th International Conference on Technologies and Innovation (CITI 2019) was held during December 2–5, 2019, in Guayaquil, Ecuador. The CITI series of conferences aims to become an international framework and meeting point for professionals who are mainly devoted to research, development, innovation, and university teaching in the field of computer science and technology applied to any important field of innovation. CITI 2019 was organized as a knowledge-exchange conference consisting of several contributions about current innovative technology. These proposals deal with the most important aspects and future prospects from an academic, innovative, and scientific perspective. The goal of the conference was the feasibility of investigating advanced and innovative methods and techniques and their application in different domains in the field of computer science and information systems, representing innovation in today's society.

We would like to express our gratitude to all the authors who submitted papers to CITI 2019, and our congratulations to those whose papers were accepted. There were 32 submissions this year. Each submission was reviewed by at least three Program Committee (PC) members. Only the papers with an average score of ≥ 1.0 were considered for final inclusion, and almost all accepted papers had positive reviews or at least one review with a score of 2 (accept) or higher. Finally, the PC decided to accept 14 full papers.

We would also like to thank the PC members, who agreed to review the manuscripts in a timely manner and provided valuable feedback to the authors.

December 2019

Rafael Valencia-García
Gema Alcaraz-Mármol
Javier Del Cioppo-Morstadt
Néstor Vera-Lucio
Martha Bucaram-Leverone

Organization

Honorary Committee

Martha Bucaram Leverone   Universidad Agraria del Ecuador, Ecuador
Javier Del Cioppo-Morstadt   Universidad Agraria del Ecuador, Ecuador
Emma Jácome Murillo   Universidad Agraria del Ecuador, Ecuador
Teresa Samaniego Cobo   Universidad Agraria del Ecuador, Ecuador

Organizing Committee

Rafael Valencia-García   Universidad de Murcia, Spain
Gema Alcaraz-Mármol   Universidad de Castilla-La Mancha, Spain
Martha Bucaram Leverone   Universidad Agraria del Ecuador, Ecuador
Javier Del Cioppo-Morstadt   Universidad Agraria del Ecuador, Ecuador
Néstor Vera Lucio   Universidad Agraria del Ecuador, Ecuador

Program Committee

Jacobo Bucaram Ortiz   Universidad Agraria del Ecuador, Ecuador
Martha Bucaram Leverone   Universidad Agraria del Ecuador, Ecuador
Rina Bucaram Leverone   Universidad Agraria del Ecuador, Ecuador
Rafael Valencia-García   Universidad de Murcia, Spain
Ricardo Colomo-Palacios   Ostfold University College, Norway
Ghassan Beydoun   University of Technology Sydney, Australia
Antonio A. López-Lorca   University of Melbourne, Australia
José Antonio Miñarro-Giménez   Medical Graz University, Austria
Catalina Martínez-Costa   Medical Graz University, Austria
Chunguo Wu   Jillin University, China
Siti Hajar Othman   Universiti Teknologi Malaysia, Malaysia
Anatoly Gladun   V.M. Glushkov of National Academy Science, Ukraine
Aarón Ayllón-Benítez   Université de Bordeaux, France
Giner Alor-Hernández   Instituto Tecnológico de Orizaba, Mexico
José Luis Ochoa   Universidad de Sonora, México
Ana Muñoz   Universidad de Los Andes, Venezuela
Miguel Ángel Rodríguez-García   Universidad Rey Juan Carlos, Spain
Lucía Serrano-Luján   Universidad Rey Juan Carlos, Spain
Eugenio Martínez-Cámara   Universidad de Granada, Spain
Gema Alcaraz-Mármol   Universidad de Castilla-La Mancha, Spain
Gustavo Zurita   Universidad de Chile, Chile

José Aguilar	Universidad de los Andes, Venezuela
Ángel García Pedrero	Universidad Politécnica de Madrid, Spain
Miguel Vargas-Lombardo	Universidad Tecnologica de Panama, Panama
Denis Cedeño Moreno	Universidad Tecnologica de Panama, Panama
Viviana Yarel Rosales Morales	Instituto Tecnologico de Orizaba, Mexico
José Javier Samper-Zapater	Universidad de Valencia, Spain
Raquel Vasquez Ramirez	Instituto Tecnologico de Orizaba, Mexico
Janio Jadán Guerrero	Universidad Indoamérica, Ecuador
Bernardo Cánovas-Segura	Universidad de Murcia, Spain
José Antonio García-Díaz	Universidad de Murcia, Spain
Noa Patricia Cruz Díaz	Hospital Universitario Virgen del Rocio, Spain
Yordani Cruz Segura	Universidad de las Ciencias Informáticas, Cuba
Gilberto Fernando Castro Aguilar	Universidad Católica de Santiago de Guayaquil, Ecuador
Freddy Mauricio Tapia León	Universidad de las Fuerzas Armadas, Ecuador
Nemury Silega Martínez	Universidad de las Ciencias Informáticas, Cuba

Local Organizing Committee

Katty Lagos Ortiz (General Coordinator)	Universidad Agraria del Ecuador
Andrea Sinche Guzmán	Universidad Agraria del Ecuador, Ecuador
Vanessa Vergara Lozano	Universidad Agraria del Ecuador, Ecuador
Maritza Aguirre Munizaga	Universidad Agraria del Ecuador, Ecuador
Carlota Delgado Vera	Universidad Agraria del Ecuador, Ecuador
Elke Yerovi Ricaurte	Universidad Agraria del Ecuador, Ecuador
Karen Mite Baidal	Universidad Agraria del Ecuador, Ecuador
Mario Cardenas	Universidad Agraria del Ecuador, Ecuador
Mitchell Vásquez Bermúdez	Universidad Agraria del Ecuador, Ecuador
Roberto Cabezas Cabezas	Universidad Agraria del Ecuador, Ecuador
Fernando León	Universidad Agraria del Ecuador, Ecuador
Evelyn Solis	Universidad Agraria del Ecuador, Ecuador
Karina Real	Universidad Agraria del Ecuador, Ecuador
Paola Grijalva	Universidad Agraria del Ecuador, Ecuador
Wilson Molina	Universidad Agraria del Ecuador, Ecuador
Willian Bazan	Universidad Agraria del Ecuador, Ecuador
Roger Freire	Universidad Agraria del Ecuador, Ecuador

Sponsor

http://www.uagraria.edu.ec/

Contents

Internet of Things and Computer Architecture

ICT in Agronomy

Pest Recognition Using Natural Language Processing

Carlos Hernández-Castillo[1] (iD), Héctor Hiram Guedea-Noriega[2] (iD),
Miguel Ángel Rodríguez-García[3] (iD),
and Francisco García-Sánchez[1(✉)] (iD)

[1] DIS, Faculty of Computer Science, University of Murcia, 30100 Murcia, Spain
`{carlos.hernandez, frgarcia}@um.es`
[2] Escuela Internacional de Doctorado, University of Murcia,
30100 Murcia, Spain
`hector.guedea@um.es`
[3] Universidad Rey Juan Carlos, Madrid, Spain
`miguel.rodriguez@urjc.es`

Abstract. Agriculture and pest control are fundamental for ensuring worldwide food provisioning. ICT-based systems have proven to be useful for various tasks in the agronomy domain. In particular, several pest recognition tools have been developed that assist in the early identification of plant pests and diseases. However, in most cases expensive devices (e.g., high-resolution cameras) are necessary in association with such tools. In general, smallholders do not have access to those sophisticated devices and so cannot benefit from those tools. In this work, we present a Web-based application that makes use of natural language processing technologies to help (inexperienced) farm workers and managers in recognizing the pests or diseases affecting their crops. End users should submit a text describing the visible symptoms in the plant, and the application returns a sorted list of the most likely causes of the described problem along with the recommended treatments. The prototypical implementation is restricted to the known pathogens infecting almond trees, a crop very rooted in the Spanish agriculture. Early tests have shown promising results.

Keywords: Pest recognition · Natural Language Processing · Integrated Pest Management

1 Introduction

Agriculture is one of the main pillars for worldwide food provisioning, especially in this age of almost exponential world population growth [1]. Experts claim that fruits and vegetables are part of a well-balanced and healthy eating plan [2, 3]. In economic terms, agriculture, as part of the primary sector, is one of the key contributors to the Gross Domestic Product (GDP) of many countries [4]. The use of ICT in agriculture, also known as 'smart agriculture', has proven effective for improving productivity while optimizing the use of external resources [5]. However, crop pests and diseases still pose a serious challenge, with new emerging pathogens causing significant yield

R. Valencia-García et al. (Eds.): CITI 2019, CCIS 1124, pp. 3–16, 2019.
https://doi.org/10.1007/978-3-030-34989-9_1

losses, partially boosted by the effects of the climate change [6]. In the last few years, a large number of computer-assisted systems have been developed that help in the identification and diagnosis of plant pests and diseases, mainly exploiting image processing capabilities and artificial intelligence techniques [7–14].

Natural Language Processing (NLP) is another powerful tool that, combined with a comprehensive plant disease-symptoms database, can assist in early crop pest recognition [15]. NLP is a field of artificial intelligence that explores the way machines can communicate with people (and vice versa) through the use of natural language text or speech [16]. NLP tools and techniques are widely used in several applications for machine translation, natural language text summarization, natural language user interfaces, information extraction and retrieval, etc. [17, 18]. Researchers in the agronomy field have just recently applied NLP for different purposes, such as extracting phenotypic data from taxonomic descriptions [19] or gathering medicinal plant knowledge from historical texts [20]. In medicine, NLP-assisted tools have also been successfully used for symptoms processing [21, 22].

In this work, we describe a responsive Web application that leverages NLP to assist in the identification of plant pests and diseases from natural language texts describing the main symptoms as perceived by end users (individual farmers). It aims at facilitate the early detection of problems affecting specific crops, which is key to avoiding important economic losses and serious damage to plants [7]. Our framework relies on a database containing the main symptoms associated to a number of crop pests and diseases, and calculates the match between those symptoms and the natural language text description provided by an external human observer. The pests and diseases, whose score is above a given threshold, are shown to the users along with the suggested treatment.

The rest of this manuscript is organized as follows. In Sect. 2, the current state-of-the-art of both NLP and pest recognition tools is briefly stated. The proposed framework and its constituting components are described in Sect. 3. The use of the prototypical application developed is exemplified in Sect. 4. Finally, conclusions and future work are put forward in Sect. 5.

2   State of the Art

The system proposed in this work rests on an NLP tool that enables the automatic processing of a textual description containing the possible effects of a given pest or disease on crops with the aim of assisting individuals with no agronomy background in identifying it. In this section, the main approaches used in natural language recognition are enumerated and some of the pest identification tools that have been developed in the last few years are studied.

2.1 Natural Language Processing

NLP is a branch of computer science that combines artificial intelligence with applied linguistics to enable the interactions between computers and human users [16]. It entails the application of algorithms with the aim to identify and extract rules so that unstructured text can be converted into a form 'understandable' by computers. Three main evolving paradigms can be distinguished in NLP research, namely, syntactic, semantic and pragmatic [23]. The syntactic analysis of the text permits to assess how the natural language aligns with grammatical rules by means of word-based techniques such as lemmatization, word segmentation, part-of-speech (PoS) tagging, etc. Problems such as the ambiguity and imprecise characteristics of the natural languages hamper the efficiency of syntactic-based NLP algorithms and suggest the need for a semantic approach. The semantic analysis involves understanding the meaning and interpretation of words and how sentences are structured, and requires the use of techniques such as named entity recognition (NER) or word sense disambiguation. Finally, in order for NLP solutions to become more adaptive, open-domain, context-aware and intent-driven, a pragmatic paradigm is necessary which is based on the narrative under-standing of the text. Nowadays, the exploitation of deep learning models and methods for numerous NLP tasks has become a popular choice [24].

Among the most well-known NLP toolkits [25], it is possible to outline the fol-lowing six: (i) Stanford CoreNLP, (ii) Natural Language Toolkit (NLTK), (iii) SpaCy, (iv) Apache OpenNLP, (v) FreeLing, and (vi) GATE. Stanford NLP software (https://nlp.stanford.edu/software/index.shtml) include statistical NLP, deep learning NLP, and rule-based NLP tools for major computational linguistics problems. In particular, Stanford CoreNLP (https://stanfordnlp.github.io/CoreNLP/) is a Java library optimized for speed with functions like PoS-tagging, pattern learning parsing, titled entity recognition, etc. NLTK (http://www.nltk.org/) is one of the most widely used NLP library for Python applications. It offers access to over 50 corpora and lexical resources as well as a number of libraries for text processing tasks such as classification and tokenization. SpaCy (https://spacy.io/) is free, open-source library for advanced NLP in Python. Unlike NLTK, it has a single implementation for each NLP component with the focus on production-level performance. Tokenization, PoS-tagging, lemmatization or NER are some of the supported features and capabilities. OpenNLP (https://opennlp.apache.org/) is hosted by the Apache Foundation and features a general, machine learning-based NLP tool covering all common NLP processing components. It can be used from the command line or within a Java application as a library. FreeLing (http://nlp.lsi.upc.edu/freeling/) is a set of C++ tools providing language analysis capabilities such as morphological analysis, NER, PoS-tagging. It provides support for many different languages (English and Spanish among others) and is easily extensible to deal with new languages. Finally, the GATE framework ('General Architecture for Text Engineering', https://gate.ac.uk/) is a Java based toolkit that assists in building text processing pipelines. Besides a Java library, GATE includes a desktop client for developers, a workflow-based Web application, and architecture and a process. It is integrated and interoperates with other tools such as OpenNLP.

In this work, a very simplistic approach to NLP is required, since only the key-words included in the natural language text description of the visible pest/disease symptoms present in the field are required (i.e., a very restricted, well-known appli-cation domain is concerned). Consequently, we opted for the use of GATE, an intu-itive, open source NLP toolkit easily integrable in Java applications. With the utilization of GATE, the input text (after some processing) is matched against a list of known keywords, which are associated to different crop pests and diseases.

2.2 Pest Recognition Tools

As in most sectors of today's society, there are a large number of ICT-based appli-cations in the field of agriculture to provide support in daily work. Technology boosts the innovation process in this domain, with solutions that seek increasing the overall yield in crop plants [5]. For example, mobile applications in the agronomy domain can be classified categories [26, 27]: (i) weather apps, (ii) soil preparation apps, (iii) sowing scheduling apps, (iv) farms management apps, (v) soil fertility and crop nutrition apps, (vi) pest management apps, (vii) irrigation and drainage apps, (viii) precision agri-culture apps, and (ix) teaching and research apps.

Research has also been done extensively on the detection of pests and diseases in crops [7, 10–12, 28–32]. In most cases, these are technological solutions that require the use of sophisticated high-resolution image capture devices or other types of sensors that are not usually available to individuals responsible for agricultural holdings. On the other hand, decision support systems have also been developed to recommend the best treatment to face the crop pests/diseases once they have been detected [33, 34].

In this work, we introduce a tool aimed at (inexperienced) farm workers and managers to assist them in identifying pests affecting their crops and suggest them the recommended treatment. It does not require any special or expensive equipment, since it can be used from any device with a Web browser. It is also very easy to use since users are expected to communicate the visible symptoms in the plants by means of natural language text.

3 Proposed Framework

The framework proposed in this work is composed of two main building blocks (see Fig. 1), namely, the front end, which represents the user interface, and the back end, which includes both the business logic and the database. A REST API [35] enables the communication between the presentation layer and the logic layer in this Model-View-Controller (MVC) architecture [36]. jQuery (https://jquery.com/) has been used to ease the burden of invoking the REST services from the client through AJAX calls by means of JSON (https://www.json.org/) formatted messages. The server side of the application has been built in Java using the Spring Framework (https://spring.io/) to handle the business logic, and Hibernate (http://hibernate.org/) to manage the con-nection to the PostgreSQL database (https://www.postgresql.org/). Finally, the GATE framework has been employed for text analysis and language processing.

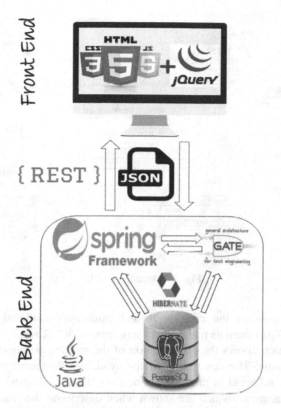

Fig. 1. Proposed framework functional architecture.

In a nutshell, the system works as follows. Users write in natural language the symptoms observed on plants. Then, the text is sent to the server for processing. Using the GATE framework, the main keywords in the inputted text are gathered. Next, the list of retrieved keywords are compared against the keywords associated to each pest/disease in the database, and a matching score is calculated. Users are shown then an ordered list with the pests or diseases that are most likely affecting the crop along with its matching score. Users are enabled then to get details about each listed pest/disease. Images, brief description, and recommended treatments are revealed to users.

Next, the main components of the proposed framework are described in some detail.

3.1 Domain Model

The framework here proposed encompasses just the necessary to deal with diseases and their prevention and treatments. As such, the conceptual model represents the most basic representative entities and their relationships (see Fig. 2).

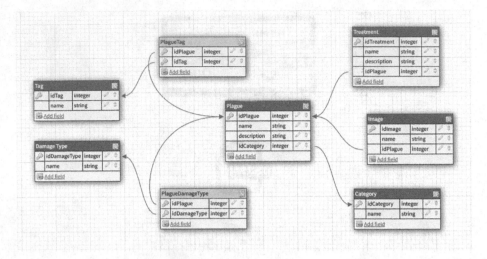

Fig. 2. Domain model.

'Plague' represents the crop pests and diseases considered in a particular implementation. Apart from its name and description, each 'Plague' is associated to a 'Category', which allows the classification of the causing pathogen in terms of its scientific order name. The description of the available 'Treatments' for a given 'Plague' is also reflected in the model. For each 'Plague', there are a number of characterizing 'Images', which are shown when describing the diseases to illustrate them. Finally, a 'Tag' (i.e., simple or composite terms) is linked to a particular 'Plague' when the term is part of the pest's symptoms description.

3.2 Database Population

A manual process has been employed to populate the database. The information introduced in the database was gathered from official guides published by the Spanish government as part of its Integrated Pest Management (IPM) movement[1]. In particular, for the purposes of our prototypical development, we focused on the pests and diseases affecting the almond tree [37], a crop very rooted in the Spanish agriculture. Besides, we enhanced pathogen description with the information available in [38].

The GATE component described in Sect. 3.3, once initially configured, has been used to establish the tags (in the 'Tag' table of the database) that should be associated to each pest/disease (in the 'Plague' table of the database). The pests/diseases' symptoms descriptions included in the documentary resources identified above were processed by the GATE component and the keyword-pest relations were stored in the database.

---

[1] https://www.mapa.gob.es/es/agricultura/temas/sanidad-vegetal/productos-fitosanitarios/guias-gestion-plagas/default.aspx.

Given that these natural language text-based documents have a standard structure and organization, for future work we plan to build a tool to automatically gather the relevant information from them and populate the database. As a result, the system would be easily useful for crops beyond almond trees.

3.3 GATE

GATE is the text processing framework used in this work. It is available in the form of an object library optimized for inclusion in diverse applications giving access to a number of services. For the purposes of this work, we defined a corpus in the form of a gazetteer, namely, a set of lists containing names of relevant entities. These lists are then used to find occurrences of these names in the input texts (i.e., named entity recognition). Therefore, it is first necessary to properly set up the environment by defining the file with the list of keywords considered. For that, the aforementioned documents [37] and [38] have been manually processed and the relevant entities have been gathered.

Once the GATE component has been correctly configured, it is leveraged for two different purposes. First, during design GATE assists in establishing the relationships between the existing tags ('Tag' table of the database) and pests/diseases ('Plague' table of the database). Then, at execution time GATE is used to annotate the text inputted by the end user finding occurrences of the relevant names in the text. The *HashGazetter* plugin has been used to complete those tasks.

3.4 Pest Recognition Service

The service layer, built using the Spring Framework, holds the main business logic. The main functionality provided by our application is to show relevant information about the pest and diseases that might be affecting the crop according to a detailed description of the plant and immediate surroundings current status. In order to do so, the pest recognition service rely on the previously mentioned GATE component, which analyzes the inputted text and returns a list of keywords as output. The keywords found in the text are then matched against the tags available in the 'Tag' table of the database (see Sect. 3.1). The 'PlagueTag' association in the database is finally leveraged to gather the pests/diseases attached to each found 'Tag'. With that information, the matching score is calculated as follows:

```
total = 0
pest_subtotal = empty_dictionary # 'string - int' map
result = empty_dictionary # 'string - float' map
for keyword in input_text:
    tag = find_tag_in_database(keyword)
    for pest in pest_with_tag_in_database(tag):
        pest_subtotal[pest] = pest_subtotal[pest] + 1
        total = total + 1
for pest in pest_subtotal:
    result[pest] = pest_subtotal[pest]/total
```

In the code above, 'pest_subtotal' retains the number of times each pest/disease is found given the retrieved tags associated to the keywords in the inputted text, and 'total' holds the total number of all pests/diseases that are somehow linked to the input text. The 'result' map contains the matching score for each pest/disease calculated by dividing the total number of times that pest/disease has been found by the total number of pests/diseases found (i.e., 'total').

The pest recognition service does also provide support for retrieving, for each pest/disease with a matching score above a given threshold, all the information associated to it, namely, damage types, images, tags, and suggested treatments.

3.5   Responsive User Interface

The front-end side of the application can be divided into two main parts: the user interface provided by the HTML+CSS code, and the interaction with the back-end that happens via Javascript code. In order for the Web application to be responsive (i.e., pages render well on a variety of devices and screen sizes), we made use of jQuery, which allows to fit the application visible area to the Web browser visible area.

In Fig. 3, a representative mock-up of the Web application is depicted. It has been designed so that it is simple, functional and well-structured. There is an initial screen for the user to input the text describing the symptoms noticed in the crop. Then, an initial list of pests and their matching score are shown to the user. Finally, more detailed information about each listed pest can be obtained.

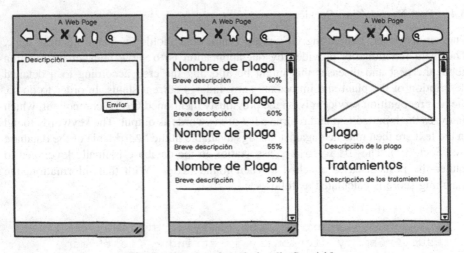

Fig. 3. User interface design [in Spanish].

jQuery is also exploited in order to make the AJAX request to the REST service. In particular, two different calls are enabled, one for getting the list of pests/diseases given the inputted symptoms, and another for getting the details of a given pest/disease (see Fig. 4).

```
findAllByText: function (text, callback) {
    $.ajax({
        type: 'POST',
        contentType: "application/json",
        url: '/plaguedetector/api/findAllByText',
        data: text,
        success: callback
    });
},

findOneById: function (idPlague, callback) {
    $.ajax({
        type: 'GET',
        contentType: "application/json",
        url: '/plaguedetector/api/findOneById?idPlague=' + idPlague,
        success: callback
    });
}
```

Fig. 4. AJAX requests.

4 Discussion

A proof-of-concept implementation of the framework has been developed. It is available as a Web application accessible from both computers and mobile devices through a Web browser (see Figs. 5 and 6). The database for this prototypical implementation has been populated with information about the main pests and diseases related to almond trees. The matching threshold has been set up to 1% so as to check the total number of pests/diseases identified for each query, and how they are sorted. Different queries have been issued with text describing the symptoms of the most recurring pests and diseases. The results have been analyzed finding that, in most cases, the actual pest/disease described appears in the first or second position (i.e., it has the first or second highest matching score).

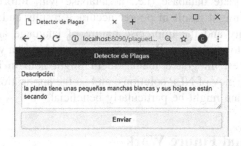

Fig. 5. Exemplary natural language pest's symptoms description [in Spanish].

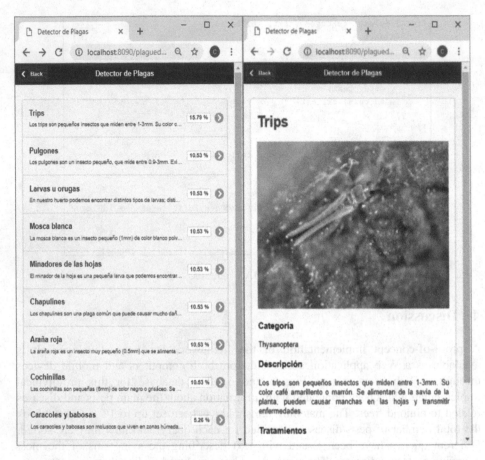

Fig. 6. Exemplary matching score list (left) and pest detailed description (right) [in Spanish].

A more in-depth analysis is planned for future work. It is necessary to check whether a more complete database (i.e., a database with information about crops besides almond tree) might result in poorer accuracy results and how it affects execution time. Ambiguity and the imprecise nature of language are what make NLP difficult for machines to implement. We believe that working in a very specific domain application such as pest integrated management might help in improving both the effectiveness and efficiency of NLP solutions, and so the application of this technology in the agronomy domain might be particularly beneficial.

5   Conclusions and Future Work

Agriculture and pest control are key elements for ensuring world food provision. Climate change, among other factors, is causing the outbreak of virulent pests and disease resulting in dramatic crop yield losses. The early identification and discrimination of (emerging) plant diseases is essential to, first, eradicate them and, second, prevent their spread and major losses. Several ICT-based tools have been conceived to assist in pest identification and control but, in most cases, sophisticated and expensive devices and techniques are required. In this work, we present a proto-typical implementation of a framework that leverages natural language processing technology to enable (inexperienced) smallholders to identify the pests and diseases affecting their crops. The text describing the main visible symptoms in the plant is processed and the gathered keywords are compared against a pest control database. As a result, a list with the most likely causes of the problem is displayed. Then, detailed information about the recommended treatments can be obtained.

The developed prototype is constrained to the pathogens affecting almond trees, but it can be easily augmented with other crops. In the few tests performed so far, the system behaved correctly including the actual pest/disease among the highest scored results. However, it is yet to be studied the impact of a more complete database containing information about the pathogens relevant to other plants besides almond tree. Ambiguity and the imprecise nature of language might interfere with the results, resulting in significant variations in accuracy. The use of ontologies and semantic Web technologies can help alleviate some of these issues [15, 39].

For future work, we plan to develop a software component to assist in the (semi) automatic population of the database [40]. The somehow standard structure of the documents describing the plant diseases and their symptoms can facilitate their auto-matic analysis by NLP tools. On the other hand, the framework proposed in this work is easily integrable with other pest recognition tools. The integration with, for example, image-based pest identification systems can result in efficiency and effectiveness gains. Finally, our current prototype is only valid for Spanish-speaking users. We aim to extend it to support other languages.

Acknowledgements. This work has been partially supported by the Spanish National Research Agency (AEI) and the European Regional Development Fund (FEDER/ERDF) through project KBS4FIA (TIN2016-76323-R), and Seneca Foundation-the Regional Agency for Science and Technology of Murcia (Spain)- through project 20963/PI/18.

References

1. Current World Population. https://www.worldometers.info/world-population/. Accessed 04 Aug 2019
2. How to Use Fruits and Vegetables to Help Manage Your Weight. https://www.cdc.gov/healthyweight/healthy_eating/fruits_vegetables.html. Accessed 04 Aug 2019
3. Healthy Eating Plate & Healthy Eating Pyramid. https://www.hsph.harvard.edu/nutritionsource/healthy-eating-plate/. Accessed 04 Aug 2019
4. Loizou, E., Karelakis, C., Galanopoulos, K., Mattas, K.: The role of agriculture as a development tool for a regional economy. Agric. Syst. **173**, 482–490 (2019). https://doi.org/10.1016/J.AGSY.2019.04.002
5. Woodard, J., et al.: ICT in Agriculture (Updated Edition): Connecting Smallholders to Knowledge, Networks, and Institutions. The World Bank (2017). https://doi.org/10.1596/978-1-4648-1002-2

6. Velásquez, A.C., Castroverde, C.D.M., He, S.Y.: Plant-pathogen warfare under changing climate conditions. Curr. Biol. **28**, R619–R634 (2018). https://doi.org/10.1016/j.cub.2018. 03.054
7. Pan, L., et al.: Early diagnosis of plant disease via NIR spectroscopy: a study in Bursaphelenchus Xylophilus disease. Int. J. Robot. Autom. **33** (2018). https://doi.org/10. 2316/Journal.206.2018.3.206-5535
8. Iqbal, Z., Khan, M.A., Sharif, M., Shah, J.H., ur Rehman, M.H., Javed, K.: An automated detection and classification of citrus plant diseases using image processing techniques: a review. Comput. Electron. Agric. **153**, 12–32 (2018). https://doi.org/10.1016/j.compag. 2018.07.032
9. Ferentinos, K.P.: Deep learning models for plant disease detection and diagnosis. Comput. Electron. Agric. **145**, 311–318 (2018). https://doi.org/10.1016/j.compag.2018.01.009
10. Cui, S., Ling, P., Zhu, H., Keener, H.: Plant pest detection using an artificial nose system: a review. Sensors **18**, 378 (2018). https://doi.org/10.3390/s18020378
11. Aasha Nandhini, S., Hemalatha, R., Radha, S., Indumathi, K.: Web enabled plant disease detection system for agricultural applications using WMSN. Wireless Pers. Commun. **102**, 725–740 (2018). https://doi.org/10.1007/s11277-017-5092-4
12. Sun, G., Jia, X., Geng, T.: Plant diseases recognition based on image processing technology. J. Electr. Comput. Eng. **2018**, 1–7 (2018). https://doi.org/10.1155/2018/6070129
13. Labaña, F.M., Ruiz, A., García-Sánchez, F.: PestDetect: pest recognition using convolutional neural network. In: Valencia-García, R., Alcaraz-Mármol, G., Cioppo-Morstadt, J., Vera-Lucio, N., Bucaram-Leverone, M. (eds.) CITAMA2019 2019. AISC, vol. 901, pp. 99–108. Springer, Cham (2019). https://doi.org/10.1007/978-3-030-10728-4_11
14. Garcerán-Sáez, J., García-Sánchez, F.: SePeRe: semantically-enhanced system for pest recognition. In: Valencia-García, R., Alcaraz-Mármol, G., Cioppo-Morstadt, J., Vera-Lucio, N., Bucaram-Leverone, M. (eds.) CITAMA2019 2019. AISC, vol. 901, pp. 3–11. Springer, Cham (2019). https://doi.org/10.1007/978-3-030-10728-4_1
15. Lagos-Ortiz, K., Medina-Moreira, J., Paredes-Valverde, M.A., Espinoza-Morán, W., Valencia-García, R.: An ontology-based decision support system for the diagnosis of plant diseases. J. Inf. Technol. Res. **10**, 42–55 (2017). https://doi.org/10.4018/JITR.2017100103
16. Gelbukh, A.: Introduction to the thematic issue on natural language processing. Computación y Sistemas **22**, 721–727 (2018). https://doi.org/10.13053/cys-22-3-3032
17. Chowdhury, G.G.: Natural language processing. Ann. Rev. Inf. Sci. Technol. **37**, 51–89 (2005). https://doi.org/10.1002/aris.1440370103
18. Paredes-Valverde, M.A., Valencia-García, R., Rodríguez-García, M.Á., Colomo-Palacios, R., Alor-Hernández, G.: A semantic-based approach for querying linked data using natural language. J. Inf. Sci. **42**, 851–862 (2016). https://doi.org/10.1177/0165551515616311
19. Endara, L., Burleigh, J.G., Cooper, L., Jaiswal, P., Laporte, M.-A., Cui, H.: A natural language processing pipeline to extract phenotypic data from formal taxonomic descriptions with a focus on flagellate plants. In: Jaiswal, P., Cooper, L., Haendel, M.A., Mungall, C. J. (eds.) Proceedings of the 9th International Conference on Biological Ontology (ICBO 2018), CEUR Workshop Proceedings 2285, Corvallis, Oregon, USA, pp. 1–4 (2018). http:// www.CEUR-WS.org
20. Sharma, V., Law, W., Balick, M.J., Sarkar, I.N.: Harnessing biomedical natural language processing tools to identify medicinal plant knowledge from historical texts. In: AMIA Annual Symposium Proceedings, Washington, DC, USA, pp. 1537–1546. American Medical Informatics Association (2017)
21. Dreisbach, C., Koleck, T.A., Bourne, P.E., Bakken, S.: A systematic review of natural language processing and text mining of symptoms from electronic patient-authored text data. Int. J. Med. Informatics **125**, 37–46 (2019). https://doi.org/10.1016/j.ijmedinf.2019.02.008

22. Koleck, T.A., Dreisbach, C., Bourne, P.E., Bakken, S.: Natural language processing of symptoms documented in free-text narratives of electronic health records: a systematic review. J. Am. Med. Inform. Assoc. **26**, 364–379 (2019). https://doi.org/10.1093/jamia/ocy173

23. Cambria, E., White, B.: Jumping NLP curves: a review of natural language processing research. IEEE Comput. Intell. Mag. **9**, 48–57 (2014). https://doi.org/10.1109/MCI.2014.2307227

24. Young, T., Hazarika, D., Poria, S., Cambria, E.: Recent trends in deep learning based natural language processing. IEEE Comput. Intell. Mag. **13**, 55–75 (2018). https://doi.org/10.1109/MCI.2018.2840738

25. Academic and Open Source Natural Language Toolkits. http://alias-i.com/lingpipe/wcb/competition.html. Accessed 09 Aug 2019

26. Ramos Gourcy, F.: Una lista de la gama de las aplicaciones móviles ("apps") para la agricultura. https://www.hortalizas.com/proteccion-de-cultivos/61807/. Accessed 12 Aug 2019

27. Lagos-Ortiz, K., Medina-Moreira, J., Sinche-Guzmán, A., Garzón-Goya, M., Vergara-Lozano, V., Valencia-García, R.: Mobile applications for crops management. In: Valencia-García, R., Alcaraz-Mármol, G., Del Cioppo-Morstadt, J., Vera-Lucio, N., Bucaram-Leverone, M. (eds.) CITI 2018. CCIS, vol. 883, pp. 57–69. Springer, Cham (2018). https://doi.org/10.1007/978-3-030-00940-3_5

28. Yue, Y., et al.: Deep recursive super resolution network with Laplacian Pyramid for better agricultural pest surveillance and detection. Comput. Electron. Agric. **150**, 26–32 (2018). https://doi.org/10.1016/j.compag.2018.04.004

29. Goodridge, W., Bernard, M., Jordan, R., Rampersad, R.: Intelligent diagnosis of diseases in plants using a hybrid multi-criteria decision making technique. Comput. Electron. Agric. **133**, 80–87 (2017). https://doi.org/10.1016/j.compag.2016.12.003

30. Patil, J.K., Kumar, R.: Analysis of content based image retrieval for plant leaf diseases using color, shape and texture features. Eng. Agric. Environ. Food **10**, 69–78 (2017). https://doi.org/10.1016/j.eaef.2016.11.004

31. Zhang, S., Wu, X., You, Z., Zhang, L.: Leaf image based cucumber disease recognition using sparse representation classification. Comput. Electron. Agric. **134**, 135–141 (2017). https://doi.org/10.1016/j.compag.2017.01.014

32. Singh, V., Misra, A.K.: Detection of plant leaf diseases using image segmentation and soft computing techniques. Inf. Process. Agric. **4**, 41–49 (2017). https://doi.org/10.1016/j.inpa.2016.10.005

33. del Águila, I.M., Cañadas, J., Túnez, S.: Decision making models embedded into a web-based tool for assessing pest infestation risk. Biosys. Eng. **133**, 102–115 (2015). https://doi.org/10.1016/J.BIOSYSTEMSENG.2015.03.006

34. Cañadas, J., del Águila, I.M., Palma, J.: Development of a web tool for action threshold evaluation in table grape pest management. Precision Agric. **18**, 974–996 (2017). https://doi.org/10.1007/s11119-016-9487-0

35. Fielding, R.T.: Architectural Styles and the Design of Network-based Software Architectures (2000). https://www.ics.uci.edu/~fielding/pubs/dissertation/top.htm

36. Krasner, G.E., Pope, S.T.: A cookbook for using the model-view controller user interface paradigm in smalltalk-80. J. Object-Oriented Program. **1**, 26–49 (1988)

37. Ministerio de Agricultura, Alimentación y Medio Ambiente: Guía de Gestión Integrada de Plagas. Almendro. https://www.mapa.gob.es/es/agricultura/temas/sanidad-vegetal/guiadealmendroweb_tcm30-57951.pdf. Accessed 12 Aug 2019

38. Ministerio de Medio Ambiente y Medio Rural y Marino: Patógenos de plantas descritos en España. Sociedad Española de Fitopatología, Madrid, Spain (2010)

39. Lagos-Ortiz, K., Medina-Moreira, J., Morán-Castro, C., Campuzano, C., Valencia-García, R.: An ontology-based decision support system for insect pest control in crops. In: Valencia-García, R., Alcaraz-Mármol, G., Del Cioppo-Morstadt, J., Vera-Lucio, N., Bucaram-Leverone, M. (eds.) CITI 2018. CCIS, vol. 883, pp. 3–14. Springer, Cham (2018). https://doi.org/10.1007/978-3-030-00940-3_1
40. García-Sánchez, F., García-Díaz, J.A., Gómez-Berbís, J.M., Valencia-García, R.: Financial knowledge instantiation from semi-structured, heterogeneous data sources. In: Silhavy, R. (ed.) CSOC2018 2018. AISC, vol. 764, pp. 103–110. Springer, Cham (2019). https://doi.org/10.1007/978-3-319-91189-2_11

Comparison Between Two Deep Learning Models for Temperature Prediction at Guayaquil

Charles M. Pérez-Espinoza[1](✉), Johanna Sanchez-Guerrero[2] (iD),
Teresa Samaniego-Cobos[2] (iD), and Nuvia Beltran-Robayo[2]

[1] Universidad de Guayaquil, Guayaquil, Ecuador
charles.pereze@ug.edu.ec
[2] Universidad Agraria del Ecuador, Guayaquil, Ecuador
{jsanchez,tsamaniego,nbeltran}@uagraria.edu.ec

Abstract. Weather prediction is a subject that is constantly changing everywhere in the world because of the different methods that are applied. This study is done in the city of Guayaquil remembering that weather forecast has played a very important role for many people who belong to different fields of research because it needs to have a minimum margin of error in order to meet the different objectives of each researcher. This paper aims to find the best type of MLP or LSTM neural network model that has a lower margin of error when predicting the weather at a specific weather station in the aforementioned city. In order to assess the accuracy between these prediction models, the Euclidean estimation standard was used. With the results of this comparison, it is hoped to contribute to the prediction of the climate to be able to help not only the researchers but also the farmers, tourists, and people in general whose work depends on this topic.

Keywords: Meteorology · Deep learning · Artificial intelligence · Neural networks · Guayaquil · Supervised algorithms

1 Introduction

Ecuador has a rainy equatorial climate. Because of its different biomes, this country has varied microclimates, as the Fig. 1 [15], and each main city of commerce has a different climatic subzone. One of these cities is Guayaquil (warm-cool-dry), a city close to the coast. Every day, different travelers, farmers, among others, need the results of predictive modeling with a minimum percentage of error in order to plan their day. This paper compares three types of machine learning prediction models using the National Institute of Meteorology and Hydrology (INAMHI[1]) database.

One of these models was taken from work already done for temperature and precipitation prediction [12], and a second carried out by the authors. The first model is MultiLayer Neural Networks (MLP) [11], and the second one is Long Short Term

---

[1] Instituto Nacional de Meteorología e Hidrología.

© Springer Nature Switzerland AG 2019
R. Valencia-García et al. (Eds.): CITI 2019, CCIS 1124, pp. 17–29, 2019.
https://doi.org/10.1007/978-3-030-34989-9_2

Memory [1–3]. For experimental validation, 8157 data of temperature, precipitation, humidity of two stations in the city of Guayaquil were analyzed. Only two stations have all the necessary senses and actuators as they had the sensors that calculate these variables to be able to download them.

There were some inconveniences when collecting data because some samples were incomplete, but an imputation technique was used [4] to obtain them and then to obtain the complete bases to demonstrate which of these models are the most recommended when predicting the weather in this area.

Fig. 1. Ecuador climates

Guayaquil is one of the most populous cities in Ecuador. Located on the Ecuadorian coast, it has about 3 million inhabitants and is known as the Pearl of the Pacific. Guayaquil is also a city that lives from daily commerce, since it has land to sow -which makes it possible for it to sell its own vegetables and fruits- a seaport and an air terminal from where it can import or export its products, among other economic activities that help the economy grow. This city is therefore in constant motion, and, as many people depend on daily activities such as agriculture or transportation, it is necessary for them to be able to predict the weather -temperature and precipitation- in order to be able to carry out their duties.

The climate of Guayaquil is influenced by two types of Pacific currents: the Humboldt current -a cold current- and El Niño -a hot current. The winds also affect the climate, as they blow in different directions in February (summer) and in July (winter). According to [7], the annual average of temperature is of 25 °C, and the annual rainfall is an average of 500 mm to 2000 mm of rain a year, taking into account that it is a dry, savanna tropical climate.

This peculiarity of behavior in the climate is a subclass of tropical climate that occurs when the dry season predominates most of the year, while the wet season is very short but with rains that can often become torrential. It is a climate that is located between the humid tropical and the semi-arid climate (Fig. 2).

M1096   GUAYAQUIL U.ESTATAL (RADIO SONDA)

MES	HELIOFANIA (Horas)	TEMPERATURA DEL AIRE A LA SOMBRA (°C)							
		ABSOLUTAS				MEDIAS			
		Máxima	dia	Mínima	dia	Máxima	Mínima	Mensual	M
ENERO	46.1	34.4	1			30.2	23.1	26.0	
FEBRERO	63.4	32.8	7			30.9	23.3	26.1	
MARZO	98.8	34.6	17			32.3	24.1	27.3	
ABRIL	114.7	34.5	12	22.8	8	32.2	24.4	27.6	
MAYO	115.3	33.8	18	22.7	13	32.2	23.7	27.8	
JUNIO	95.8	34.6	16	21.9	14	31.7	23.2	27.4	
JULIO	108.3			20.2	28	30.5	21.8	26.3	
AGOSTO	116.3	32.1	14	19.2	10	29.8	20.9	25.0	
SEPTIEMBRE	143.4	33.3	8			30.4	21.6	25.4	
OCTUBRE	115.6	34.6	5	20.6	2	30.3	21.7	25.5	
NOVIEMBRE	141.9	35.0	26	20.5	16	31.9	22.2	26.2	
DICIEMBRE	124.2	35.6	29	21.7	2	32.5	23.3	27.3	
VALOR ANUAL	1283.8					31.2	22.8	26.5	

Fig. 2. Data from the M1096 station granted by INAMHI

Normally, the annual rainfall decreases very rapidly towards the south until it reaches a desert area on the border of Ecuador. This is why the Humboldt current, a cold current from Antarctica, turns west towards the Galapagos Islands, creating the same dry climate. To the north of the city of Guayaquil, a warm current predominates, with a humidity which falls in the form of rain.

This work is divided into different sections: (a) The first is the introduction and theoretical framework of what will be used in the publication, such as the specifications of the type of climate, artificial intelligence and the types of neural networks to be used; (b) The second part is the methodology that the authors used for the experimentation, including what type of databases were chosen, the method used for imputation of data, and the software that was developed so that these predictive models could be used; (c) The final section offers the results of the study, with comparative tables between the models used for prediction, in addition to the estimation of errors, conclusions, and a summary of a future study.

In this study, the authors will only create prediction models based on temperature.

1.1   Artificial Intelligence and the Weather

Artificial intelligence (AI) has helped prediction for a long time, but obviously, year after year, the models for such prediction are improving [4–6]. It all started from, that informed about mathematical equations and the standard error to calculate it, and even publications that evidence that the best ways to calculate the climate is through artificial neural networks.

Artificial neural networks (ANN) have an extensive classification; therefore, each work that the authors have reviewed has met with two or three specific ones for the prediction of the climate, specifically of the temperature.

The authors, in their research based on ANNs, found that for the construction of a good network it was necessary to test and select the input variables. The behavior and solution of the network depends on the quantities of inputs chosen. The creation and the result of the model with the use of these variables must demonstrate a high statistical correlation. It must be remembered that known weather patterns [12] have a significant impact on the weather forecast. Therefore, the use of these weather patterns as inputs can significantly improve network performance. The following variables were used as inputs to the proposed network:

- Weather-related entries: temperature is the most important meteorological variable, which represents the strongest correlation with the variation of climate-related precipitation. The maximum and minimum daily temperature values were used as the inputs in the model. Normally, for the training stage, the authors took the bases by INAMHI, which helped to obtain the necessary weights for the final model.
- Historical values: 31 values registered for the 21 months of historical reading were used as 31 inputs to the proposed network. In Fig. 3 shows the output values for the training of the networks.

Another question about this prediction according to [13], is that it depends on other factors for weather prediction such as whether it is in the countryside or in the city. If it is in the countryside, the prediction is much simpler since it only has to do with the weather and precipitation of rains, wind, and natural factors. On the other hand, in the city, it is not only based on these variables, but it is often affected by the pollution of the city such as car smoke, the use of electric energy, and other variables that often affect weather. Figure 3 presents the final values for the training of the networks.

```
[[30.   29.3 29.1 29.7 30.6 29.9 27.5 32.2 32.2 32.4 31.9 31.6
  29.4 31.5 33.4 33.5 32.2 32.5 30.6 32.5 33.5 33.6 30.4 30.4
  30.1 31.6 30.9 30.6 38.8 31.2 31.44]]
```

Fig. 3. Outputs for the neural networks

1.2 Deep Learning and Neural Networks

Deep learning is a part of machine learning born when AI began studying intelligent computing solutions through feature extraction. This began in 1943 when scientists Walter Pitts and Warren McCulloch created the first neural network model [14]. Currently, deep learning is one of the most frequent topics in AI for different classification and prediction topics. Deep learning is based on the unmonitored, known neural networks. Most branches of AI focus on emulating the learning of human beings to obtain solutions to complex problems and create basic knowledge through predictions if another similar problem appears. In other words, deep learning can be considered as a way to automate predictive analysis.

A normally supervised simple neural network has an input layer and an output layer to make decisions, but deep learning decisions are different. An example of deep learning models would be the most used multilayer neural networks. These networks, also called MLP, have some layers that help to create autonomous learning. These are more complex and, in addition to the input and output, have "hidden" layers where the processing for prediction is centered, and the more layers of this type the more powerful neural network becomes (Fig. 4).

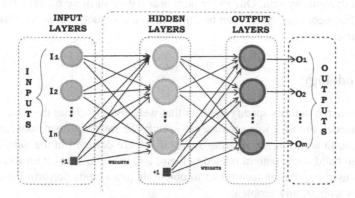

Fig. 4. Neuronal network system

Deep learning networks learn by detecting complex structures in the data they receive. By creating computational models composed of several layers of processing, networks can create several levels of abstraction that represent the data.

1.3 BackPropagation Method (MLP) and LSTM Method (Recurring)

ANNs provide a methodology to solve many types of nonlinear problems that are difficult to solve using traditional techniques [8]. Most meteorological processes often exhibit temporal and spatial variability and are plagued with problems of nonlinearity of physical processes, spatial and temporal scale conflicts and uncertainty in parameter estimates. With ANNs, there is the ability to extract the relationship between the inputs and outputs of a process, without the physics being explicitly provided [19]. Therefore, these ANN properties adapt well to the weather forecast problem under consideration.

Among these different ANN architectures for the weather forecast problem, the ones selected are the so-called Multilayer Perceptron (MLP) and recurring links. Currently, dynamic and recurring architectures are also interesting to research. Some of the articles [4–6] use applications of these models for the weather forecast problem. The incorporation of feedback connections (BackPropagation) in an MLP network results in significant changes in the operation and learning processes of the networks compared to their static counterparts. They have greater computing power over conventional MLP networks. Instead, recurring networks can make assignments that are functions of time and/or space or converge at one of several limit points. As a result, they are able to perform more complex calculations than static power networks. For example, they are able to learn sequences of temporal patterns, that is, sequences of patterns that depend on context or time.

The Long/Short Term Memory (LSTM) architecture is similar to a recurrent neural network with the difference that it introduces memory neurons [7]. These consist of a special type of neuron that can process data when there are interruptions or delays. In addition, these are members of a class of neural network models that exhibit inherent dynamic behavior and can be used to construct empirical models for weather forecasting as a dynamic system. Due to the nonlinear nature of these models, the behavior of the weather prediction system can be captured in a compact, robust and more natural representation.

2 Methodology

In this section, the authors specify the data that were used to create the neural network prediction model. For this, it is necessary to specify the ranges, dimensions, and type of each variable. In addition, the missing values that were detected in the databases were quantified to build some pattern related to them, and when meeting with these patterns the authors used imputation techniques to obtain them and thus perform the prediction experiments without any problem.

2.1 Database and Resources

Obtaining a good database to be able to generate an accurate result is a task that takes some time to obtain, but after obtaining this data and carrying out the predictive analysis it is essential that this database has a considerable amount of both past and current values. These data are necessary to establish patterns of behavior, not only for prediction but also for imputation. Thanks to these prediction models, computers can obtain "autonomous learning" and thus develop knowledge, but for all this to work, it is always necessary to provide them with the best natural resource of modern technological society: data.

The database was granted by the National Institute of Meteorology and Hydrology, which was of two different stations in Guayaquil which are the most complete that INAMHI uses for its predictions or for its investigations. One of them is located near the university citadel of the University of Guayaquil (Fig. 5) and is called M1096-GYE. The other is located in the Faculty of Natural Sciences within the University of Guayaquil (Fig. 6) and is called M1271-GYE.

The database of M1096 has data between the dates February 1992 to November 2015, of which it presents a total of 8,516 data corresponding to the precipitation of rain taking a daily sample. It also presents 8.397 values corresponding to the minimum temperature, and 8,397 values corresponding to the maximum temperature. These values were taken once a day.

For this study, the authors only chose the database corresponding to the temperature.

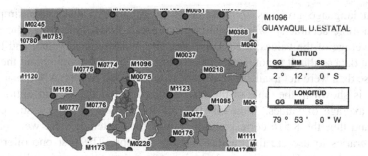

Fig. 5. Location of M1096

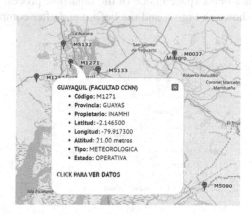

Fig. 6. Location of M1271-GYE

2.2 Imputation of Data

In the current study, the authors relied on using a simple imputation method. Although it is recognized that multiple imputation methods are more adequate, in some situations, they deliver very precise results without much error estimation. Despite the aforementioned, it is not possible to define rules to decide when it is feasible to use a method of simple imputation or not, so it is recommended to test the methods carefully to reproduce a prediction [9, 10].

Regarding simple temperature data imputation obtained in the behavior in coastal climates, during the last years at INAMHI, the problem of bias due to lack of data and its correction has been an issue that has not been taken into account during the predictions. These problems have arisen due to the lack of sending data in the sensors. Many times no answers are received because they are very old or because at that time there was no good communication with the place that stored the data. In the database, some values were eliminated because the training analysis could not have something incomplete, and the sample size was greatly reduced, which often causes a drastic loss of information. For this inconvenience regarding certain values that are missing, the imputation of data that was not sent is usually the best solution. However, the methods to impute data are still taken theoretically to be able to test whether the prediction is better or not.

Python language gives us some samples to be able to make this simple data imputation more accurately, which could be categorized into three types: the first one uses the average of the values; the second uses the most frequent value; and the third deletes that data so that it is not used. The first test was done by eliminating the days in which these data were not available, but there were no good results. A summary of that prediction is shown in the table of the results chapter, and the second option was to place the average of values. With this type of imputation, a better result could be obtained and thus the 8,516 corresponding values for the temperature were obtained.

The libraries to use are the Pandas and the Numpy. The first one offers us the function of calling an Excel page, and placing it in a data frame and replacing it with the average value of each column. On the other hand, the second one is able to use the NAN value that means a blank space in one of the data. The process of performing this imputation of data is shown in Fig. 7, and the before and after comparison is shown in Fig. 8.

```
import pandas as pnd
import numpy as np
#Load the Excel Sheet
xls = pnd.ExcelFile('BASE_DATOS_M_CNN.xlsx')
#Print the names of the sheets to choose
print(xls.sheet_names)
#Put in a dataframe the sheet
dtf = xls.parse('tempMax')
#Obtain the transponse of the dataframe
dtfT = dtf.T
#Obtain the mean of the 278 days of the dataframe
#and replace it for the imputation
for i in range(0,278):
    prom = dtfT[i].mean()
    prom = round(prom,2)
    dtfT[i] = dtfT[i].replace(np.nan, prom)

print(dtfT)
```

Fig. 7. Process to do the imputation in Python

	0	1	2	3	4	5	...	273	274	275	276	277	278
1	31.9	31.9	31.4	30.5	32.4	33.5	...	32.8	34.2	30.4	29.7	29.5	29.3
2	28.7	32.0	31.8	31.0	30.0	32.3	...	33.0	32.5	32.0	32.6	31.1	31.6
3	30.5	30.4	32.8	32.8	31.4	32.2	...	32.8	33.6	31.3	33.0	29.7	30.7
4	32.2	29.5	30.0	33.0	31.6	29.2	...	31.4	28.5	31.4	31.9	33.2	31.4
5	30.0	31.2	31.3	33.4	30.3	30.7	...	31.6	32.1	30.8	28.0	32.9	32.6
6	30.5	32.6	32.8	31.7	31.2	30.0	...	32.1	34.1	30.3	34.1	28.9	31.0
7	32.6	31.0	32.3	32.7	32.5	28.2	...	30.0	32.7	29.7	32.1	30.7	29.5
8	30.7	32.0	33.0	NaN	33.0	28.0	...	30.2	31.5	29.5	30.2	29.8	29.6
9	29.7	31.0	32.6	32.0	30.0	28.7	...	32.0	30.2	30.1	31.0	32.1	33.6
10	30.9	29.4	30.0	32.2	30.3	30.6	...	30.5	31.7	29.1	29.2	33.0	33.5
11	28.6	30.6	29.0	28.6	31.6	29.2	...	32.3	30.3	31.9	31.1	32.4	32.5
12	30.7	29.0	32.1	31.6	29.2	31.6	...	32.9	30.9	31.7	34.0	29.2	33.6
13	31.8	29.6	31.6	33.0	29.0	31.3	...	33.0	32.4	32.3	34.4	33.2	33.7
14	31.8	31.2	34.0	30.5	30.6	30.0	...	30.7	31.4	29.4	30.1	29.3	29.4
15	29.1	32.9	32.5	32.1	29.8	26.9	...	30.1	32.5	31.2	31.0	27.3	34.0
16	30.2	32.0	31.8	32.7	30.6	31.2	...	32.0	34.0	28.4	32.1	32.4	30.5
17	30.5	30.6	32.0	32.0	30.1	29.8	...	33.1	32.4	30.7	33.6	30.8	32.2
18	29.4	29.0	32.6	33.0	30.0	30.2	...	29.9	28.1	31.8	31.4	29.9	NaN
19	30.5	29.5	32.4	31.3	29.5	29.1	...	33.7	28.6	28.5	32.2	30.5	NaN
20	33.3	32.0	33.1	33.4	31.6	28.9	...	33.5	28.5	27.0	31.4	34.3	NaN
21	33.5	32.4	31.6	29.7	30.0	27.6	...	31.3	32.3	32.7	33.3	28.0	NaN
22	32.3	31.2	32.0	30.8	32.5	30.5	...	32.4	32.2	30.0	32.6	31.7	NaN
23	30.7	33.0	31.1	31.9	30.2	29.6	...	31.0	29.7	30.4	29.5	32.0	NaN
24	32.5	33.4	33.5	32.4	28.9	29.5	...	33.6	31.0	30.8	33.4	34.6	NaN
25	31.2	29.6	32.1	32.6	29.6	28.0	...	32.8	30.4	31.6	30.4	33.2	NaN
26	31.5	32.6	30.3	31.5	28.3	30.2	...	31.6	30.3	27.5	32.4	31.3	NaN
27	32.4	32.8	32.0	30.5	33.1	27.3	...	32.1	28.7	29.2	32.7	33.5	NaN
28	32.2	30.5	32.2	31.5	30.7	26.8	...	31.5	29.0	32.7	30.5	31.7	NaN
29	32.2	30.0	32.5	32.6	29.6	26.7	...	30.6	31.1	31.6	33.5	34.5	NaN
30	NaN	29.8	33.0	31.0	28.9	30.4	...	32.1	32.5	33.4	29.6	31.0	NaN
31	NaN	31.3	NaN	29.0	NaN	30.9	...	NaN	27.9	26.4	NaN	32.8	NaN

(a)

	0	1	2	3	4	5	...	273	274	275	276	277	278
1	31.90	31.9	31.40	30.5	32.40	33.5	...	32.80	34.2	30.4	29.7	29.5	29.3
2	28.70	32.0	31.80	31.0	30.00	32.3	...	33.00	32.5	32.0	32.6	31.1	31.6
3	30.50	30.4	32.80	32.8	31.40	32.2	...	32.80	33.6	31.3	33.0	29.7	30.7
4	32.20	29.5	30.00	33.0	31.60	29.2	...	31.40	28.5	31.4	31.9	33.2	31.4
5	30.00	31.2	31.30	33.4	30.30	30.7	...	31.60	32.1	30.8	28.0	32.9	32.6
6	30.50	32.6	32.80	31.7	31.20	30.0	...	32.10	34.1	30.3	34.1	28.9	31.0
7	32.60	31.0	32.30	32.7	32.50	28.2	...	30.00	32.7	29.7	32.1	30.7	29.5
8	30.70	32.0	33.00	31.7	33.00	28.0	...	30.20	31.5	29.5	30.2	29.8	29.6
9	29.70	31.0	32.60	32.0	30.00	28.7	...	32.00	30.2	30.1	31.0	32.1	33.6
10	30.90	29.4	30.00	32.2	30.30	30.6	...	30.50	31.7	29.1	29.2	33.0	33.5
11	28.60	30.6	29.00	28.6	31.60	29.2	...	32.30	30.3	31.9	31.1	32.4	32.5
12	30.70	29.0	32.10	31.6	29.20	31.6	...	32.90	30.9	31.7	34.0	29.2	33.6
13	31.80	29.6	31.60	33.0	29.00	31.3	...	33.00	32.4	32.3	34.4	33.2	33.7
14	31.80	31.2	34.00	30.5	30.60	30.0	...	30.70	31.4	29.4	30.1	29.3	29.4
15	29.10	32.9	32.50	32.1	29.80	26.9	...	30.10	32.5	31.2	31.0	27.3	34.0
16	30.20	32.0	31.80	32.7	30.60	31.2	...	32.00	34.0	28.4	32.1	32.4	30.5
17	30.50	30.6	32.00	32.0	30.10	29.8	...	33.10	32.4	30.7	33.6	30.8	32.2
18	29.40	29.0	32.60	33.0	30.00	30.2	...	29.90	28.1	31.8	31.4	29.9	NaN
19	30.50	29.5	32.40	31.3	29.50	29.1	...	33.70	28.6	28.5	32.2	30.5	NaN
20	33.30	32.0	33.10	33.4	31.60	28.9	...	33.50	28.5	27.0	31.4	34.3	NaN
21	33.50	32.4	31.60	29.7	30.00	27.6	...	31.30	32.3	32.7	33.3	28.0	NaN
22	32.30	31.2	32.00	30.8	32.50	30.5	...	32.40	32.2	30.0	32.6	31.7	NaN
23	30.70	33.0	31.10	31.9	30.20	29.6	...	31.00	29.7	30.4	29.5	32.0	NaN
24	32.50	33.4	33.50	32.4	28.90	29.5	...	33.60	31.0	30.8	33.4	34.6	NaN
25	31.20	29.6	32.10	32.6	29.60	28.0	...	32.80	30.4	31.6	30.4	33.2	NaN
26	31.50	32.6	30.30	31.5	28.30	30.2	...	31.60	30.3	27.5	32.4	31.3	NaN
27	32.40	32.8	32.00	30.5	33.10	27.3	...	32.10	28.7	29.2	32.7	33.5	NaN
28	32.20	30.5	32.20	31.5	30.70	26.8	...	31.50	29.0	32.7	30.5	31.7	NaN
29	32.20	30.0	32.50	32.6	29.60	26.7	...	30.60	31.1	31.6	33.5	34.5	NaN
30	31.11	29.8	33.00	31.0	28.90	30.4	...	32.10	32.5	33.4	29.6	31.0	NaN
31	31.11	31.3	31.98	29.0	30.55	30.9	...	31.89	27.9	26.4	31.7	32.8	NaN

(b)

Fig. 8. (a) The original database, (b) the database transformed by mean imputation

2.3   Neural Network Training

In order to train the types of neural networks, it was necessary to use the Python programming language in version 3.6.4, downloading the numpy, tensorflow, time, random, pandas, keras, matplotlib, scikit-learn libraries. Finally, to interpret this language, the authors used the Pycharm Community Edition IDE to develop this software, and all information was saved in text files for future use.

The training of neural networks was based on two parts, one for MLPs, and the other for LSTM. Tests were made with different months of the years that were available for information. First, the authors used the MLP (Fig. 9).

Fig. 9. Training for the BackPropagation in python

The training was based on using the data of the different months of the year, that is, the authors had information from 1992 to 2015, a total of 24 years. It could be said that 21 years of information were used and the other three were tested in prediction. In Fig. 8, a part of the MLP model with Back Propagation that the authors used is shown with the due transformation, and the result is in the same figure but at the bottom. If we compare these values with Fig. 3, it is evident that they have certain proximity and that their error is low. This training was used with different weights and iterations until an acceptable estimation error was reached compared to what was sought.

For the LSTM, all other points are considered, such as the number of hidden nodes for the neural network. In the same way as the MLP, the authors tested with some numbers of nodes, until they concluded that between 50 and 70 hidden nodes were necessary to reach a training that does not have an error estimate lower than that of the MLP. In the same way as the previous method, the 21 input neurons were used. After obtaining the desired weights in the training sessions of each of the methods, predictions with the other 2 years left for the test begun, obtaining favorable results for the investigation. Tests were made with each of the 12 months of the 24 years that were obtained in the database so a comparison table was constructed between these months. This concluded the training part.

Fig. 10. Training for the LSTM in python

2.4 Prediction Model

In the same way of training, each of the methods used in Python had its function of predicting. The *predict* function used in the MLP was based on using the weights found in training and predicting through the same sigmoid function and sigmoid_derivating the weights through the BackPropagation. On the other hand, in the *predict* function of LSTM, it was obtained through the scikit-learn library that already has this neural network function of the Sequential type model created, which is created at the time of making its algorithm.

3 Results

To obtain the results, the authors compared the two types of neural networks already used in other publications to obtain a good prediction. A moderate amount of data was applied that helped better prediction. The database that the authors used was standardized and imputed since some data was not complete or was misinterpreted. In the first network, a hidden layer of 31 neurons each was used while the sigmoid formula was applied to transform them and, in the end, only one was obtained with the derived sigmoid transformation. The following linear graph (Fig. 10) shows the comparison between the average maximum and minimum temperatures obtained by the database for each month, and the results of the MLP outputs and LSTM outputs are also shown. In order to represent this pre-process and testing process, and make the definitive comparison in the training of the 8,517 data obtained by the INAMHI with their corresponding accusations, the authors used a Windows 10 computer with 8 GB of RAM, Core i7 7th Generation. Table 1 shows the estimated time in each of the phases of this process:

Table 1. Total time that the pre-process and process took

Phase	Day	Hours	Minutes
DataBase order	2	12	0
Database Imputation	0	0	16
Training MLP	3	18	0
Training LTSM	4	2	0
Test MLP	0	0	7
Test LSTM	0	0	13
Total	10 days 8 h y 36 min		

Like is shown in the Table 1, the preprocess (training) was the largest step, because the authors have to compare, different types of layers configurations, and different mathematical expressions, in MLP was sigmoidal and linear, but the best combination was sigmoidal and the sigmoidal derivation. Instead the LSTM had the configuration of the hidden layers. Also the iterations were a problem at the moment of the training, in MLP was 500000 and in the LSTM was 50000. For the test the authors obtained the next results (Fig. 11):

Table 2. Results by months

	Temperature values						
	Max	Min	Avg	MLP	Error	LSTM	Error
January	30.1	22.41	26.26	29.34	11.75	27.51	4.78
February	31.43	20.63	26.03	28.89	10.99	27.14	4.26
March	30.31	21.18	25.75	29.55	14.78	26.89	4.45
April	31.86	21.67	26.77	30.87	15.34	27.53	2.86
May	32.57	22.16	27.37	31.3	14.38	29.68	8.46
June	30.23	23.25	26.74	30.1	12.57	28.52	6.66
Julio	30.91	23.7	27.31	29.03	6.32	29.2	6.94
August	32.29	23.79	28.04	26.58	5.21	29.23	4.24
September	32.22	24.28	28.25	31.64	12.00	29.69	5.10
October	31.01	23.72	27.37	28.83	5.35	29.07	6.23
November	28.88	22.42	25.65	28.88	12.59	26.8	4.48
December	30.75	23.67	27.21	24.11	11.39	28.15	3.45
Mean error estimation					11.06%		5.16%

The Table 2 presents the average values of all 24 years each month and compare with the results of the MLP test and LSTM test. In August in MLP appeared a lower temperature this because the first random weight was very low, and in March it was very high. The estimation error average was about 11%, this represent that the MLP was not a good predict estimator. In LSTM the estimation error average was 5%, this value represents that this method is better than the other, but is not so good.

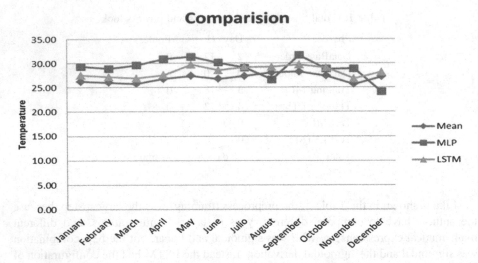

Fig. 11. Comparision between the average and the LSTM and MLP values

4 Conclusion and Future Works

The conclusion of this work, it is that always is better to use LSTM method to predict the temperature, because it has less estimated error. The LSTM had more hidden layers that improved the training and gave to the authors' better precision. The result shows that in all months the LSTM had better accuracy.

Another conclusion is that this method was tested in Guayaquil's weather, maybe in other cities this method is not so useless, and always researchers have to test it. To improve the MLP for a future research is put more hidden layers for the backpropagation method that transforms the weights in a better way. Also it is important to know that when the authors chose the first weights they noticed that this step was primordial to have a good prediction.

As a future development, it should be taken into account that these models could be tested in other types of climates. An example would be in the mountains of Ecuador, which are cold. Another example would be in the east, warmer, of more arid climate, or even in the Galapagos Islands.

References

1. Connor, J.T., et al.: Recurrent neural networks and load forecasting. In: Proceedings of the 1st International Forum on Applications of Neural Networks to Power System, pp. 22–25 (1991)
2. Lee, K.Y., et al.: Short-term load forecasting using diagonal recurrent neural network. In: Proceedings of the 2nd International Forum on Applications of Neural Networks to Power System, pp. 227–232 (1993)
3. Khan Muhammad, R., Ondr˚ U˚Sek, ˚C.: Recurrent neural network technique for one-day ahead load forecasting. In: Proceedings of the 3rd International Conference on Prediction

(NOSTRADAMUS), pp. 93–99, Technical University, Faculty of Technology, Zl'ın, Czech Republic, October 2–3 (2000)
4. Bravo, C.E., et al.: State of the art of artificial intelligence and predictive analytics in the E&P industry: a technology survey. SPE J. **19**(4), 547–563 (2014)
5. Choudhurya, S.K., Bartarya, G.: Role of temperature and surface finish in predicting tool wear using neural network and design of experiments. Int. J. Mach. Tools Manuf **43**(7), 747–753 (2003)
6. López, T., Pérez, A., Rivas, F.: Data analysis techniques for neural networks- based virtual sensors. In: Proceedings of 8th WSEAS International Conference on Neural Networks. Vancouver, Canada (2007)
7. Vermaak, J., Botha, E.C.: Recurrent neural networks for short-term load forecasting. IEEE Trans. Power Syst. **13**(1), 126–132 (1998)
8. Hagan, M., Demuth, H., Beale, M.: Neural Network Design. Hagan Publishing, Boston (2002)
9. Little, R., Rubin, D.: Statistical Analysis with Missing Data. Wiley, New York (1987)
10. Madow, W., Nisselson, H., Olkin, I.: Incomplete Data in Sample Surveys, vol. I. Report and case Studies. Academic Press, New York (1983)
11. Kung, S.Y.: Digital Neural Networks. Prentice-Hall (1993)
12. Maqsood, I., Khan, M.R., Abraham, A.: Neural Comput. Appl. **13**, 112 (2004). https://doi.org/10.1007/s00521-004-0413-4
13. Rivas, F., Recalde, E., Bedon, I.: Environmental temperature prediction using a Data analysis and Neural Networks methodological approach (2010). Mapas de climas
14. McCulloch, W.S., Pitts, W.: A logical calculus of the ideas immanent in nervous activity (1943). Pages 15–27 MIT Press Cambridge, MA, USA
15. CLIMA DEL ECUADOR POR REGIONES Hong Kong Observatory. https://www.cuyabenolodge.com/turismo-amazonas/clima-de-ecuador.htm

Prototype of an Embedded System for Irrigation and Fertilization in Greenhouses

Karen Mite-Baidal$^{(\boxtimes)}$, Carlota Delgado-Vera ,
Maritza Aguirre-Munizaga , and Kleber Calle-Romero

Faculty of Agricultural Sciences, Computer Science Department,
Agrarian University of Ecuador, Av. 25 de Julio y Pio Jaramillo,
P.O. BOX 09-04-100, Guayaquil, Ecuador
{kmite, cdelgado, maguirre, kcalle}@uagraria. edu. ec

Abstract. The main objective of the research is the automation of current agricultural practices using technology for better performance. This study is based on the hardware-software codesign methodology applied for embedded systems which allows to fully exploit the synergy between both elements. As a result of the study, a prototype was designed for helping farmers to carry out the work in greenhouses in a more automatic way avoiding much of the manual handling. The prototype includes both environmental temperature and soil moisture sensors, which will activate the irrigation or fertigation through nebulizers. These specific sensors are able to detect percentages of nitrogen, phosphorus, potassium and other minerals in the soil. It also includes an ultrasonic sensor that measures the current water level in the tanks for water rationing and a solar panel is used as an energy supply. Data from the sensors are read by the farmer from a mobile application to then be stored on a server in the cloud and keep records. The designed prototype is an excellent alternative for the agricultural sector as it lowers costs and automates the processes. It also gives the farmer access to the information as it keeps daily data records, but the most important benefit is that allows to give an optimal treatment for the plants in the greenhouses.

Keywords: Embedded system · Prototype · Irrigation · Fertigation · Sensor

1 Introduction

In the machine design procedure, it is fundamental the experimentation on proto-types that are the product of the application of both: a design methodology and simulation models at an experimental level are established in order to contribute developing low-cost systems that can be useful for the automation of various tasks.

The design process of the construction of large-scale prototypes is expensive, therefore the importance of the research in small-scale systems that considerably reduces the time and costs of manufacturing and start-up. Clearly, the results to be obtained from the small-scale model should be, if possible, very close to those that would produce the full-scale model.

© Springer Nature Switzerland AG 2019
R. Valencia-García et al. (Eds.): CITI 2019, CCIS 1124, pp. 30–40, 2019.
https://doi.org/10.1007/978-3-030-34989-9_3

Theories of similarity and likeness are used to achieve these small-scale models [1]. In this research, it will be explained the general considerations and physical sustenance that must be taken into account for the design and construction of scale models of embedded systems for automation of irrigation and fertilization in greenhouses.

According to research, it is known that a greenhouse is a closed structure that protects plants from extreme weather conditions, in this case: wind, ultraviolet radiation and attacks of pests and insects. Irrigation of the agricultural field is carried out by automatic drip irrigation, which operates according to the soil moisture threshold which is established for having an optimum amount of water applied to the plants [2, 3].

With the global rise of the internet of things technology (IoT), Ecuador aims to be one of the South American countries from 2020 will carry out performance checks for the 5G network, it is expected that with the implementation of this service, automation in various areas will increase its relevance for the process of systematization of key areas of the country's economic conditions. In the south region, Uruguay is the only country that has a 5G network. Chile, Brazil, Mexico, Argentina, Colombia, and Peru are in a trial period and old networks still work here in Ecuador, like 2G and 3G.

In this article, it was presented the design of an embedded system for automation of the irrigation and fertilization system in a greenhouse. As background, it is emphasized that drip irrigation was named in Israel in 1959. Modern agricultural industries based on greenhouses are the recent requirement worldwide in every part of the agriculture domain. In this technology, the humidity and temperature of the plants are accurately controlled [20].

As part of this study is important to mention that water is very valuable for all humans and for plants or trees. The agricultural industry uses the largest amount of freshwater for irrigation. By using nebulizers, the water will remain at a constant level, it means that the water will reach the roots of the plants without damaging them. This is very important because it can guarantee the survival of plants.

The concept of agricultural IoT uses networking technology in agricultural production, the hardware of this agricultural IoT includes temperature, humidity and light sensors that are connected to a data processing center which helps the monitoring and care of crops; these hardware devices are connected by various types of wireless communication technology for short distance, such as Bluetooth, WiFi or Zigbee. In fact, according to research ZigBee technology due to its convenient network and low power consumption, it is widely used in agricultural IoT. The network is combined to remotely control and monitor sensor data [4].

The Internet of Things (IoT) and data analysis (DA) are used in agriculture to improve mainly operational efficiency and productivity. The IoT integrates several existing technologies such as WSN, radio frequency identification (RFID), cloud computing, middleware systems, and end-user applications [3].

This document proposes an embedded greenhouse management system based on the Internet of Things using networks of sensors and web-based technologies. This is different from other works mentioned in the literature due to its low cost and accessibility to the agricultural sector that is still growing in Ecuador. Therefore, it is introduced as an automation option for SMEs that are engaged in the Ecuadorian agricultural sector.

2   Related Work

Inventions in the robotics domain exist and can be applied directly to the agricultural sector, especially for vehicles used in this activity. The application of new popular robotic technologies will increase the manufacture of agricultural vehicles in the future such as mobile robots, flying robots, and forest robots, which are used exclusively for improving the accuracy and precision in the different activities [5]. Research [6], proposed a mechanism for automatic control and fertilization and irrigation management to improve the porosity and soil nutrients through timely application of fertilizers and the necessary water level for the growth and development of crops. The operation is controlled by the interface of several components and intelligence units such as ISE sensors, DHT11 sensor, actuator, AT89C52 microcontroller and other components to automatically apply soluble agrochemical fertilizer and water according to the needs of the plant. In India, an automatic watering system was developed for detecting the moisture content of the soil through PV (photovoltaic cell progression) and GSM [7], it is a system that automatically activates a water pump via SMS in response to a real-time alert system and after reaching the proper humidity level the farmer can disconnect the water pump by sending an SMS or by a manual task. The components are fed through photovoltaic cells. Chung-Liang Chang and Kuan-Ming Lin [8], proposed a scheme that combines computer vision and multitasking processes to develop a small-scale intelligent machine that can automatically remove the weeds and perform irrigation with a variable rate within a cultivated field using fuzzy logic. The experimental results show that the system can classify plants and weeds in real-time with an average rate of 90% classification. Xue et al. [9], designed a novel method of artificial vision with variable field of view that allows a robot to navigate between rows of maize fields, the artificial vision hardware consisted of a camera with motion control for pitch and yaw. Image processing algorithm was also used for the morphological characteristics and the robot was guided along these lines using fuzzy logic control, showing a maximum error of 15.8 mm and stable navigation behaviour. At work proposed by Shama and Borse [10] they designed and built an autonomous mobile robot for sensing plant diseases, for growth monitoring and spraying mechanism of pesticides, fertilizers, and water with application in agriculture or greenhouses; it has a compact platform that allows spraying pesticides, fertilizers and water directly to the plant. This approach will help farmers make the right decision by providing real-time information about the plant and its environment using basic principles of the Internet, sensors technology and image processing. Researchers Walter Schmidt and Yucel Toprak [11], they patented a mobile device with the process to adequately irrigation of the soil, in which the movable carriage has a control unit for irrigation of the soil and a mobile unit for measuring by microwaves determine the water content of the soil along a measuring path; furthermore it has a water tank to irrigate the land autonomously.

In this study, we have developed an automatic control and management of irrigation and fertilization system that can automate the supply of water and soluble fertilizer to the crop, according to its needs. This system can determine the condition of the environment, temperature, and soil moisture before taking the decision to irrigate and it also can complement the sample with measurements of chloride, nitrate, and ammonia.

3 Embedded System

In software engineering, embedded systems [12] refer to every digital electronic circuit that is able to perform computing operations, usually in real-time, which serves to fulfil a particular or specific task.

Embedded systems consist of limited resources and own applications that make them productive and useful in multiple environments that are commonly used nowadays, for example, modern cars, mobile phones, medical and agricultural equipment.

3.1 Features and Architecture of an Embedded System

The most important characteristics of an embedded system lie in the low production cost and low power consumption. These should automatically respond to stimuli from the environment where they are. Embedded systems design [13] faces hardware limitations since they usually have no hard drives, keyboards or monitors; a flash memory replaces the disks and some buttons, and an LCD screen normally replaces the interface device. Programming these devices is done in assembly language or C language.

3.2 Architecture of an Embedded System

Figure 1 shows the architectural specification of an embedded system [14] which consists of the following elements: a microprocessor and software running on it. But this software needs a place to be stored before being executed by the processor, this is

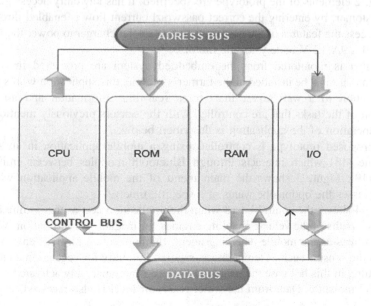

Fig. 1. The architecture of an embedded system

called RAM or ROM memory. Every embedded system needs a certain amount of memory that even can be located within the same processor chip and additionally, a number of inputs and outputs necessary to communicate with external devices. The work performed by embedded systems is relatively easy, processors commonly use records of 8 or 16 bits. In its memory, it only remains the program to master a particular application. Its input/output (I/O) lines support the connection of the sensors and actuators of the device to control and all additional available resources are intended to meet its requirements. This is the common architecture of embedded systems, everything else will be totally different for each of them in particular due to the variety of available applications.

4 Hardware/Software Co-design Methodology

The hardware/software co-design methodology is the ideal methodology for embedded systems [15, 16], it is a design process to break a problem into a hardware component (usually designed and optimized for special purposes) and software component (usually by controlling the hardware part). The main objective of the HW/SW design methodology is to get most of the benefits from the microcontroller's features so that the software controls the highest percentage of functionalities of the device [17].

4.1 Architectural Specification of the Prototype Embedded System for Irrigation and Fertilization

The embedded system has been structured on a physical level with an Arduino microcontroller, which programming language is based on C++. Its coding enabled the connection of each of the sensors in the structure of the prototype.

In Fig. 2 elements of the prototype are specified, it has key entry access generated by the customer, by entering the correct password current flow is enabled through the relay to access the features of the prototype. It has a solar charger to power the Arduino boards and a 9A 12 V battery for the motors.

Data that is monitored from the embedded system are processed in a mobile application that must be installed in the farmer's mobile, this application works through the connection to a web server that stores real-time information and allows the automation of the tasks that are controlled with the sensors previously mentioned.

The operation of the application is described below:

The proposed prototype is controlled using a mobile application in an Android smartphone [18] which interacts through Bluetooth modules between emitter and receiver [19]. Figure 3 shows the main menu of the mobile application where the farmer accesses the options he wants at a specific time.

Figure 4 shows the control board when the application acts as the issuing agent, it controls the paths of the vehicle enabling engines for irrigation or fertigation. When the application acts as the mobile receiving agent, the application receives environmental data from the sensors such as temperature, relative humidity for vegetation control, and soil moisture, in this last case the irrigation system is automatically activated in case of lack of soil moisture. Data from the water reservoir level is also received.

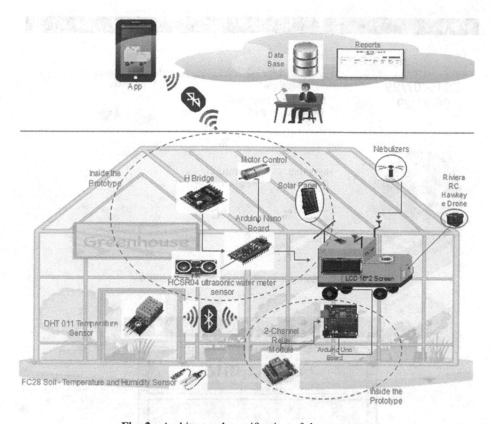

Fig. 2. Architectural specification of the prototype

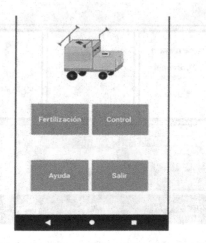

Fig. 3. Main menu of the mobile application

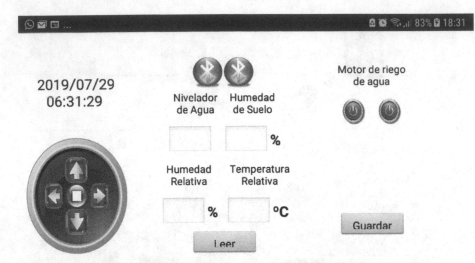

Fig. 4. Main menu of the mobile application

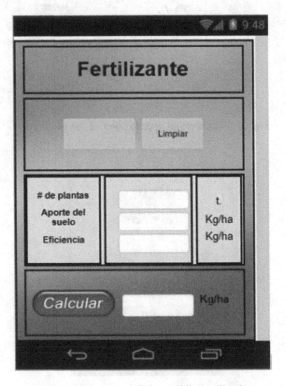

Fig. 5. Main menu of the mobile application

Figure 5 shows an option where the farmer can specify the number of plants available in the greenhouse. As soon as, the farmer has made a study of the soil quality, he can determine the contribution and efficiency needed so that the system automatically will calculate the amount of fertilizer to be applied in the greenhouse.

Finally, the mobile application sends the data to a web server and then to a database, MySQL. These data are received by the designed software which function is to generate reports allowing to use filters, search by date or by name, and printed if necessary.

The system features an embedded HD Rivera camera for viewing, recording or taking pictures inside the greenhouse.

5 Experiment

It was claimed that the prototype of the embedded system for irrigation and fertilization allowed the water supply for plants in a greenhouse promoting the growth of the roots and avoiding the soil saturation. Plants needed to be nebulized seventeen times a day, for 5 min each time. Nebulizers allowed this type of irrigation and with the help of a timer, it was possible to give nebulizations in scheduled times within the day. Nebulizers maintain constant pressure, so that water comes out simultaneously by each nozzle forming a mist which prevents excessive watering.

It is intended to improve the uniformity and coverage of the water distribution, by placing each nebulizer according to the spacing of the plants in the greenhouse. The flow rate of each nebulizer is 5.5 L/h per nozzle, according to the technical specifications of the pump. For this study, it was used a submersible pump of 0.5 HP of power, with a flow rate of 6500 L/h, and with a maximum suction height of 8 m. The embedded system worked in a stationary process, with a 200 L tank fed by a water source, which is a limiting factor in its coverage area. On the other hand, the power of the system was notorious due to the usage of the solar panel, reducing significantly the energy consumption. In addition, the prototype was able to be connected to a Venturi injector which allowed the timed fertigation.

Another advantage of the prototype is that it was able to monitor the environmental temperature, the relative humidity and the soil moisture with sensors connected to an Arduino microcontroller. In terms of data collection, the results obtained were good; data were transmitted in real-time to the mobile application by which they were sent for storage in the online database, and they were available for issuing the reports requested by the user about fertigation or daily watering, during a certain period of time. With this experiment, better root development was achieved for the plants in the greenhouse.

Table 1 shows the investment for the development of embedded system prototype.

There is a huge difference in the investment used for the development of the prototype and the traditional cost of a 50×20 m greenhouse, equivalent to 100 m^2. The investment for the prototype is around $255 and the price for the traditional greenhouse would vary from $1000 to $1200. The budget includes the pump, pipes and other connections transmitters without sensors.

Table 1. Embedded system materials

Number	Materials	Prices
1	DHT 011 temperature sensor	$2,00
1	HC SR04 ultrasonic water level sensor	$3,00
1	FC 28 soil humidity and temperature sensor	$4,00
1	HC 05 Bluetooth module	$6,50
1	HC 06 Bluetooth module	$6,50
1	16 × 2 LCD display screen	$4,50
1	3 × 4 keypad	$5,00
8	12 V 5-pin relay	$5,60
2	2-channel module relay	$9,60
2	Arduino Uno microcontroller board	$30,00
1	Arduino Nano microcontroller board	$18,00
4	DC 12 V 5 A motors	$23,00
1	Motorcycle battery 12 V 9[a]	$20,80
1	Solar panel	$15,00
1	Water pump	$9,50
1	DC motor adapted to a water pump	$14,50
1	I2c module	$2,40
3	Protoboard 400 points	$11,40
2	Potenciometer	$1,00
10	1 K resistance	$1,00
4	Mosfet IRFZ44 N transistor	$1,60
8	TIP 31c transistor	$4,00
8	1N4001 diodes	$1,40
3	Male to male jumper wire	$5,00
3	Male to female jumper wire	$5,00
3	Female to female jumper wire	$5,00
1	Switch	$5,00
2	Computer fan	$5,00
2	Nebulizers	$5,00
1	Riviera RC Hawkeye Drone-WiFi Streaming	$24,00
	Total	**$254,30**

6 Tests - Results

Tests were focused on analysing the operation of an Embedded System prototype for irrigation and fertilization in warehouses, first in a real environment and then at the implementation site of the prototype, establishing a comparison of water use and fertilizer application efficiency and its effect on the improvement of the vegetative part of the plants.

Irrigation using the prototype is much more accurate since it is not based on a fixed parameter but responds to soil moisture changes by means of sensors. However, with traditional irrigation, the system would water during a certain time without taking into account the temperature of the environment, which could harm the plants.

Due to the timer, the time and work of turning the pump on and off is optimized, since it is possible to program waterings paused throughout the day, keeping the soil always in harvest capacity and the baskets with a favourable temperature, achieving energy savings and optimizing the water consumption.

7 Conclusions and Future Work

The system allowed data monitoring and storage of the environmental variables of temperature (T) and relative humidity (RH), inside the greenhouse. Monitoring and control allow the farmer to ensure a smooth process for the maintenance of the vegetative area.

One of the limitations is the water supply system for the prototype as it restricts the irrigation coverage for the warehouse.

Future work is taken as reference, therefore the recognition of the person who will use the prototype can be improved with the use of fingerprints [21], also a specialized pattern recognition software would be configured for this purpose.

One might also consider not only capture but also processing the images with the Android Studio platform [22].

Recent developments in the field of communications for embedded systems are focused on the acquisition and control of high-speed data [23] using optical fiber because they have shown that longer transmission distances for data acquisition can cause errors.

Embedded systems today are a significant contribution [24] mainly in the different sectors where they intensify their use.

Acknowledgments. We thank researchers from the Agricultural University of Ecuador, for seeking timely information for the study.

References

1. Righi, E., Dogliotti, S., Stefanini, F.M., Pacini, G.C.: Capturing farm diversity at regional level to up-scale farm level impact assessment of sustainable development options. Agric. Ecosyst. Environ. **142**, 63–74 (2011). https://doi.org/10.1016/J.AGEE.2010.07.011
2. Jiang, J., Moallem, M.: Development of greenhouse LED system with RedlBlue mixing ratio and daylight control. In: 2018 IEEE Conference on Control Technology and Applications (CCTA), pp. 1197–1202. IEEE (2018). https://doi.org/10.1109/CCTA.2018.8511374
3. Elijah, O., Rahman, T.A., Orikumhi, I., Leow, C.Y., Hindia, M.N.: An overview of Internet of Things (IoT) and data analytics in agriculture: benefits and challenges (2018). https://doi.org/10.1109/JIOT.2018.2844296
4. Li, Z., Wang, J., Higgs, R., Zhou, L., Yuan, W.: Design of an intelligent management system for agricultural greenhouses based on the Internet of Things. In: 2017 IEEE International Conference on Computational Science and Engineering (CSE) and IEEE International Conference on Embedded and Ubiquitous Computing (EUC), pp. 154–160. IEEE (2017). https://doi.org/10.1109/CSE-EUC.2017.212

5. Yaghoubi, S., Akbarzadeh, N.A., Bazargani, S.S., Bazargani, S.S., Bamizan, M., Asl, M.I.: Autonomous robots for agricultural tasks and farm assignment and future trends in agro robots. Int. J. Mech. Mechatronics Eng. **13**, 1–6 (2013)
6. Adegboye, M.A., Lukman, A., Folorunso, T.A.: Automatic fertilized-irrigation control and management (2017)
7. Chilumula, R.: Automatic irrigation system on sensing soil moisture content using PV and GSM **4**, 955–961 (2018)
8. Weeding, V.: Smart agricultural machine with a computer (2018). https://doi.org/10.3390/robotics7030038
9. Xue, J., Zhang, L., Grift, T.E.: Variable field-of-view machine vision based row guidance of an agricultural robot. Comput. Electron. Agric. **84**, 85–91 (2012). https://doi.org/10.1016/j.compag.2012.02.009
10. Sharma, S., Borse, R.: Automatic Agriculture Spraying Robot with Smart, pp. 743–758. https://doi.org/10.1007/978-3-319-47952-1
11. Application, F., Data, P.: Process and apparatus for adequately irrigating soil (2015)
12. Oshana, R., Kraeling, M.: Software Engineering for Embedded Systems: Methods, Practical Techniques, and Applications. Elsevier Science (2019)
13. Zurawski, R.: Embedded Systems Design and Verification. CRC Press, Boca Raton (2018)
14. Platunov, A., Penskoi, A., Kluchev, A.: The architectural specification of embedded systems. In: Proceedings - 2014 3rd Mediterranean Conference on Embedded Computing MECO 2014 - Incl. ECyPS 2014, pp. 48–51 (2014)
15. Bartík, M., Pichlová, D., Kubátová, H.: Hardware-software co-design: a practical course for future embedded engineers. In: 2016 5th Mediterranean Conference on Embedded Computing MECO 2016 - Incl. ECyPS 2016, BIOENG.MED 2016, MECO Student Chall. 2016, pp. 347–350 (2016). https://doi.org/10.1109/MECO.2016.7525779
16. Sampson, A., Bornholt, J., Ceze, L.: Hardware-software co-design: Not just a clich. Leibniz Int. Proc. Informatics, LIPIcs **32**, 262–273 (2015). https://doi.org/10.4230/LIPIcs.SNAPL.2015.262
17. Lugou, F., Apvrille, L.: Toward a methodology for unified verification of hardware/software co-designs. J. Cryptogr. Eng. 1–12 (2016)
18. Hana, R.E.: Apply android studio (SDK) tools. Int. J. Adv. Res. Comput. Sci. Softw. Eng. **5** (2015)
19. Vyas, S., Chaudhari, U., Chinmay, V., Thakare, B.: Access control application using android smartphone, arduino and bluetooth. Int. J. Comput. Appl. **142**, 16–20 (2016). https://doi.org/10.5120/ijca2016909902
20. Prathyusha, K., Chaitanya Suman, M.: Design of embedded systems for the automation of drip irrigation. Int. J. Appl. Innov. Eng. Manag. **1**, 254–258 (2012)
21. Sumit Singh, D.K.Y.: Fingerprint based attendance system using microcontroller and LabView. Int. J. Adv. Res. Electr. Electron. Instrum. Eng. **04**, 5111–5121 (2015). https://doi.org/10.15662/ijareeie.2015.0406029
22. Thakker, S., Kapadia, H.: Image processing on embedded platform Android. In: IEEE 2015 International Conference on Computer, Communication and Control IC4 (2016). https://doi.org/10.1109/IC4.2015.7375672
23. Di Paolo Emilio, M.: Embedded systems design for high-speed data acquisition and control (2015). https://doi.org/10.1007/978-3-319-06865-7
24. Stepanić, J., Kasać, J., Merkač, M.: A contribution to considerations of the role of embedded systems. Bus. Syst. Res. J. **5**, 47–56 (2014). https://doi.org/10.2478/bsrj-2014-0004

Control and Monitoring System
for Edaphoclimatic Variables in Rice
Cultivation: Case Study

Carlota Delgado-Vera[1(✉)], Evelyn Solis-Aviles[1],
Andrea Sinche-Guzman[1] (iD), and Yoansy Garcia-Ortega[2] (iD)

[1] School of Computer Engineering and Computer Science,
Faculty of Agricultural Sciences, Agrarian University of Ecuador,
Av. 25 de Julio and Pio Jaramillo, PO BOX 09-04-100, Guayaquil, Ecuador
{cdelgado,esolis,asinche}@uagraria.edu.ec
[2] Agronomic Engineering School, Faculty of Agricultural Sciences,
Agrarian University of Ecuador, Av. 25 de Julio and Pio Jaramillo,
PO BOX 09-04-100, Guayaquil, Ecuador
ygarcia@uagraria.edu.ec

Abstract. The project consists of monitoring edaphoclimatic parameters that influence the development of rice, in order to avoid that the crop is affected by these factors which are, PH, salinity, temperature, humidity, water level, and rainfall intensity. Soil salinity is one of the most important parameters that need our especial attention, because side effects can affect greatly the rice crops according to the vegetative phase, it can be very harmful in the initial phase but the damage will last until the latter phase. This paper presents a case study of a system implementation which aims to improve the edaphic environment, in order to optimize the crop production system. Different types of sensors were used in hardware development, and they were integrated with the microcontroller. Regarding the development of software, some programming languages are integrated such as Phyton, MySql and Arduino IDE interface which works for the acquisition, processing, and display of data.

Keywords: Rice · Soil · Climate · Monitoring system · Sensors

1   Introduction

According to studies conducted by the National Financial Corporation (CFN), the largest concentration of Ecuadorian companies is in Guayas and Los Rios provinces. During 2013-2017, Ecuador exported most of its rice production to Colombia (49%), followed by Peru [1, 2]; and mainly small producers got the highest participation in the production schema. Its share in the Gross Domestic Product (GDP) represents only 1.55% (average during 2014–2017). Most of the rice production is destined for domestic consumption (96%), leaving very little product for exportation (4%) [3].

R. Valencia-García et al. (Eds.): CITI 2019, CCIS 1124, pp. 41–52, 2019.
https://doi.org/10.1007/978-3-030-34989-9_4

INIAP[1] states that soil analysis is a basic and necessary tool in the diagnosis of soil conditions, which includes any physical, chemical or mineralogical test performed on soil samples. Fertility diagnostic of soil is determined by the amount of nutrients available in it which can lead on recommendations for improving fertilization. These recommendations might be adjusted by the experimental information and experience of the user about crop management and his knowledge about soil or climate conditions of the specific region.

Globally, climate variability represents approximately one-third of the yield variability; the relationship between both of them is based on parameters of temperature, precipitation, and their interaction explains the crop yield variability [4, 5].

Rice is currently in high demand and due to its production process, in order to get a good harvest, it is important to pay special attention to the growing phase of the crop. Nowadays, there are already established values that ensure the optimal development of rice crops.

On the other hand, the crop care is essential in order to avoid that external and influential factors cause any harm to the plants. Often the rice is marketed without having adequate control during the cultivation phase, and there are also many losses due to damage to the plantations which directly affects the income of the farmer. The physiological parameters that influence rice yield are the index of foliar area, plant height and dry matter in the phenological stages of rice. In addition, the productivity of rice cultivation is influenced by weather conditions as solar radiation, temperature, and availability of water during the vegetative and reproductive stages [6].

This paper presents a prototype with a monitoring system for edaphoclimatic variables of rice cultivation. The system integrates Arduino technologies and mobile applications through a graphical interface, thus allowing to store the information in a database where the user can access from the interface, and facilitates the generation of graphics according to the recommended standard parameters. The remainder of this paper is structured as follows: Sect. 2 describes research related to monitoring systems, Sect. 3 details the components of the hardware and software used for the water monitoring system presented in this paper, Sect. 4 presents the evaluation results of the effectiveness of this system, and finally Sect. 5 includes conclusions and future work.

2 Related Work

There are currently technological innovations for the agricultural sector, in the mechanisms applied to crop control, the mechanisms for damage prevention, and the machines that monitor the different stages of the cultivation. With the integration of ICTs in the different stages of rice cultivation, the aim is to increase productivity and to improve the socio-economic impact of the process in comparison to conventional methods. Research [7] showed that using remote sensing applications to identify critical points in the area of rice planting would help forecast production. This approach is based on the integration of meteorological parameters with remote sensing.

---

[1] Instituto Nacional de Investigaciones Agropecuarias. https://eva.iniap.gob.ec.

In Ecuador, in the town called Babahoyo, researchers used GIS in-training (GIS) to generate a map of drought risk (DRM) for rice cultivation [8]. The map represented the production risks incurred by the onset of a drought. The vulnerability of the rice crop was determined through a soil evaluation and water availability during the crop cycle rather than addressing the problem in terms of drought indices.

Other methods used for real time monitoring is via wireless sensors [9, 10] which can obtain values of leaf humidity, soil moisture, soil pH, and atmospheric pressure which activate the water sprayer and dose the effective amount of fertilizer achieving precision agriculture and thus increasing the production of rice. Automated systems for monitoring soil properties using an Arduino interface are gaining popularity because of their benefits of low costs of implementation [11]. The growing environment of rice cultivation is complex, some important parameters such as carbon dioxide, oxygen, temperature and moisture, pH value and content of microbial in the black soil would affect the growth of plants and the quality of the rice in other areas for which it is used [12].

The proposal [13] is based on a system which uses sensors for identifying values of environmental conditions such as humidity, temperature, and quantity of water required by crops. Among the sensors that constitute the system, we have the sensor of water flow, the temperature sensor, and the soil humidity sensor; in addition, it is used an Arduino microcontroller which collects and receives the data. It contains designs of interfaces such as PC Lab VIEW [14] that allow the storage, graphics display, processing, and analysis in real time suitable for detecting changes in environmental temperature, moisture, and pH of the rice crop. The parameters can also be linked to an interactive website that displays real time values versus standard values for some specific crop to greatly reduce development costs and provide an easy way for implementation [15].

3 Experimental Section - Monitoring System for Rice Crops

3.1 Platform

The system works with an Arduino-based device [16] that allows obtaining information of the environment in real time through programmable sensors, some of these parameters are: soil pH, electrical conductivity, water layer meter, rain sensor, temperature and humidity of air, and soil moisture.

In addition, the data transmission is executed by Phyton with the Tkinter library [17] which is responsible for the program design and allows users to view the data collected. Finally, the system relates to a database based on MySQL [18] to store all the data collected by sensors.

Figure 1 shows the model implemented able to measures the different parameters and/or variables through various sensors.

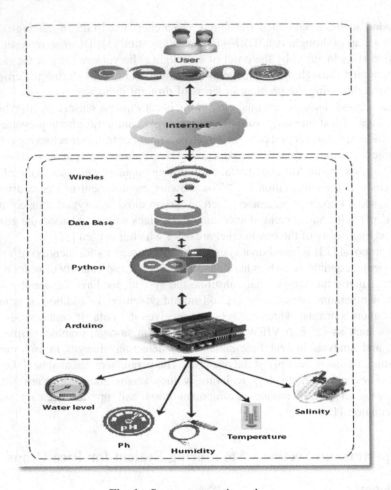

Fig. 1. System connection scheme

3.2   Microcontroller and Sensors

The technical specifications of the platform to be built with the microcontroller Arduino for field and laboratory measurements are detailed below in Table 1.

Table 1. Technical details of the microcontroller and sensors

Hardware	Specifications
Arduino Mega 2560	Microcontroller: ATmega256
	Operating voltage: 5 V
	Input voltage (recommended): 7–12 V
	Input voltage (limits): 6–20 V
	Digital I/O pins: 54 (of which 14 provide Analog input pins: 16
	DC current per I/O pin: 40 mA.
	DC current for 3.3 V pin: 50 mA
	Flash memory: 256 KB of which 8 KB SRAM: 8 KB
	EEPROM: 4 KB
	Clock speed: 16 MHz
Sensors	Yl-83 sensor, Analogous ph, DHT-11, FC-28, HC-SR04

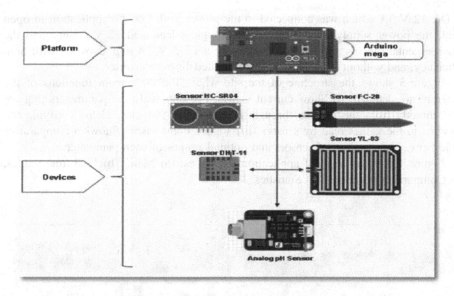

Fig. 2. Scheme of arduino prototype & sensors

In Fig. 2, the connections between the microcontroller and sensors are shown, and they are assembled in a removable module capable of being transported to different areas of the agricultural land; these sensors are controlled by an Arduino board which is pre-programmed for this project. A continuous stream 7-12 V (CC) is recommended to feed the platform. For the testing phase, an electronic adapter was used 110-220 V AC

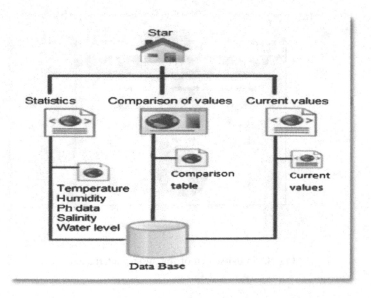

Fig. 3. Structure of the site

to DC 12 V 3A which was connected to the power grid. For the application in open field, the power supply can be provided through a lead-acid 12 V battery and the environmental sensors are supplied directly by a 12–5 V 3A digital switch with high efficiency, and without bypassing the incorporated linear converter.

Figure 3 shows the structure of the site where the three main functions of the program are detailed: (i) Show current values: Presents real-time parameters that are read directly from the module through graphics; (ii) Statistics: Helps verifying the changes in the values read by sensors (iii) Values comparison: Shows a comparative table between the values of sensors and optimal ranges of each parameter.

Figure 4 presents a set of application interfaces: (a) Main, (b) Real-time values, (c) Comparison of values, (d) Statistics

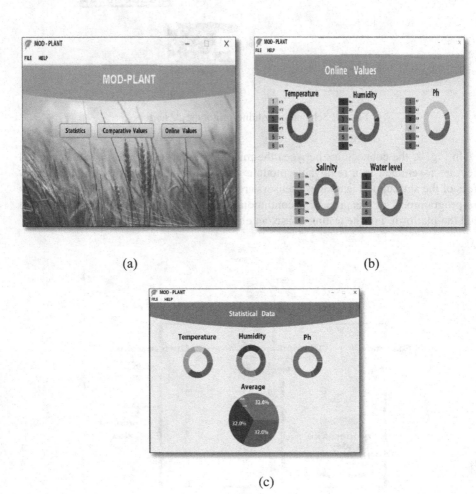

(a)   (b)

(c)

Fig. 4. Initial screen of the system interface

3.3   Sensor Calibration

The data were modelled using a calculation function with two parameters, therefore the importance of setting parameters and the error adjustment [19]. For calibration of the pH electrode and the electrical conductivity, the pH sensor was tested in two types of solutions: water of rice crop and NaCl (liquid); with these results the pH values were obtained with a margin of error of 0.3%. Moreover, the conductivity value was calculated by using appropriate correction factors from the margin of error. Once the electrode and conductivity have been correctly calibrated and calculated, the value for the rice crop solution was 348 μS/cms. The equations used to obtain the values are the following:

$$NewValue = \frac{(2301) * NewVoltios}{pHValue})$$ (1)

$$NewVoltios = (7 - pHValue) * 59.16$$ (2)

$$Conductance = (NewVoltios + NewValue) * 10$$ (3)

The pH is the measurement of acidity or alkalinity of a liquid, it is one of the most common measuring parameters and is applied in various types of industry such as: Drinking water plant and wastewater treatment plant, chemical production, agriculture, research, environmental monitoring, Biotechnology & pharmacy, and food & beverage processing.

$$f(x) = A - e^{\ln\left(\frac{mV}{B}\right)}$$ (4)

Where B is a constant value which can be obtained using the table of the electric potential related to the pH; A is a reference value by taking tests to obtain the pH from the electrical potential.

Figure 5 shows the pH concentration and the electrical potential dissolved in the soil, according to a set of samples used in this work and the results are shown in Table 2. This sampling of values has been taken with a minimum margin of error between 1% and 3% for each liquid solution sample. When the pH value is elevated by

Table 2. Values for pH and electrical potential

Voltage (mV)	pH Value
414,12	0,00
354,12	1,00
295,80	2,00
236,64	3,00
177,48	4,00
118,32	5,00
59,16	6,00
0,00	7,00

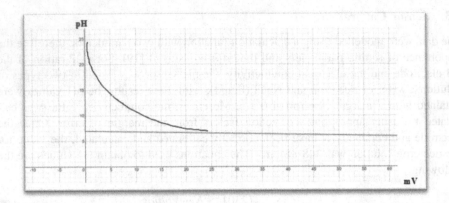

Fig. 5. pH behavior and electrical conductivity

the increased concentration of oxydryl ions (OH–), negative charges increase and thus the voltage decreases, and when the pH is acidic because of the increase of hydronium ions (H+) in the dissolution, the positive charges increase and therefore the voltage decreases.

4   Results and Discussion

Several tests were performed for the system implemented at the Hacienda Miraflores, Parroquia Tarifa, Samborondon, Guayas province. Located within the UTM coordinates: 17 M 637089 9781207. These results were useful for validating the effectiveness of the sensors and for comparing them with the test results obtained in the laboratory executed by professionals. In order to validate the reliability, usability and installation complexity as shown in Table 3, a survey was conducted, and 85% of farmers determined that the system facilitates monitoring and obtaining values of edaphoclimatic parameters. In addition, 72% of researchers believe that the information collected is reliable.

Table 3. Results of the survey of researchers

Factor	Not suitable at all		Not so suitable		Something suitable		Very suitable		Extremely suitable		Users
Reliability	0	0%	0	0%	0	0%	2	33%	4	67%	6
Utility	0	0%	0	0%	0	0%	1	17%	5	83%	6
Installation complexity	0	0%	0	0%	0	0%	2	33%	4	67%	6
Median	0	0%	0	0%	0	0%	3	28%	3	72%	6

Another fact that was considered in this evaluation is the cost of implementing the hardware. Table 4 presents the average cost of the hardware used in the system to cover one hectare (ha) of crop, thus determining that the project is feasible to work with several hectares.

Table 4. Hardware costs

Sensor name	Module scope	Quantity device	Cost per unit	Cost per one ha
Arduino mega 2560	Depending on the module	9	$ 20,00	$ 180,00
Rain sensor	For an area of 9 mts^2	9	$ 2,00	$ 18,00
Ultrasonic sensor	Surface reach of 2 mts^2	9	$ 3,50	$ 31,50
Humidity sensor (solids)	For an area of 9 mts^2	9	$ 3,00	$ 27,00
Ambient temperature sensor	For an area of 9 mts^2	9	$ 2,00	$ 18,00
Wi-Fi module ESP8266	10 mts^2	9	$ 10,99	$ 98,91
Router Wireless N Wifi Linsksys E2500 4 Internal antennas	For one hectare	5	$ 80,00	$ 400,00
Total		**59**	**$441,49**	**$773,41**

This kind of research is useful in agriculture as it allows to keep control of the most important chemical properties such as detecting levels of soil salinity. Several authors suggest that from a conductivity of 3.0 dS/m, the yields start to decrease and for every unit of electrical conductivity it increases 12% [20]. Salinity is a component that should be properly handle since the detrimental effects vary according to the vegetative growth cycle, being the early stages the most affected ones but the damage is maintained until harvest [21, 22]. So, with the proposed system and if the earlier state of salinity is known, important actions can be taken.

The pH is an important indicator since when it is high in rice cultivation, it can lead to increased accumulation of toxic elements such as Fe+2, and decreased absorption of potassium, calcium, and magnesium. Also by precipitation, it decreases availability of manganese and zinc [23]. This causes decreased performance and profitability of the crop. However, these authors suggest that the absorption of phosphorus and copper are not affected by the influence of this specific parameter.

The results achieved are shown in Table 5, and they indicate that this system is a tool with high applicability, because the difference compared with lab results regarding the pH was 0.2, which is about an error of about 3%. The electrical conductivity also expresses an error of 3%.

The present authors successfully developed an automated control system for the quality of the soil environment which optimizes the productive system of rice culti-vation. This investigation is extremely important in Ecuador, where there is a serious problem with the degradation of agricultural soils, especially those for the cultivation of this specific grain.

Table 5. Parameters

Variable	Real value (Measuring from professional laboratory equipment)	Value obtained with the Arduino system	% of mistake
pH	6.8	6.6	3
Electric conductivity	0.33 dS/m	0.34 dS/m	3
Water layer meter	10 cm	11 cm	1.11
Rain sensor	s/m	s/m	0
Temperature and humidity of the environment	31 °C, 62% humidity	30.5 °C, 60% humidity	1.13 1.6
Soil moisture	50% Saturate	50% Saturate	0

Using the obtained data, corrections of the pH can be planned in order to ensure greater availability of nutrients. It can also give clues to the appearance of sodicity which leads to the destruction of the structure and based on that, the user can take early action [24]. Furthermore, measuring the water layer, a maintenance plan can be achieved based on adequate levels of water resources for the plantation. Lower or higher levels can be detrimental for the crop.

With humidity, rain, and temperature sensors, the user can monitor the possible incidence of pests and diseases and take preventive actions when critical levels are about to be reached. Advances in science and technology have made it possible to integrate a large number of these instruments to be used for this purpose such as sound or ultrasonic sensors, among others. This optimizes the application of agrochemicals which leads to reduce production costs and obtain healthier foods, which is the main requirement nowadays in agriculture.

Soil moisture measurement allows irrigation planning and reflects the different energy states in which water is retained. However, this study was not very useful for this parameter because the rice cultivation usually has a water layer that varies from 10 to 20 cm.

The soil of the rice crop where the sensors were tested has optimal conditions to achieve high yields according to the results obtained by the laboratory and compared with the Arduino system.

This research is of great impact on the rice sector of the country since the majority of rice producers have limited resources, implementation of this low-cost system could improve the productivity and living standards of small farmers.

5 Conclusion and Future Work

The designed system includes an Arduino microcontroller and provides a fairly complete monitoring station where soil and environmental information are integrated in real-time, this facilitates the work of producers as they can make timely decisions through reliable data analysis. The reliability of the data will depend on the calibration of the sensors, so it is important to have this process standardized and to keep a preventive maintenance plan for them.

In addition, it provides a framework for the replication and updating of a low-cost custom platform for all components, it allows the visualization of applications where many sensors are required and must of them would be located in places where they cannot be easily recovered.

As an improvement to the proposed system, recommendations modules using diffuse rules can be included in order to facilitate the prevention of damage caused by soil salinity or sodicity, according to established parameters through the generation of alerts for the user. With this information, we will proceed to recommend processes that actually prevent the negative effects that the crop can experiment.

References

1. Corporacion Financiera Nacional: FICHA SECTORIAL : Arroz (2018)
2. Proaño Ramírez, G.A., Vega Jaramillo, F.Y.: Gasto en el consumo de cereales y derivados frente al índice de precios del arroz en el Ecuador, 2009 – 2014. Espacios, 38 (2017)
3. Viteri Viteri, G.I., Edison Zambrano, C.: Comercialización de arroz en Ecuador: Análisis de la evolución de precios en el eslabón productor-consumidor. Cienc. y Tecnol. 9, 11 (2017)
4. Ray, D.K., Gerber, J.S., MacDonald, G.K., West, P.C.: Climate variation explains a third of global crop yield variability. Nat. Commun. 6, 5989 (2015)
5. Mondal, M.S., et al.: Simulating yield response of rice to salinity stress with the AquaCrop model. Environ. Sci. Process. Impacts 17, 1118–1126 (2015)
6. Quevedo Amaya, Y.M., Beltrán Medina, J.I., Barragán Quijano, E.: Identification of climatic and physiological variables associated with rice (Oryza sativa L.) yield under tropical conditions. Rev. Fac. Nac. Agron. Medellín 72, 8699–8706 (2019)
7. Mosleh, M., Hassan, Q., Chowdhury, E.: Application of remote sensors in mapping rice area and forecasting its production: a review. Sensors 15, 769–791 (2015)
8. Valverde-Arias, O., Garrido, A., Valencia, J.L., Tarquis, A.M.: Using geographical information system to generate a drought risk map for rice cultivation: case study in Babahoyo canton (Ecuador). Biosyst. Eng. 168, 26–41 (2018)
9. Sakthipriya, N.: An effective method for crop monitoring using wireless sensor network. Middle East J. Sci. Res. 20, 1127–1132 (2014)
10. Masriwilaga, A.A., Munadi, R., Rahmat, B.: Wireless Sensor Network for Monitoring Rice Crop Growth. 5, 47–52 (2018)
11. Spinelli, G.M., Gottesman, Z.L.: A low-cost Arduino-based datalogger with cellular modem and FTP communication for irrigation water use monitoring to enable access to CropManage. HardwareX 6, e00066 (2019)
12. Li, Y., Zhang, Y.F., Wu, C.H., Wang, J.F.: Analysis of black soil environment based on Arduino. In: IOP Conference Series Earth and Environmental Science, vol. 67, p. 012008 (2017)
13. Singh, P., Saikia, S.: Arduino-based smart irrigation using water flow sensor, soil moisture sensor, temperature sensor and ESP8266 WiFi module. In: IEEE Region 10 Humanitarian Technology Conference 2016, R10-HTC 2016 - Proceedings (2017)

14. Li, Y., Zhang, Y.-F., Wu, C.-H., Wang, J.-F.: The application of data acquisition system of rice planting environment based on the Arduino and LabVIEW. J. Anhui Agric. Sci. **12**, 65 (2017)

15. Fajar, M., Halid, A., Arfandy, H., Munir, A.: Development of a low cost wireless sensor network for a real time paddy field monitoring system. Int. J. u- e- Serv. Sci. Technol. **9**, 397–408 (2016)

16. Arduino: Arduino Control-Structure If. https://www.arduino.cc/reference/en/language/structure/control-structure/if/ (2019)

17. Gui, T., Tk, B.: Python interface to Tcl/Tk. https://docs.python.org/2/library/tkinter.html (2016)

18. Mico, O.M., Santos, P.B.M., Caldo, R.B.: Web-based smart farm data monitoring system : a prototype. 3, 85–96 (2016)

19. Bitella, G., Rossi, R., Bochicchio, R., Perniola, M., Amato, M.: A novel low-cost open-hardware platform for monitoring soil water content and multiple soil-air-vegetation parameters. Sensors (Switzerland) **14**, 19639–19659 (2014)

20. Shereen, A., Mumtaz, S., Raza, S., Khan, M.A., Solangi, S.: Salinity effects on seedling growth and yield components of different inbred rice lines. Pakistan J. Bot. **37**, 131–139 (2005)

21. Huang, L., et al.: Interactive effects of pH, EC and nitrogen on yields and nutrient absorption of rice (Oryza sativa L.). Agric. Water Manag. **194**, 48–57 (2017)

22. Ghosh, B., Ali Md, N.: Response of rice under salinity stress: a review update. Rice Res. Open Access. **4**, 2–9 (2016)

23. Morales, C., Brzovic, F., Dascal, G., Aranibar, Z., Mora, L.: Measuring the economic value of land degradation/ desertification considering the effects of climate change. A study for Latin America and the Caribbean La valeur économique de la dégradation des terres/ désertification considérant les effets du change. Sci. Chang. planétaires/ Sécheresse, 23 (2012)

24. Ruiz-Sannchez, M., Muñoz-Hernndezndez, Y.: Manejo del agua de riego en el cultivo de arroz (Oryza sativa L.) por trasplante, su efecto en el rendimiento agrícola e industrial. Cultiv. Trop. **37**, 178–186 (2016)

Prediction of the Yield Per Hectare of the Crop of Chili Pepper (Capsicumchinense), by Means of a Simulation Model with GIS. A Case Study in Santo Domingo - San Jacinto Del Bua

Sergio Merchán-Benavides⃝, Katty Lagos-Ortiz⁽⊠⁾⃝,
Fanny Rodríguez-Jarama⃝, and Robin Vera-Chica⃝

Faculty of Agrarian Science, Universidad Agraria del Ecuador,
Av. 25 de Julio, Guayaquil, Ecuador
{smerchan, klagos, frodriguez}@uagraria.edu.ec,
robinvl609@gmail.com

Abstract. The present investigation refers to the application of a model of prediction of the yield per hectare of the pepper crop (Capsicumchinense), with the help of GIS tools. Results are delivered in maps which are easy to interpret. The main independent variables will be number, weight and fruit diameters. In addition, the Normalized Difference Vegetation Index (NDVI) will be included as a variable. This index will be extracted from an aerial image captured by a drone with multispectral camera. The aim is to observe the statistical correlation that exists between the Performance and the NDVI. Also a validation of the model is made comparing the estimated performance vs. the real performance. In case there is a deficit in production, corrective measures will be recommended. The methodology begins with the processing of the NDVI index. It will be treated and reclassified. Later regression will be applied in the ArcGis software. The results show that the prediction achieved a visual similarity which is very close to reality, offering ranges of (4125 to 580 kg/Ha) Estimated yield (3594 to 694 kg/Ha) Real yield and a difference of (1039 to −353 Kh/Ha); the R2 in general gave as a result 0.9 in the multivariate regression; the exponential regression between the NDVI and the real yield gave R2 of 0.068, so there is a linear dispersion of data. In general the prediction was very close to reality, and it was very similar in visual terms between the resulting images.

Keywords: Chili pepper · NDVI · Prediction · Regression · Yield

1 Introduction

Crop yield prediction models are fundamental tools that allow to estimate production according to the agronomic management that is used in agricultural farms. This is done by interpreting available management hypotheses, understanding the ecosystem as a whole. These allow for technological, economic and environmental impact studies, in addition to evaluating productive strategies and crop yield forecasts. They are generally used for better understanding of the problems and anticipating the reality being investigated.

© Springer Nature Switzerland AG 2019
R. Valencia-García et al. (Eds.): CITI 2019, CCIS 1124, pp. 53–65, 2019.
https://doi.org/10.1007/978-3-030-34989-9_5

Geographic Information Systems (GIS) have become an effective tool for making important decisions to improve production. This is known as "Precision Agriculture", which is gaining a lot of strength within the agricultural context. Its multiple applications have led to better decision-making that leads to the solution of many problems that arise in agriculture. For this, it is recommended the application of techniques that help to develop research on the estimation in the production of crops, predicting in some way the possible amount (kg/ha).

An orthomosaic represents a set of images, which unite to form a continuous mosaic dataset. Its main benefit is that the geometric distortion is corrected and there is a better balance of colors, which are also orthorectified [1]. He assures [2] that orthomosaics are indispensable when it comes to processing digital terrain models. If only common images were used, the accuracy, range, and quality of the image would not be valid for GIS work.

The use of Vegetation Indices (IVs) is very effective for the diagnosis of the state of a given vegetation. Thanks to the use of satellite images, certain study areas can be identified and classified by categories, which is very useful for any type of research aimed at Vegetation analysis. With the indices, plus the relationship that exists between the equation of yield (R2), it will be possible to obtain a prediction of estimated harvest, which together with the comparison of the real harvest, it will be able to validate the proposed model.

In recent years there have been attempts to include many predictive models for different crops, which have worked well, and have offered very similar results to the real ones.

The authors [3], at the Marengo Agricultural Center of the National University of Colombia, applied a simple simulation model of dry mass distribution in broccoli, and also cabbage, taking as variables samples of leaf area, dry weight, average temperature and hours of sun exposure. It was integrated by means of a deterministic multiplicative mathematical model.

In 2016 [4] the crop yield was estimated by simulations with the CROPWAT model, using the irrigation requirements and the deficit in banana yield when grown under safe conditions. All metrological data were used and entered into the above program. With this they obtained the yield variations in each treatment that was implemented depending on the degree of humidity used.

This research project is structured as follows. Section 2 presents a review of the literature about systems for the predictions of crop yields based on agroclimatic parameters and satellite images. Section 3 presents the methods and the methodology established for the investigation began with the recognition of the study area to know the location, shape, surface and perimeter, and later it would be treated in a CAD vector modeling software. Sections 4 and 5 presents the analysis of the results obtained in the investigation. Finally, Sect. 6 presents our conclusions and depicts future directions to design new projects.

2 Related Works

Nowadays the use of GIS (Geographical Information Systems) for multiple investigations and even for the prediction of crop yields is common in many countries. Inifap [5] is a Mexican company that specializes in crop predictions for different crops such as corn, sorghum, wheat, barley, soybean, rice, chili, among others, through the application of simple models. These models are based on agroclimatic parameters, physiological behaviors, and mainly the use of satellite images.

The authors [6] made a crop prediction for cereal, barley and wheat crops. They used as independent variables the index (NDVI), extracted from satellite images, rainfall data, land and air surface temperature data, surface surveys and yields for the different crops. The methodology used was the interpolation of rainfall data by Thinsen's polygons, interpolation with the inverse of the potential distance factor using a digital terrain model. The results gave a variation of less than 7% with respect to real yields.

There are also other alternatives such as the one applied by Rivas, Ocampo and Carmona [7], their research being the basis on which this thesis will be developed. They demonstrated the feasibility of the crop prediction simulation model in wheat cultivation with the help of foliar area indexes (IAF), specifically the Normalized Difference Vegetation Index (NDVI), which is a very versatile index for vegetation assessment and cover change dynamics. This index has been studied and evaluated with a series of satellites for many years, changing its method of calculation with respect to the number and type of satellite bands [8].

The collection of samples was based on the number of spikes, grains per spike and an average was established, obtaining the weight of 1000 seeds. For the estimation of yield (R2), the relationship of these two parameters would result in a future estimate of production in kg/ha. To finish validating the model, a mapping of the real crop georeferenced with GPS was obtained and compared with the estimated crop. Its results show that there is a direct relationship between the prediction of yield and the NDVI index, with an estimation error of 12%, tending to overestimate low yields of 168 kg/Ha and underestimate yields above 4800 kg/Ha.

They also [9] carried out a precision Vermiculture project in which they used the NDVI index and field sampling of different variables such as number of buds, number of shoots, number of bunches, and pruning weight after harvest. A geostatistical process called "kriging" was used. The variogram turns out to be a very efficient tool to predict these values, and to map in a very practical way the yield that was obtained.

Its results show that there is a prediction with little variability in yields. In the case of Cabernet Sauvignon the prediction was 12.7 Tn/Ha and the real harvest was 11.6 Tn/Ha, which indicates that it is possible to use the prediction model, although having used a statistical multivariate regression the relation coefficients R and R2 provided low values. This does not mean that having a higher NDVI will always lead to more production, as some agroclimatic variables are needed to supplement the model.

3   Methods

This section shows the variables used, identifies the data sources and explains the methods adopted to achieve our aim.

3.1   Area of Study

This research was carried out in the province of Santo Domingo de los Tháchilas, in the rural parish of San Jacinto del Búa, geographical location 679736, 9984214 UTM projection, zone 17S, DATUM WGS84, due to the high production of chilli. This study was developed thanks to the help of companies such as ProAjí.

3.2   Data Used in the Study

In order to analyze the prediction of yield per hectare of the chilli crop (Capsicum-chinense) using a GIS simulation model, agronomic variables such as fruit weight, number of fruits, fruit diameter, NDVI index and yields were used. The same agronomic management was adopted for all the agricultural exploitation, which was carried out in the rural Parish San Jacinto del Búa, geographical location 679736, 9984214 UTM projection, zone 17S, datum WGS84. This area is highly productive of chilli peppers. The surface area of the farm is 4935 m^2, with 6666 chilli plants. For the purposes of the study, the statistical formula was used to calculate the sample size, which resulted in a sample of 164 plants. The study was carried out with samples of 4 m^2 and 8 plants per sample. In addition, the soil and climatic conditions of the crop were taken into account.

In addition, multivariate regression was used, that is, when there is more than one independent variable, and only one dependent variable, the joint of many variables helps to minimize the error that may exist in the [10] and exponential model. When we try to explain or predict the variable Y with the help of a covariable X, there is the possibility that it is not linear, and instead forms a curve, but it is convenient to transform this exponential equation into a linear one, by means of a natural logarithm [11]. As for yield estimation, the independent variables helped to predict the dependent variable in this case yield (kg/ha), and in the correlation of the two main study variables, the NDVI index (Independent Variable), and yield (Dependent Variable).

The chilli is found in America and the central Andean region, in what is currently the south of Brazil and the east of Bolivia, also Western Paraguay and north-east of Argentina. There are approximately 30 different species of the genus Capsicum. Depending on the place where it grows it can benefit economically to places where the temperature goes from 10 °C and a maximum of 35 °C, with climates that go from 0 to 2700 msnm. The required rainfall should range from 600 to 1250 mm. The humidity should be between 65% and 50%. It requires deep and well-drained soils with a texture ranging from silty to clayey. The pH should be between 6.5 and 7.0 in order not to have problems with antagonisms and synergisms. The soil should be fertile, and the slope should not be less than 8% to avoid flooding, and especially fungal diseases.

In order to delimit and analyse the area, an image was taken by a drone with a multispectral camera, which helped to extract the spectral bands, and to calculate the

NDVI. It was also necessary to use GIS software to process the images to determine the NDVI. Microsoft Excel was essential for keeping the records and statistical analysis.

In the field, it was necessary to have templates and forms where the quantity, toll and size of fruits were recorded, therefore, it was also necessary to have scales, measuring tapes, containers and plastic covers. The use of a GPS will be of great importance to be able to geolocalize each sample and each weighing.

4 Methodology

The methodology established for the investigation began with the recognition of the study area to know the location, shape, surface and perimeter, and later it would be treated in a CAD vector modeling software. With the help of a Dron, the first resolution was obtained, to later obtain the spectral images, especially those of the near infrared band and visible red band, which are the corresponding bands for the NDVI calculation formula. After having the images with the bands already mentioned, the following formula is applied:

$$NDVI = \frac{\rho_{NIR} - \rho_{RED}}{\rho_{NIR} + \rho_{RED}} \tag{1}$$

Where ρ_{NIR} means *Banda Infrarrojo cercano* and ρ_{RED} means *Banda Rojo Visible*

Samples were taken every 15 days and one day before harvest. The study ended at the end of the first harvest or the first flowering cycle which is where the highest yield percentage exists.

The estimated and actual crop yield mapping was obtained from a database used in the GIS software where the sampling data were with the coordinates of the sampled sites. A geoprocessing tool called Kriging [12] was used to interpolate the data, and to have raster images for each variable, i.e. for the number, weight and diameters of fruits, as well as for the weight of the actual crop.

The next point is the statistical part, which consists of applying multivariant regression, to find the coefficients and apply the formula in ArcGIS. The result should be a raster map with the estimated yield or prediction yield.

Statistical analysis was based on 2 types of regression, exponential and multivariate. Multivariate regression was performed to obtain the estimated yield. The independent variables will help to predict the dependent variable, which in this case is the yield (kg/ha). The equation was the following:

$$Y = \alpha + \beta_1 X_1 + \beta_2 X_2 + \beta_3 X_3 + \beta_4 X_4 \tag{2}$$

Where Y is the dependent variable, X the independent variable, α the coefficient Alfa and β the coefficient Beta.

The exponential regression was based on the correlation of the two main variables: the NDVI index (Independent Variable), and the yield (Variable De-pending). For this, the adjusted exponential model was used, using the following formulas:

The relation between R and NDVI is the following exponential expression:

$$Y = \alpha . e^{\beta . X} \tag{3}$$

Where Y is the dependent variable, X the independent variable, α the coefficient Alfa and β the coefficient Beta.

5 Results

The drone flight took 11 min. Its trajectory had previously been traced, in which it was able to capture 21 hectares of surface. The drone flew at an approximate height of 159 m to the surface. The camera used was "CanonPo-werShotS110_5.2_4048 × 3048 (Red, Green,NIR)". The resolution according to their average ground sampling distance was 5.59 cm/2.20 in. 54 photographs were taken along the way, of which 48 were processed to form the Ortomosaic.

With the help of the multispectral camera, the infrared and visible red bands were extracted and used for the corresponding treatment using the NDVI formula. The next step was to provide it with a characteristic vegetation colouring. For the reclassification of the image the range obtained from the original NDVI image was taken into account, which is from 0.312775 to −0.061164. With the categorization of NDVI according to Garcia [13], it was improved and a new reclassification was obtained in which the plant coverage present in the area can be seen (Table 1).

Table 1. Reclassification Ranges

No	Range	Classification
1	−0.06–0.15	No vegetation soil
2	0.15–0.18	Light vegetation
3	0.18–0.23	Medium vegetation
4	0.23–0.26	Healthy vegetation
5	0.26–0.31	Vigorous vegetation

In ArcMAP with the ArcToolbox tool (where all modifications were made), 3D Analyst Tools were used. The Raster Reclassification option was selected, and the Reclassify option was executed. The next step was to introduce the values reflected in the table, and then the new raster was saved.

It is very important to transform the raster into a polygon. In Conversion Tools the Raster option was executed, and finally clicked on Raster to polygon. We proceeded to fill in the fields and the location where the Shapefile was saved. In the attributes table we proceeded to calculate areas and perimeters of the polygons.

Once the image was reclassified using GIS conversion tools, this was passed on to a polygon shapefile for the calculation of surfaces and perimeters (Table 2).

In order to validate the exponential model adjusted with the proposed formulas, comparisons between yield maps, harvest samples were carried out. A total of 4 harvests were obtained, being thus the same number of samplings, which were carried out

Table 2. Tables of perimeters and areas

No	Classification	Permeter (m)	Area (m^2)
1	No vegetation soil	7650.7	1922.2
2	Light vegetation	15191.5	1344.3
3	Medium vegetation	10304.2	1628.6
4	Healthy vegetation	2754.9	235.7
5	Vigorous vegetation	179.4	14.7

fortnightly. The distribution of the samples in the field was made in the form of a grid. Each plant had its own numbering and therefore its respective UTM coordinate, in order to be able to record the study variables in detail.

The records were summarized by harvest, to have the data sorted and to be able to process them, both with Excel and in the GIS software. The NDVI variable could be extracted quantitatively in each plant with the Geospatial tool Spatial Analyst, executing the extraction option and selecting the option Extract Multiple Values to Points. These values were included in the Excel sheets, where the values of the variables from other study are already present. The performance of each of the samples was calculated to obtain a reference in the statistical regression.

For the regression, the Excel tables of the sample records described above were used, but the spreadsheet was configured first. In Options, then in add-ins, the Go To button was selected. For this it was necessary to leave the tool tabs active for analysis, analysis - VBA, euro and solve. The statistical regressions, specifically the multivariate, were calculated with the help of the menu bar. In the data option, there is the Data Analysis tab. When it was executed, the Regression option was already found. Finally, the data corresponding to the variables "X" and "Y" were filled in (Fig. 1).

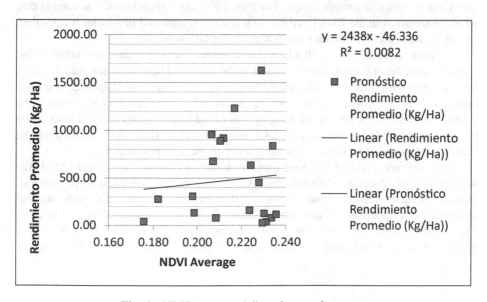

Fig. 1. NDVI Average Adjusted regression curve

The scatter diagrams corresponding to each independent variable with the dependent variable showed that there is a relationship between crop yield variables (Kg/ha) with number of fruits harvested and fruit weight. However, there is no relationship between the variables crop yield (Kg/ha), fruit diameter and average NDVI. Correlation coefficients for fruit weight and number of fruits harvested in relation to crop yield were close to 1. It should be noted that this trend was sustained in the 4 harvest periods of the crop (Fig. 2).

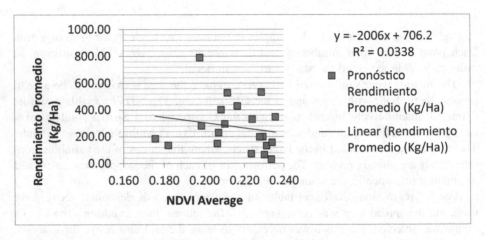

Fig. 2. NDVI Average Adjusted regression curve

In order to apply the formula of the multivariate regression that was performed for each harvest, it was necessary that the data of the field variables were transformed from quantitative values to a raster image. For this, a Kriging interpolation was carried out, which -together with the NDVI variable that is already captured in a raster image- then joined to make the performance prediction in the GIS software.

The process is the same in all 4 harvests. It began by entering the excel tables of the samples, with the option to add data that is in the file tab. Then select the Add XY data option. Once the points were observed, they were transformed to shapefile. The Data option was selected, then Export data was executed. Once the entity was saved, the points were ready to be processed. Kriging was found in the Spatial Analyst tools in the Interpolation tab. It is necessary to take into account as limit the boundary of the terrain, so that the geoprocessing is carried out in the 4 interpellations.

The estimated yield of the four harvests between February and April 2019 was 4125.62 to 580.52 kg/ha, while the actual yield measured and weighed during the four harvests in the months mentioned above is 3594.22 to 694.36 kg/ha. This indicates that at the time of comparison we can say that there was a deficit or prediction error of 13%. The statistical correlation between the two values shows a high relationship according to Pearson, which is reflected in a linear line. The final R2 coefficient was 0.95 (Fig. 3).

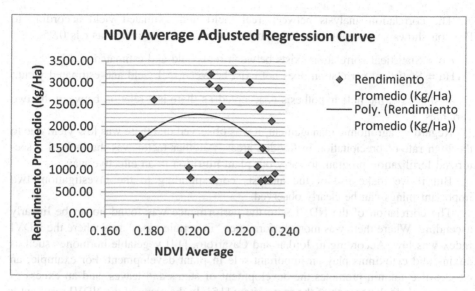

Fig. 3. Dispersion diagram R. Real vs NDVI

According to Pearson coefficient there is very low correlation between the two variables, as r is 0.24.

IIo = Statistical correlation exists between real performance and NDVI.

Ha = Statistical correlation does not exist between real performance and NDVI.

Nule hypothesis is rejected as there is no relation between the two variables (Fig. 4).

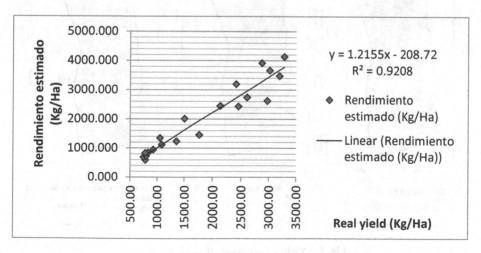

Fig. 4. Real yield (Kg/Ha) Adjusted regression curve

The correlation analysis between real yield and estimated yield according to Pearson shows very strong correlation between these two variables, as r is 0.95.

Ho = Statistical correlation exists between real yield and estimated yield.
Ha = Statistical correlation does not exist between real yield and estimated yield.

In this case, the nule hypothesis is accepted as there is a relation between the two variables.

Regarding agronomic management, it was observed that there was low yield due to the high rate of precipitation in flooded areas. Another factor was the lack of a sectorized fertilization program to carry out plant nutrition in an effective way.

But if we make use of the analysis corresponding to the investigation, two important things can be clearly observed.

The correlation of the NDVI with the performance was found not to be linearly ascending. Where there was more performance "in certain cases" was where the NDVI index was low. According to Jordan and Casarreto, [14] vegetable hormones such as auxins and cytokinins play an important role in plant development. For example, an excess of cytokinin promotes the development of stems and leaves, and an excess of auxins can help the growth of the root system [15]. In the plane of the NDVI resultant it can be observed that where there is more leaf area is where casually the yield was low (Fig. 5).

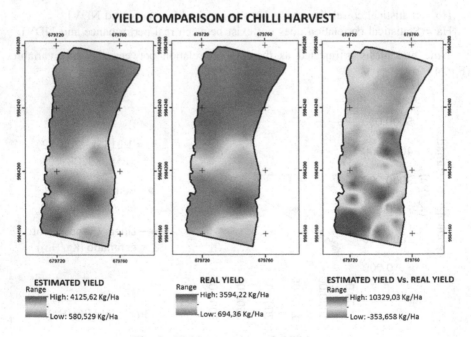

Fig. 5. Yield comparison of chilli harvest

6   Analysis

Considering the results of the investigation it was determined that the orthomosaic with which it was worked had a resolution of 5.59 cm per pixel. Comparing this with the work of Inifap [16], it is commented that in general the resolution of satellite images is 50 cm per pixel onwards. The reason why the resolution of the image should be of better quality is that the analysis of data per cm^2 will be more accurate. Satellite images are very useful for bigger works and are more general; on the other hand the images captured by a drone can be used for more specific works and their analysis is more exhaustive.

It must be made clear that so far there are few predictions that are linked to the cultivation of chilli peppers, since most of the predictions were made in crops such as corn, soya, wheat, barley, soybeans, rice and grapes among others, but almost all crops were of a single crop in its life cycle according to Inifap.

But predictive models are usually the same or very similar and each one adapts to its characteristics. I agree with Rivas, Ocampo and Carmona [7] that statistical regression is one of the best ways to make predictions, using parameters and variables of the crop itself, obtaining an estimation error of 12%. In the case of the present study, there was a margin of error between yield calculations of 13%, but it would be interesting to try other types of methodologies such as the one used by Román, Calle, and Delgado [6]. They used Thinsen polygons, interpolation with the inverse of the potential factor of distance. Their variation with respect to the real yield was 7%, using agroclimatic parameters and surveys among others.

With respect to the statistical part, almost all the models in which the NDVI was used as the study variable show a linear regression, that is, the higher the index, the higher the yield per hectare, which did not happen in the present research. But according to Martínez and Bordes [9], they show that it should not always be so for all crops, because their correlation coefficient R and R2 moved away from 1, however the prediction they made was still quite close to reality, even visually in the planes, there is too much similarity. They obtained predicted yield of 12.7 Tn/Ha and the real harvest was 11.6 Tn/Ha. The present investigation obtained values of 4125.62 to 580.52 kg/ha of prediction and 3594.22 to 694.36 kg/ha for the real yield.

7   Conclusions

In conclusion, the prediction of the yield per hectare of the crop of chilli (Capsicum chinense) turned out to be very close to reality.

The estimated yield or total prediction of the four harvests that were made between the months of February and April 2019 was 4125.62 to 580.52 kg/ha, while the real yield measured and weighed during the 4 harvests already mentioned is 3594.22 to 694.36 kg/ha, which indicates that at the time of making a comparison we can say that there was a deficit or prediction error of 13%. The statistical correlation between the two values, according to Pearson shows a strong relation, and the coefficient of final R2 was 0.95.

The index calculated thanks to multispectral images gave a range of 0.312775 to −0.061164, which according to the bibliography, as it is a short cycle crop in general the vegetation is in good condition. It was expected that there would be a linear regression between the NDVI and the actual yield, i.e. the hypothesis was that the higher the index the higher the yield, however on many occasions it turned out to be the opposite. This explains the low correlation and is reflected in the coefficient of R2: 0.24. This is attributed to the fact that the chilli plants, in their physiological process presented a greater development of the foliar area, but not an incentive to flowering that is later summarized in fructification.

Statistical regression is more accurate when more independent variables are included. In this case the variables weight of fruits, number of fruits and average diameter of fruits per plant, are more linked to production and yield, which improved their correlation in the statistical regression.

As stated at the beginning, the prediction turned out to be very close to reality. With this type of models we seek to have a more exact reference of what happens in our agricultural property, it is like making an X-ray that will help us make future decisions. Thus we can say that the yield planes obtained from prediction in comparison with the real yield planes turned out to be very similar to each other, which gives a clear idea of the areas where there will be greater yield and where there will be a low yield.

The low yields were due to excessive rainfall, which made drainage difficult in those areas and the plant did not flower as expected, it is estimated that in the next harvest this percentage will improve.

Future work is oriented to establish, based on the analysis of this research, the study of the prediction of yields in perennial crops, such as cocoa, mango, grape. This research also establishes a basis for a future study of prediction of yields with irrigation and fertilization management.

References

1. Escalante Torrado, J.O., Cáceres Jiménez, J.J., Porras Díaz, H.: Orthomosaics and digital elevation models generated from images taken with UAV systems. Tecnura **20**, 119–140 (2016)
2. Gutierrez, S., Hernandes, L.: Analisis de imagenes multiespectrales adquiridas con vehiculos aereos no tripulados (2018)
3. Carranza, C., Lanchero, O., Miranda, D., Salazar, M.R., Chaves, B.: Modelo simple de simulación de distribución de masa seca en brócoli (Brassica sp.) variedad Coronado y repollo (Brassica oleracea) híbrido Delus cultivados en la Sabana de Bogotá. Agron. Colomb. **26**, 23–31 (2008)
4. Toro-Trujillo, A.M., Arteaga-Ramírez, R., Vázquez-Peña, M.A., Ibáñez-Castillo, L.A.: Irrigation requirements and yield prediction of bananas growing through a simulation model in Urabá Antioqueño. Tecnol. y ciencias del agua. **7**, 105–122 (2016)
5. Inifap: Sistemas de prediccion de Cosecha de cultivos agricolas basados Modelos de Simulacion Dinamica II, Maiz, Ajo, Frijol, Cebada y Chile (2006)
6. Román, L.J., Calle, A., Delgado, J.A.: Modelos de Estimación de Cosechas de Cereal Basados en Imágenes de Satélite y Datos Meteorológicos. In: Teledetección y Desarrollo Regional. X Congreso de Teledetección, Cáceres, pp. 31–34 (2003)

7. Rivas, R., Ocampo, D., Carmona, F.: 2011, undefined: Wheat yield prediction model from NDVI: application in the context of precision agriculture. An. XV Simpósio Bras. Sensoriamento Remoto - SBSR, Curitiba, PR, Bras. INPE, vol. 30, pp. 584–590 (2011)
8. Bisquert, M., Sánchez, J., Caselles, V., Paz Andrade, M.I., Legido, J.L.: undefined: Los índices de vegetación como indicadores del riesgo de incendio con imágenes del sensor TERRA_MODIS (2010). http://aet.org.es
9. Martínez Casasnovas, J.A., Bordes Aymerich, X.: Viticultura de precisión: predicción de cosecha a partir de variables del cultivo e índices de vegetación. Rev. teledetección. **24**, 67–71 (2005)
10. Newbold, P., Carlson, W., Thorne, B.: Estadística para administración y economía. Pearson Educacion, London (2008)
11. Damodar, G., Dawn, P.: Regresion y Correlacion. En Econometria. - Buscar con Google. McGraw-Hill, New York (2010)
12. ArcMap: Cómo funciona Kriging, http://desktop.arcgis.com/es/arcmap/10.3/tools/3d-analyst-toolbox/how-kriging-works.htm
13. Melendres García, M.B.: Análisis de Series de Tiempo de los Índices de Vegetación EVI y NDVI a partir de Datos Imágenes del Sensor MODIS-TERRA (250 m) y el seguimiento de la producción y rendimiento de los cultivos agrícolas en la cuenca Chancay Lambayeque (2001 – 2014). Univ. Nac. Pedro Ruiz Gall. (2018)
14. Jordán, M., Casaretto, J., Squeo, F.A., Cardemil, L.: Hormonas y reguladores del crecimiento: auxinas, giberelinas y citocininas (2006)
15. Villatoro, E.: Efecto de la citoquinina (CPPU) sobre el cuaje y rendimiento de minisandía (Cytrullus lannatus, cucurbitaceae); estanzuela, zacapa (2014)
16. INIFAP: Sistemas de prediccion de Cosecha de cultivos agricolas basados Modelos de Simulacion Dinamica II, Maiz, Ajo, Frijol, Cebada y Chile (2006). http://www.inifap-nortecentro.gob.mx/files/proyectos/6586608a.pdf

A Brief Review of Big Data
in the Agriculture Domain

William Bazán-Vera$^{(\boxtimes)}$ ⓘ, Oscar Bermeo-Almeida ⓘ,
Mario Cardenas-Rodriguez ⓘ, and Enrique Ferruzola-Gómez ⓘ

Faculty of Agricultural Sciences, Agrarian University of Ecuador, Av. 25 de
Julio y Pio Jaramillo, P.O. Box 09-04-100, Guayaquil, Ecuador
{wbazan, obermeo, mcardenas, rcabezas,
eferruzola}@uagraria.edu.ec

Abstract. Agriculture is one of the most important sectors in the world. Agricultural productivity is important for a country's economy. Big Data technology has been successfully used to solve problems from several sectors such as health, finance, and energy for mention a few. In agriculture, Big data is being used for making better decisions and improving productivity. The increasing interest of Big Data technology in agriculture calls for a clear review. The objective of this review is to collect all relevant research on Big Data technology in agriculture to detect current research topics, benefits of Big Data in Agriculture, Big Data sources, algorithms, approaches, and techniques used. We have extracted 18 primary studies from scientific repositories published between 2017 and 2019. The results show that 67% of the studies are dominated by Indian and China research community. The results also show that half of the studies are focused on crop quality and productivity.

Keywords: Agriculture · Big data · Review

1 Introduction

As the world's population grows, farmers need to increase yields and lower costs. Also, consumers around the world demand high-quality food. Several sources of data are being used in the agricultural world to increase efficiency and at the same time decrease the impact on the environment. The integration of new technologies such as Big Data allows increasing the capacity to collect, exchange, and process data in order to make better decisions and improving the productivity, for example, in the optimization of inputs such as seeds, water, fertilizer, and pesticides.

Big data analysis is successfully being used in various domains, such as health [1, 2], energy [3, 4], finance [5, 6] to mention but a few. In the agriculture sector, Big Data is being applied for several objectives such as (1) increasing crop production, (2) making better farming decisions, (3) improving the quality of information about agricultural soils, (4) identifying anomalies, detecting fraud and improving performance of food supply chain, among others.

It is important to identify topics related to the agriculture sector that they have been already studied and addressed in Big Data, the main benefits of Big Data in Agriculture, Big Data sources, algorithms, approaches, and techniques used. In this sense,

© Springer Nature Switzerland AG 2019
R. Valencia-García et al. (Eds.): CITI 2019, CCIS 1124, pp. 66–77, 2019.
https://doi.org/10.1007/978-3-030-34989-9_6

we presented a review to identify relevant papers related to Big Data in agriculture. The review presented was performed by following the methodology proposed by Brereton et al. [7]. This information could help other researchers to identify possible areas for future research as well as farmers and companies to know how big data technology is been used in the agricultural sector.

The rest of this paper is organized as follows: Sect. 2 presents the research methodology which is divided into four parts: question formulation, search strategy, select primary studies and data extraction, while Sect. 3 presents the results of the review and a discussion. Finally, our conclusions are presented in Sect. 4.

2 Research Methodology

The review presented in this paper aims to detect relevant literature in the subject area. We followed the methodology proposed by Brereton et al. [7]. The process consists of three major phases: planning, execution, and result analysis. The first phase refers to planning the review, identifying its needs and defining its protocol which involves (a) research questions, (b) search strategy and (c) select primary studies. The second phase consists of the execution of the established plan extracting relevant information. Finally, the third phase consists of providing results and conclusions.

2.1 Question Formulation

In this section, we present the four research questions that guided us throughout the research and helped us meet the objectives of the review. The research questions that were addressed by our work are:

RQ1 What research topics have been addressed in current research on Big Data for agriculture?
RQ2 Which sources of big data are used for agriculture?
RQ3 What are the main benefits of the Big Data in the agriculture?
RQ4 Which are the main algorithms, approaches and techniques used?

2.2 Search Strategy

The search strategy is the main part of a review. Firstly, repositories must be identified wherein the search for primary studies would be carried out. In this review, we selected three digital libraries (IEEE Xplore Digital Library, ACM Digital Library, and Springer) and two Web sources (Google Scholar, and Web of science).

Secondly, a keyword-based search was performed. Therefore, we identified a set of keywords related to our research topic; and synonyms for the keywords and related concepts (see Table 1).

The search strings were built by combining the keywords presented in Table 2 with the connectors "AND" and "OR". It is important to mention that we considered the period from 2017 to 2019. Thus, the search chain that we use is the following:

Table 1. Keywords used during the review.

Area	Keywords	Related concepts
Agriculture	Agriculture, Agricultural	e-agriculture
		agribusiness
		farming
Big Data	Big Data	Big Data

((Agriculture OR e-agriculture OR Agribusiness OR Farming OR Agricultural) AND Big Data) Year: 2017–2019.

2.3 Select Primary Studies

Regarding the selection of primary studies, these were selected based on inclusion and exclusion criteria.

First, we selected only studies that included at least one keyword referring to the Agricultural, and the other one concerning to Big Data.

Second, we applied three exclusion criteria (1) papers written in other languages than English, (2) Master and doctoral dissertations, and (3) duplicated articles detected on web sources, which are also indexed in primary sources (IEEE, ACM, Springer).

The goal of this step was to ensure the study was related to the topic of the publication. When there was no certainty about this relation, the full-paper was downloaded and sections such as introduction and conclusions were reading.

Figure 1 shows that 78% of the primary studies were published in conferences, and 22% in journals. Specifically, 7 papers studying big data in Agriculture were published

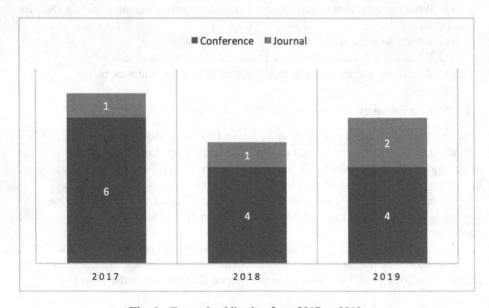

Fig. 1. Type of publication from 2017 to 2019.

in 2017 (six in conferences and one in a journal), 5 papers were published in 2018 (four in conferences and one in a journal), and until now 6 has been published in 2019 (four in conferences, and two in journals).

Figure 2 presents the geographical distribution of the selected papers. As can be seen, there is a great interest by universities or companies in India with 44% of the

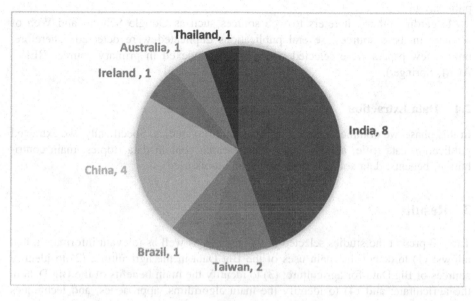

Fig. 2. Geographical distribution.

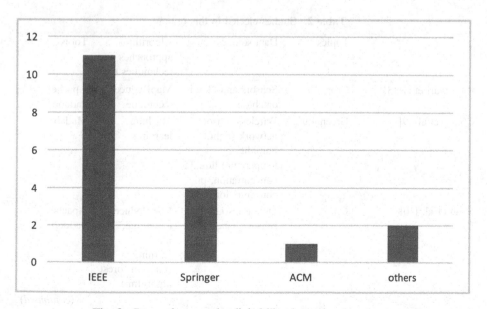

Fig. 3. Research papers by digital libraries and web sources.

papers published. Other countries with great interest in this area were China (22%) and Taiwan (11%). Meanwhile, the rest of the countries (Thailand, Australia, Ireland, and Brazil) had one paper published.

According to Fig. 3, IEEE is the publisher with the greatest number of articles published about Big Data in agriculture. Springer also has an important number of publications about this topic. Meanwhile, ACM digital library has only a few publications.

Regarding others, it refers to web sources such as Google Scholar and Web of science. In these sources, several publications duplicated were detected. Therefore, only a few papers were selected which are not indexed in primary sources (IEEE, ACM, Springer).

2.4 Data Extraction

In this phase, we obtained relevant information from studies. Specifically, we extracted publication data (title, authors, year) and research content data (topics, main contribution, benefits, data sources, approaches and tools used).

3 Results

Table 2 present the studies selected in this review, as well as relevant information that allows: (1) to detect the main uses of the Big Data in the agriculture; (2) to identify sources of Big Data for agriculture; (3) to identify the main benefits of the Big Data in the agriculture; and (4) to identify the main algorithms, approaches, and techniques used.

Table 2. Studies elected in this review.

	Topics	Data sources	Algorithms, approaches and techniques used	Tools
Rajeswari et al. [8]	Crop	Sensors and cloud database	MapReduce technique	Apache hadoop
Chang et al. [9]	Greenhouse	Wireless sensor network (light, humidity, temperature liquid concentration, ph concentration)	Machine learning	Matlab
Sahu et al. [10]	Crop	Online resource and sensors data	MapReduce technique, machine learning (random forest algorithm)	Apache hadoop

(continued)

Table 2. (*continued*)

	Topics	Data sources	Algorithms, approaches and techniques used	Tools
Tseng et al. [11]	Crop	IoT sensors	3D cluster correlation	XMPP, Python, MySQL server
Sharma et al. [12]	Crop	Historical data (crop pattern, yield monitoring, climate condition, etc.) Agricultural equipment's and sensor data (remote sensing devices, wireless sensors, drones, etc.) Social data Business, industries, and External Data (billing and forecast system, manufacturing departments, etc.)	MapReduce technique, machine learning (GWO_SVM)	Apache hadoop
Kumar and Nagar [13]	Farming decision making	Sensor data, social media, operational data, web service, spatial data	MapReduce technique	Pentaho BI, Apache hadoop
Alves and Cruvinel [14]	Soil	Agricultural tomographs	MapReduce technique	Apache hadoop, Hive, Pig, HBase, and Zookeeper
Bhosale et al. [15]	Crop	Electronic devices	Data analytics and machine learning (K-means, a priori, Naïve Bayes)	–
Li et al. [16]	Agricultural engineering machinery	Floor metadata (data of the agricultural machinery when performing agricultural operations)	MapReduce technique, CART (Category Regression Tree) analysis model	Apache hadoop, Spark

(*continued*)

Table 2. (*continued*)

	Topics	Data sources	Algorithms, approaches and techniques used	Tools
Sekhar et al. [17]	Productivity improvement	Meteorological dept about the atmosphere conditions, pesticide data and new seeds in the market. Pictures through cell phones Master and specialists' recommendations	MapReduce technique, machine learning (K-means)	Apache hadoop, Microsoft HDInsight, NoSQL, Hive, SQOOP
Shah et al. [18]	Crop	Open datasets and digital data available over the web and Internet	Machine learning	MongoDB, cassandra, Spark, GeoSpark, Shiny, Sparklyr
Ji et al. [19]	Food supply chain	Food consuming (Retailers, Suppliers, Government, Third-party data brokers, Customers) food logistic (government, transportation operators, individuals, third-party data providers)	Bayesian network and deduction graph model	–
Ngo et al. [20]	Agricultural data warehouse	User data, logs, sensor data or queries from Products module, such as web application, web portal or mobile app	Data mining	Cassandra, MongoDB, Hive
Chen and Gong [21]	Agricultural products	Mobile device data source, radiofrequency data source, sensor data source, databases store data	statistical analysis, data mining	Apache hadoop

(*continued*)

Table 2. (*continued*)

	Topics	Data sources	Algorithms, approaches and techniques used	Tools
Parvin et al. [22]	Food security	RFID and Wireless Sensors data, auto and semi-automated asset tracking data; warehousing and transportation communication data; GPS, GPRS and position location systems for vehicle and shipment tracking; Surveillance Systems for situation awareness; public communications related to goods and assets' local and international movement; containers and contents tracking systems; and vehicle and engineering tracking systems such as black-boxes on the heavy vehicles	Semantic annotation and XML profiling	–
Huang and Zhang [23]	Agricultural data	Sensors, videos, picture collection equipment (light, temperature, air humidity, carbon dioxide content, soil conductivity, photos, and video)	MapReduce technique	Apache hadoop, storm, cassandra
Chandra et al. [24]	Crop	Structured Data, Unstructured Data (Audio, text files, social media), Semi-Structured Data (data represented in XML file)	Data analytics, MapReduce technique	Apache hadoop, R

(*continued*)

Table 2. (*continued*)

	Topics	Data sources	Algorithms, approaches and techniques used	Tools
Kliangkhlao and Limsiroratana [25]	Agricultural market	Environmental Data Service Product Trading Data Warehouse Commodity Exchange Market Crude Oil Market, and Petroleum Price Service in Thailand Crop Exporting Trading Prices	Machine learning	–

3.1 Discussion

The results obtained from this review shows that several researches are focusing their efforts mainly on crop quality and productivity.

Regarding benefits of Big Data in agriculture, it has been applied with positive results. Some of its benefits are:

(1) To improve crop production with a reduction in the cost of fertilizer requirements keeping soil with health intact [8].

(2) To improve agricultural quality and make efficient decisions [9].

(3) To improve the productivity, growth, and quality of the plants [10].

(4) To Increase crop production and help analyze cultivation techniques of farmers [11].

(5) To Acquire precise information about the expected amount of rainfall, the moisture of soil and infer accurately whether it is a suitable time to sow the fresh seeds [12].

(6) More effective marketing, new revenue opportunities, better agriculture planning, improved farmer's production [13].

(7) To reconstruct the greatest number of agricultural soil tomographic images in the same time-frame. Improve the quality of information about agricultural soils [14].

(8) To increase the yield of their crops [15].

(9) To reduce maintenance time and maintenance costs during farm hours [16].

(10) To get an optimal decision in farming, crop recommendations, farming practices, pest prediction, forecast the Agri commodity prices ahead of the season [17].

(11) To improve the productivity in agricultural practices [18].

(12) To create transparency; identify anomalies, detect fraud and improve performance; Micro-segmentation to customize actions; find unknown patterns that occur in food network in a time-efficient and cost-effective manner; Innovate new business models, products, and services [19].

(13) Flexible schema; data integration from real agricultural multi datasets; data science and business intelligent support; high performance; high storage; security; governance and monitoring; consistency, availability and partition tolerant; cloud deployment [20].
(14) To achieve efficient docking of agricultural production and sales, and further to meet the growing high-quality demand of consumers [21].
(15) To avoid food loss in order to ensure food security [22].
(16) To improve the crop's quality and production ability [23].
(17) To increase crop productivity [24].
(18) To understand the market factors that shape and drive the Agricultural Market [25].

Considering the analysis performed, the sources of big data used by the different authors are historical data (cropping pattern, soil test, field monitoring, yield monitoring, and climate condition); agricultural equipment's and sensor data (remote sensing devices, GPS based receiver, variable-rate fertilizers, temperature sensor); social and Web-based data (farmer and customers feedback, social media group web pages, data from search engines); streamed data (data from crop monitoring, mapping, wireless sensors, drones, security surveillance); and Business, industries, and External Data (forecast system, manufacturing departments, and other agricultural)

All the 18 studies analyze big data according to some techniques or combination of methods. Machine Learning is the approach more used. MapReduce technique is widely used to process large data sets.

4 Conclusions and Future Work

The goals of this study were to detect the main uses of the Big Data in the agriculture, to identify sources of Big Data for agriculture; to identify the main benefits of the Big Data in the agriculture; and to identify the main algorithms, approaches, and techniques used. We obtained and analyzed 18 primary studies from scientific databases and web sources.

The review papers on Big Data in agriculture is very dominated by Indian and China research community. We attribute this to the fact that agriculture plays a vital role in the Indian and china economy.

This review demonstrates that Big Data plays an important role in the agricultural sector. A large amount of data can be obtained from sensors, drones, cameras, mobile applications for mention a few. The analysis of this Big Data enables farmers and companies to extract value from it, making better decisions, and improving their productivity. For analysis of Big Data, there are several frameworks supporting effective parallel processing in distributed modes. Apache Hadoop has been the most popular framework for big data processing. It provides a parallel computation technique known as MapReduce.

As future work, we plan to extend this work by including a wider set of repositories such as the Wiley Online Library and ScienceDirect (Elsevier). Furthermore, we are interested to carry out a more specialized analysis of frameworks and programming languages for Big Data analysis to provide more detailed information about the features, benefits, and limitations. Finally, we plan to identify the Big Data "V" dimensions in general agricultural research areas.

References

1. Elhoseny, M., Abdelaziz, A., Salama, A.S., Riad, A.M., Muhammad, K., Sangaiah, A.K.: A hybrid model of Internet of Things and cloud computing to manage big data in health services applications. Futur. Gener. Comput. Syst. **86**, 1383–1394 (2018). https://doi.org/10.1016/J.FUTURE.2018.03.005
2. Wang, Y., Kung, L., Wang, W.Y.C., Cegielski, C.G.: An integrated big data analytics-enabled transformation model: application to health care. Inf. Manag. **55**, 64–79 (2018). https://doi.org/10.1016/J.IM.2017.04.001
3. Liang, Y.C., Lu, X., Li, W.D., Wang, S.: Cyber physical system and big data enabled energy efficient machining optimisation. J. Clean. Prod. **187**, 46–62 (2018). https://doi.org/10.1016/J.JCLEPRO.2018.03.149
4. Zhang, Y., Ma, S., Yang, H., Lv, J., Liu, Y.: A big data driven analytical framework for energy-intensive manufacturing industries. J. Clean. Prod. **197**, 57–72 (2018). https://doi.org/10.1016/J.JCLEPRO.2018.06.170
5. Begenau, J., Farboodi, M., Veldkamp, L.: Big data in finance and the growth of large firms. J Monet. Econ. **97**, 71–87 (2018). https://doi.org/10.1016/J.JMONECO.2018.05.013
6. Müller, O., Fay, M., vom Brocke, J.: The effect of big data and analytics on firm performance: an econometric analysis considering industry characteristics. J. Manag. Inf. Syst. **35**, 488–509 (2018). https://doi.org/10.1080/07421222.2018.1451955
7. Brereton, P., Kitchenham, B.A., Budgen, D., Turner, M., Khalil, M.: Lessons from applying the systematic literature review process within the software engineering domain. J. Syst. Softw. **80**, 571–583 (2007). https://doi.org/10.1016/j.jss.2006.07.009
8. Rajeswari, S., Suthendran, K., Rajakumar, K.: A smart agricultural model by integrating IoT, mobile and cloud-based big data analytics. In: 2017 International Conference on Intelligent Computing and Control (I2C2), pp 1–5. IEEE (2017)
9. Chang, H.-Y., Wang, J.-J., Lin, C.-Y., Chen, C.-H.: An agricultural data gathering platform based on Internet of Things and big data. In: 2018 International Symposium on Computer, Consumer and Control (IS3C), pp. 302–305. IEEE (2018)
10. Sahu, S., Chawla, M., Khare, N.: An efficient analysis of crop yield prediction using Hadoop framework based on random forest approach. In: 2017 International Conference on Computing, Communication and Automation (ICCCA), pp. 53–57. IEEE (2017)
11. Tseng, F.-H., Cho, H.-H., Wu, H.-T.: Applying big data for intelligent agriculture-based crop selection analysis. IEEE Access **7**, 116965–116974 (2019). https://doi.org/10.1109/ACCESS.2019.2935564
12. Sharma, S., Rathee, G., Saini, H.: Big data analytics for crop prediction mode using optimization technique. In: 2018 Fifth International Conference on Parallel, Distributed and Grid Computing (PDGC), pp. 760–764. IEEE (2018)
13. Kumar, M., Nagar, M.: Big data analytics in agriculture and distribution channel. In: 2017 International Conference on Computing Methodologies and Communication (ICCMC), pp. 384–387. IEEE (2017)
14. Alves, G.M., Cruvinel, P.E.: Big data infrastructure for agricultural tomographic images reconstruction. In: 2018 IEEE 12th International Conference on Semantic Computing (ICSC), pp. 346–351. IEEE (2018)

15. Bhosale, S.V., Thombare, R.A., Dhemey, P.G., Chaudhari, A.N.: Crop yield prediction using data analytics and hybrid approach. In: 2018 Fourth International Conference on Computing Communication Control and Automation (ICCUBEA), pp. 1–5. IEEE (2018)

16. Li, D., Zheng, Y., Zhao, W.: Fault analysis system for agricultural machinery based on big data. IEEE Access 7, 99136–99151 (2019). https://doi.org/10.1109/ACCESS.2019.2928973

17. Sekhar, C.C., Sekhar, C.: Productivity improvement in agriculture sector using big data tools. In: 2017 International Conference on Big Data Analytics and Computational Intelligence (ICBDAC), pp. 169–172. IEEE (2017)

18. Shah, P., Hiremath, D., Chaudhary, S.: Towards development of spark based agricultural information system including geo-spatial data. In: 2017 IEEE International Conference on Big Data (Big Data), pp. 3476–3481. IEEE (2017)

19. Ji, G., Hu, L., Tan, K.H.: A study on decision-making of food supply chain based on big data. J. Syst. Sci. Syst. Eng. 26, 183–198 (2017). https://doi.org/10.1007/s11518-016-5320-6

20. Ngo, V.M., Le-Khac, N.-A., Kechadi, M.-T.: Designing and implementing data warehouse for agricultural big data. In: Chen, K., Seshadri, S., Zhang, L.-J. (eds.) BIGDATA 2019. LNCS, vol. 11514, pp. 1–17. Springer, Cham (2019). https://doi.org/10.1007/978-3-030-23551-2_1

21. Chen, X., Gong, J.: Research on precision marketing model of Beijing agricultural products under big data environment. In: Xhafa, F., Patnaik, S., Tavana, M. (eds.) IISA 2018. AISC, vol. 885, pp. 805–812. Springer, Cham (2019). https://doi.org/10.1007/978-3-030-02804-6_105

22. Parvin, S., et al.: Smart food security system using IoT and big data analytics. Advances in Intelligent Systems and Computing, vol. 800, pp. 253–258. Springer, Cham (2019). https://doi.org/10.1007/978-3-030-14070-0_35

23. Huang, J., Zhang, L.: The big data processing platform for intelligent agriculture. In: AIP Conference Proceedings, p. 20033. AIP Publishing LLC (2017)

24. Chandra Sekhar, Ch., Uday Kumar, J., Kishor Kumar, B., Sekhar, Ch.: Effective use of big data analytics in crop planning to increase agriculture production in India. Int. J. Adv. Sci. Technol. 113, 31–40 (2018)

25. Kliangkhlao, M., Limsiroratana, S.: Towards the idea of agricultural market understanding for automatic event detection. In: Proceedings of the 2019 8th International Conference on Software and Computer Applications - ICSCA 2019, pp. 81–86. ACM Press, New York, USA (2019)

Knowledge-based Systems and Pattern Recognition

Mining Twitter for Measuring Social Perception Towards Diabetes and Obesity in Central America

José Medina-Moreira[1] , José Antonio García-Díaz[2(✉)] ,
Oscar Apolinardo-Arzube[1] , Harry Luna-Aveiga[1] , and Rafael
Valencia-García[2]

[1] Facultad de Ciencias Matemáticas y Físicas, Universidad de Guayaquil,
Cdla. Universitaria Salvador Allende, Guayaquil 090514, Ecuador
{jose.medinamo,oscar.apolinarioa,harry.lunaa}@ug.edu.ec
[2] Facultad de Informática, Universidad de Murcia,
Campus de Espinardo, 30100 Murcia, Spain
{joseantonio.garcia8,valencia}@um.es

Abstract. For a long time, diabetes and obesity have been considered a menace only in developed countries. Nevertheless, the proliferation of unhealthy habits, such as fast-food chains and sedentary lifestyles, have caused diabetes and obesity to spread worldwide causing many and costly complications. Since citizens use of the Internet to search, learn, and share their daily personal experiences, the social networks have become popular data-sources that facilitate a deeper understanding of public health concerns. However, the exploitation of this data requires labelled resources and examples; however, as far as our knowledge, these resources do not exist in Spanish. Consequently, (1) we compile a balanced multi-class corpus with tweets regarding diabetes and obesity written in Spanish in Central-America; and, (2) we use the aforementioned corpus to train and test a machine-learning classifier capable of determining whether the texts related to diabetes or obesity are positive, negative, or neutral. The experimental results show that the best result was obtained through the Bag of Words model with an accuracy of 84.30% with the LIBLinear library. As a final contribution, the compiled corpus is released.

Keywords: Diabetes · Obesity · Opinion mining · Bag of words · Natural language processing

1 Introduction

According to the World Health Organization (WHO)[1], the diabetes is a *chronic disease that occurs either when the pancreas does not produce enough insulin or when the body cannot effectively use the insulin it produces.* Insulin is a hormone

---

[1] https://www.who.int/news-room/fact-sheets/detail/diabetes.

© Springer Nature Switzerland AG 2019
R. Valencia-García et al. (Eds.): CITI 2019, CCIS 1124, pp. 81–94, 2019.
https://doi.org/10.1007/978-3-030-34989-9_7

that regulates blood sugar. Over time, diabetes affects nerves, blood vessels, eyes and kidneys. Adults with diabetes are more likely to suffer heart attacks and, in severe cases, diabetes increases the risk of suffering foot ulcers, infections, blindness, and kidney failure. For a long time, diabetes and obesity have been considered problems only for developed countries, but, due the proliferation of unhealthy habits, diabetes and obesity are now considered a global disease [6].

In Ecuador diabetes has reached a prevalence of 1.7% in the population aged 10 to 59 [22]. This increase is mainly due to: (1) unhealthy eating; (2) physical inactivity; and (3) substance abuse, such as alcohol or cigarettes. Moreover, the prevalence of obesity is increasing in all age groups. It is especially serious that 30% of school-age children presents overweight and obesity, which constitutes a threat to public health.

To prevent diabetes and obesity, some activities related to a healthy diet and regular physical activity should be promoted. In this sense, that citizens know the health risks arising from these diseases is the first step in fighting them [25]. Mobile-apps and social networks have the potential to facilitate a deeper understanding of the public health threats of obesity and diabetes [2,17]. Twitter, Facebook, or Instagram among others social networks, have become a mean where users can share their experiences and knowledge. Therefore, social networks provide a data-source to infer what is happening around the world by analysing what individuals think and do. However, to conduct analysis of the social perception of society, examples and labelled corpora are needed. Despite the fact that there are some corpus available for the diabetes domain in English [27], as far as our knowledge there are no corpora available in Spanish. Consequently, (1) we compile a balanced multi-class corpus with tweets regarding diabetes and obesity written in Spanish; and, (2) we use the aforementioned corpus to train and test a machine-learning classifier capable of determining whether the texts related to diabetes or obesity are positive, negative, or neutral.

The remainder of the paper is structured as follows. Section 2 presents background information concerning Opinion Mining and previous works related to diabetes and obesity. Materials and methods used in this experiment are described in Sect. 3. Section 4 describes the results, and, finally, Sect. 5 summarises the conclusions of this research and suggests some lines of further work.

2   Background Information

Natural Language Processing (NLP) is the subfield of Artificial Intelligence (AI) that aims to facilitate the interaction between computers and humans. Opinion Mining (OM), also known as Sentiment Analysis, is the NLP task that aims to detect the attitude of the users towards a specific topic. Despite OM is a recent research field (the first studies date from the early 2000s [23]), it has nowadays multiple applications, such as infodemiology [1,12], customer satisfaction [19], satire-detection [5,28], or the stock-market [8,13,29] to name a few.

According to the degree of specificity, OM can be classified as (1) document level [20], (2) sentence level [3], or (3) aspect level [30]. Document level classification consists in assigning a unique polarity to the document. Document level is adequate due to its simplicity and its accuracy when the goal is to measure the global perception towards a specific topic without going into details. In the real world, however, people can express different and even contradictory ideas about a topic. In this sense, sentence level and aspect level provides more understanding of the topic. Sentence level classification assigns an individual sentiment to each sentence in the text. Although sentence level classification is more detailed than document level classification, it requires manual work in order to extract fine-grained conclusions. In an aspect level classification, the topic under study is divided into aspects (or features) and the sentiments are analysed individually towards each of these aspects. For example, the attitude towards a mobile phone can vary when users are commenting the price, the battery duration, or the reliability. However, the identification and extraction of the features may require of the use of complex techniques such as ontologies [21,24].

According to the techniques, OM can be classified into two major groups. On the one hand, the semantic orientation approach (SO), which makes use of general-purpose sentiment lexicons. In this sense, SentiWordNet [4] is a popular lexicon widely used in the research community. It is based on WordNet [18] and extends it by including three scores corresponding to its positivity, negativity and objectivity. Nevertheless, the SO approach has the downside that is not effective in certain domains, such as satire identification, mainly due to the figurative language or negative clauses, which can modify the meaning of the utterances. On the other hand, the machine learning approach, relies in the construction of a machine-learning classifier capable to infer hidden patterns from the texts.

Machine-learning approaches require that the texts are encoded as numbers so computers can work with them. The Bag of Words (BoW) is a statistical-model, very popular in several NLP tasks, which consists into count the frequency of the words that compose a text. The downsides of the BoW model is that (1) it obviates the context of each word, that is, their neighbour words, and (2) it is not language independent, so it can not trivially be used in other languages without having available a large amount of training data. To solve these issues, some authors have proposed the addition of bigrams and trigrams in order to increase the context of the words [33]. Other authors, however, have proposed the usage of arbitrary sequences of characters, known as char-grams, instead of unigrams. The main idea behind this approach is that char-grams are stronger against grammatical errors. Finally, some authors have used linguistic tools to extract the frequency of some relevant psycho-logical linguistic features.

Machine-learning methods require a collection of labelled examples to train its models. Usually, labelled examples are expensive to obtain and they are domain-dependent. Concerning the diabetes and obesity domain, Salas-Zarate et al. [27] conducted an aspect-level opinion mining experiment in order to detect positive, negative and neutral utterances concerning diabetes and obesity. George Shaw, Jr. [31] proposed a framework based on opinion mining and topic modelling to discover negative topics about obesity, diet, diabetes, and exercise. However, both studies [27, 31] are focused in the English language. Consequently, we decided to compile a corpus in Spanish by ourselves.

3   Materials and Methods

Twitter, a popular micro-blogging platform, was selected as data-source. Twitter is widely used in the research community for conducting OM research [16]. Its popularity is mainly due to the length-restriction of the posts, called tweets, which makes the users to be focused in only one topic.

To compile tweets related to diabetes and obesity we use the standard Twitter Search API[2]. This API allows to obtain tweets no older than seven days from a url-encoded search query. This API also supports geo-coding, returning tweets by users located within a given radius of the given latitude/longitude. Due to the time restriction, we daily compile new tweets in central America with the following keywords or hashtags: *diabetes*, *obesidad* (obesity), *hipoglucemia* (hypoglycaemia), *hiperglucemia* (hyperglycemia), and *insulina* (insulin). Figure 1 contains an example of one tweet compiled.

Fig. 1. An example of one tweet of the corpus. In English: *connection that is created with food leads to addictions and obesity*

Once the tweets were compiled, we proceed with the classification stage. In some cases, this stage can be performed automatically by applying distant supervision, which consist in assigning a specific sentiment based on clues in the text, such as the presence of emoticons [9, 32]. However, some linguistic phenomena, such as figurative language, irony, or sarcasm, hindered this approach. Therefore, we relied in a manual classification with the help of 30 volunteers from the University of Guayaquil in Ecuador. The volunteers were provided with a self-developed tool that randomly selects unrated tweets and allow the volunteers to assign to each tweet only one of the followings values: *very-positive*, *positive*, *neutral*, *negative*, *very-negative*, and *out-of-domain*. The classification stage was monitored daily to ensure that the number of classifications was uniform among time and that all the volunteers contributed equally in order to avoid bias.

---

[2] https://developer.twitter.com/en/docs/tweets/search/overview/standard.

At the end of this process, volunteers had classified a total of 273 000 tweets. It is important to remark that each tweet was rated individually by different volunteers, so it was easy to discard tweets with contradictory ratings. By average, each tweet was rated by 17 volunteers, with a standard deviation of 1,1737.

In the bibliography, some researchers argue that neutral statements do not provide relevant information in order to build a machine-learning classifier because (1) binary problems are easier to solve than multi-class problems, and because (2) there is usually a lack of neutral documents [15]. Other researches, however, argue that the large amount of documents that contains only objective information without expressing any sentiment can not be omitted [23]. In our case, after a manual revision of the tweets, we decided to keep neutral tweets because we have a considerable amount of them. In addition, *very-positive* and *positive* tweets as well as *very-negative* and *negative* tweets were merged because a high fine-grained separation was not needed. At the end of the classification stage, the compus was composed by 1000 *positive* tweets, 1000 *neutral* tweets and 1000 *negative* tweets.

Then, we proceeded with the normalisation stage, that consisted of (1) removing hyperlinks, (2) transforming texts into lowercase; and, (3) collapsing multiple-space and line-breaks into one single space.

The last step consisted in the extraction of the frequency of unigrams, bigrams and trigrams with the BoW model. The frequency of each gram was expressed with the Term Frequency - Inverse Document Frequency (TF-IDF) formula (see Eq. 1). The Term-Frequency was expressed using the normalised term frequency (see Eq. 2), per each feature, with the aim of preventing bias for longer or shorter documents.

$$TFIDF = TF * IDF \tag{1}$$

$$TF = number\_of\_occurrences/number\_of\_grams \tag{2}$$

$$IDF = \log_2 corpus\_size/documents\_with\_terms \tag{3}$$

To prevent the large number of features generated by the BoW model, which may cause sparsity, over-fitting models and requires more time and memory to train and to evaluate each the machine-learning classifier, we applied a cut-off filter to remove those grams that do not appear more than in the 1% of all the documents in the corpus. This value was set with a trial and error process.

4   Experiments

The experiments were executed under the WEKA platform [10]. The selected classifiers were, on the one hand, Random-Forest (RF), from the family of decision trees, and the LIBLinear (LL) library [7] from the family of Support Vector Machines (SVM). Algorithms based on decision trees have proven effectiveness conducting experiments with large number of features [14]. On the other hand, LIBLinear is an open source library for large-scale linear classification, specially designed to handle data large amounts of instances and features [11].

As we are dealing with a balanced multi-class classification problem, we use the weighted accuracy to compare the reliability of the machine-learning classifiers. The accuracy is defined as the ratio of the total of correct predictions to the total of input samples. In addition, precision (P), recall (R), and F1-Measure (F1) are also included in the results.

To assess how the machine-learning classifiers behave as the number of documents in the corpus increases, we decided to divide the corpus into smaller chunks. We began with a subset of 300 tweets (100 per class), and we continued adding 100 more tweets to each class, resulting in a second subset of 600 tweets (200 per class). We continued this process until we reach to 3000 tweets (1000 per class). It is worth noting that (1) each of these subsets is balanced, that is, each subset contains the same number of positive, neutral and negative tweets, and (2) the cut-off filter was applied proportionally to the number of documents of each subset.

The first experiment consisted into measure the reliability of unigrams (see Table 1), bigrams (see Table 2) and trigrams (see Table 3) in isolation. We can observe that the unigrams achieve its best result with an accuracy of 84.20% with LL and a corpus size of 1800 tweets whereas the worst result, 79.30%, is achieved with RF and a corpus size of 300 tweets. We can observe that no classifier beats the other in all corpus size and there are no bigger differences among them.

Table 1. Performance of the Bag of Words model with unigrams for Random-Forest (RF) and LibLINEAR (LL).

Size	P	R	F1	ACC	P	R	F1	ACC
	RF				LL			
300	79.40	79.30	79.30	79.30	82.70	82.70	82.70	82.70
600	81.90	81.50	81.50	81.50	79.50	79.50	79.50	79.50
900	82.20	81.90	81.90	81.90	82.20	82.10	82.10	82.10
1200	82.40	82.10	82.10	82.10	83.30	83.20	83.20	83.20
1500	82.70	82.50	82.60	82.50	84.10	83.90	84.00	83.90
1800	83.30	83.10	83.10	**83.10**	84.30	84.20	84.20	**84.20**
2100	82.10	81.90	81.90	81.90	82.50	82.30	82.40	82.30
2400	82.30	82.20	82.20	82.20	81.70	81.50	81.50	81.50
2700	81.00	80.80	80.80	80.80	80.30	80.10	80.10	80.10
3000	80.70	80.50	80.60	80.50	80.50	80.30	80.30	80.30

Bigrams (see Table 2) and trigrams (see Table 3) have less performance than unigrams. This lower performance indicates that bigrams and trigrams are less common that unigrams. However, the accuracy of the bigrams is reasonably high, achieving an accuracy of 75.30% using LL and a corpus size of 600 tweets.

Table 2. Performance of the Bag of Words model with bigrams for Random-Forest (RF) and LibLINEAR (LL).

Size	P	R	F1	ACC	P	R	F1	ACC
	RF				LL			
300	71.20	70.70	70.50	70.70	75.50	73.70	73.50	73.70
600	70.80	70.70	70.50	70.70	77.00	75.30	75.30	**75.30**
900	73.50	73.30	73.30	**73.30**	74.60	73.20	73.10	73.20
1200	72.80	72.50	72.50	72.50	73.50	71.80	71.60	71.80
1500	72.50	72.20	72.20	72.20	73.30	71.90	71.70	71.90
1800	72.00	71.50	71.50	71.50	72.60	70.90	70.80	70.90
2100	71.20	70.70	70.70	70.70	72.10	70.40	70.40	70.40
2400	69.60	69.10	69.10	69.10	70.30	68.70	68.70	68.70
2700	69.80	69.30	69.30	69.30	69.70	68.00	67.90	68.00
3000	70.10	69.60	69.60	69.60	69.90	68.10	68.10	68.10

Trigrams (see Table 3) have the worst overall results and they behave similar to a random classifier.

It draws our attention that the accuracy does not increases linearly with the number of tweets. This fact suggests that the cut-off filter is removing rare but informative grams. In Fig. 2 and Fig. 3 we can observe how the accuracy of RF and LL varies with the corpus size. Each figure contains the unigrams, bigrams and trigrams individually. We can observe that the performance of unigrams behaves uniformly whereas bigrams and trigrams loses accuracy as the corpus size grows.

Table 3. Performance of the Bag of Words model with trigrams for Random-Forest (RF) and LibLINEAR (LL).

Size	P	R	F1	ACC	P	R	F1	ACC
	RF				LL			
300	66.00	62.30	60.30	**62.30**	64.00	60.00	57.90	60.00
600	69.10	62.00	60.70	62.00	67.40	60.50	58.70	**60.50**
900	67.60	59.10	57.30	59.10	68.50	58.90	57.10	58.90
1200	67.40	57.60	55.60	57.60	66.40	56.80	54.40	56.80
1500	67.90	57.80	55.80	57.80	66.40	56.50	53.80	56.50
1800	65.80	54.80	52.10	54.00	64.20	53.60	50.30	53.60
2100	64.70	53.60	50.70	53.60	63.50	52.50	49.00	52.50
2400	60.80	49.90	45.90	49.90	59.40	49.00	44.20	49.00
2700	59.50	50.10	45.90	50.10	60.90	50.10	45.50	50.10
3000	60.30	49.40	45.00	49.40	58.40	48.20	43.20	48.20

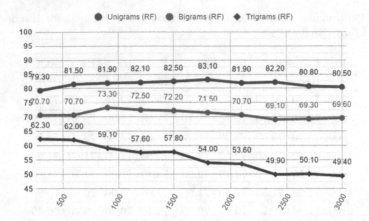

Fig. 2. Performance of unigrams, bigrams and trigrams in isolation with RF.

Next, unigrams, bigrams and trigrams were combined in order to discover if the features were disjoint. The combinations performed were: (1) unigrams and bigrams (see Table 4), (2) bigrams and trigrams (see Table 5), and (3) unigrams, bigrams, and trigrams (see Table 6). We can observe that the combination of unigrams and bigrams (see Table 4) achieves its best accuracy with 84.30% with LL and a corpus size of 300 tweets. When we compare the combination of unigrams and bigrams (see Table 4) with unigrams (see Table 1), we can observe that the accuracy is slightly lower. The same behaviour can be observed when we compare the combination of bigrams and trigrams (see Table 5) with bigrams (see Table 2), and the comparison between the combination of unigrams, bigrams and trigrams (see Table 6) with unigrams (see Table 1). These facts indicates that the bigrams and trigrams extracted in this corpus it is not relevant to distinguish between positive, neutral and negative statements. Figures 4 and 5 shows how

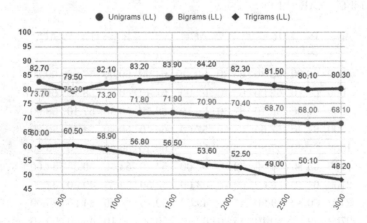

Fig. 3. Performance of unigrams, bigrams and trigrams in isolation with LL.

Table 4. Performance of the Bag of Words model with combinations of {unigrams, bigrams} for Random-Forest (RF) and LibLINEAR (LL).

Size	P	R	F1	ACC	P	R	F1	ACC
	RF				LL			
Combinations of unigrams and bigrams								
300	80.70	80.70	80.70	80.70	84.50	84.30	84.30	**84.30**
600	82.10	81.30	81.40	81.30	80.20	80.00	80.00	80.00
900	82.90	82.60	82.60	82.60	83.00	83.00	83.00	83.00
1200	82.90	82.40	82.40	82.40	83.80	83.80	83.70	83.80
1500	83.30	83.10	83.10	**83.10**	83.40	83.20	83.20	83.20
1800	83.30	83.00	83.00	83.00	83.50	83.30	83.30	83.30
2100	82.30	82.00	82.10	82.00	81.70	81.50	81.50	81.50
2400	81.90	81.70	81.70	81.70	81.00	80.80	80.80	80.80
2700	81.60	81.40	81.40	81.40	80.40	80.10	80.10	80.10
3000	80.90	80.60	80.70	80.60	79.80	79.60	79.60	79.60

the accuracy varies when the number of tweets is increased for the RF and the LIBLinear classifier respectively.

In order to verify that bigrams and trigrams do not contribute with relevant information we obtained the Information Gain measure for each gram (see Table Table 7). We can observe that some bigrams and trigrams are merely combinations of unigrams with an article or a preposition. For example, the unigram *riesgo* (risk), appears as a bigram twice: *riesgo de* (risk of) and *el riesgo* (the risk), and as a

Table 5. Performance of the Bag of Words model with combinations of {bigrams, trigrams} for Random-Forest (RF) and LibLINEAR (LL).

Size	P	R	F1	ACC	P	R	F1	ACC
	RF				LL			
300	72.80	72.30	72.10	**72.30**	74.70	72.70	72.50	72.70
600	71.30	71.00	70.80	71.00	76.00	74.20	74.00	**74.20**
900	72.20	72.10	72.10	72.10	75.40	73.40	73.40	73.40
1200	72.50	72.20	72.10	72.00	75.60	73.60	73.50	73.60
1500	72.00	71.70	71.70	71.70	75.80	74.10	74.00	74.00
1800	71.50	71.00	70.90	71.00	74.20	72.40	72.30	72.40
2100	70.90	70.40	70.40	70.40	73.70	71.80	71.80	71.80
2400	70.50	70.00	70.00	70.00	72.10	70.30	70.40	70.30
2700	69.80	69.20	69.20	69.20	71.70	69.80	69.80	69.80
3000	70.30	69.80	69.80	69.80	71.60	69.70	69.70	69.70

Table 6. Performance of the Bag of Words model with combinations of {unigrams, bigrams, trigrams} for Random-Forest (RF) and LibLINEAR (LL).

Size	P	R	F1	ACC	P	R	F1	ACC
	RF				LL			
300	80.00	80.00	80.00	80.00	83.20	83.00	82.90	83.00
600	81.60	80.80	80.90	80.80	80.60	80.30	80.40	80.30
900	83.00	82.40	82.50	82.40	82.90	82.80	82.80	82.80
1200	82.80	82.40	82.40	82.40	83.70	83.60	83.60	83.60
1500	83.30	82.80	82.90	82.80	83.60	83.50	83.50	83.50
1800	83.20	82.80	82.90	**82.80**	84.00	83.80	83.90	**83.80**
2100	82.00	81.80	81.80	81.80	82.00	81.80	81.80	81.80
2400	82.30	82.10	82.10	82.10	81.50	81.30	81.40	81.30
2700	81.20	80.90	80.90	80.90	80.30	80.00	80.10	80.00
3000	80.90	80.50	80.60	80.50	80.10	79.80	79.90	79.80

trigram three times: *el riesgo de* (the risk of), *aumentan el riesgo* (increase the risk), or *riesgo de sufrir* (risk of suffer). This fact reinforce our previous idea about the relevance of bigrams and trigrams in sentiment classification. We can assume, therefore, that this corpus does not contains enough texts with joint-words which can change the polarity of the sentiment. For example, the bigram *actividad física* (physical activity) appears mostly in positive tweets as well as the unigrams *actividad* (activity) and *física* (physical). However, in other scenarios, the words *actividad* and *física* could also be used to denote negative or informative statements. For example, *La actividad de la enfermedad ha aumentado* (The activity of the disease has increased).

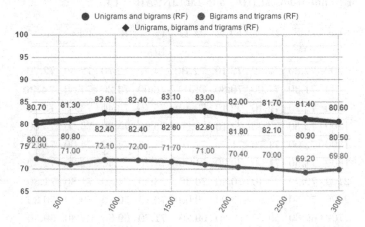

Fig. 4. Performance of unigrams, bigrams and trigrams in isolation with RF.

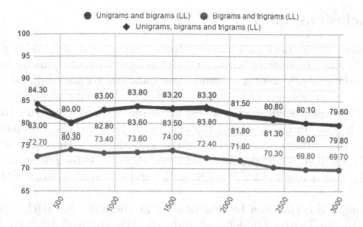

Fig. 5. Performance of unigrams, bigrams and trigrams in isolation with RF.

We can observe that unigram *me* is the most discriminatory (see Table 7). In Spanish, *me* is a first-person unstressed personal pronoun. This pronoun usually appears accompanied with a verb, forming a pronominal verbs. Usually, pronominal verbs are used in Spanish to describe first-person experiences. For example, the sentence *Me dio diabetes* (It does give me diabetes) is reporting a personal experience. We used Naive Bayes algorithm to get the mean and standard deviation for each feature and we notice that *me* is used mainly in neutral statements rather than in positive or negative statements.

Table 7. Best Information Gain (IG) scores for unigrams, bigrams and trigrams.

IG	Unigrams	IG	Bigrams	IG	Trigrams
0.11889	me	0.1042	riesgo de	0.07116	el riesgo de
0.11003	para	0.0717	el riesgo	0.06908	la diabetes tipo
0.10281	riesgo	0.06767	la obesidad	0.04226	curar la diabetes
0.09664	obesidad	0.06633	diabetes	0.02923	la obesidad infantil
0.09094	la	0.05909	diabetes tipo	0.02904	aumentan el riesgo
0.05839	insulina	0.04895	actividad física	0.02413	riesgo de sufrir
0.05723	diabetes	0.04226	curar la	0.0225	la obesidad puede
0.05469	tipo	0.03124	contra la	0.0225	la actividad física
0.05403	no	0.03068	prevenir la	0.0225	reducir la obesidad
0.05232	física	0.02904	que me	0.0225	de curar la
0.04895	fármaco	0.02904	de sufrir	0.02087	contra la obesidad
0.04895	actividad	0.02904	aumentan el	0.02087	diabetes y cáncer
0.04728	mi	0.0274	obesidad puede	0.02087	sufrir diabetes y
0.04442	prevenir	0.02671	de diabetes	0.01925	para reducir la
0.04412	sufrir	0.02481	obesidad infantil	0.01925	tipos de cáncer

5   Conclusions and Further Work

In this paper, we conduct an Opinion Mining experiment to build a machine-learning classifier capable of extracting the subjectivity of opinions regarding diabetes and obesity. Moreover, a multi-class balanced corpus composed by 3000 tweets written in Spanish concerning diabetes and obesity was compiled and released. The experiments showed a best accuracy of 84.20% applying LibLincar library with a balanced subset of the corpus of 1800 tweets. Compared with [27], where the authors performed a similar experiment with tweets related to diabetes in English, our experiment achieves slightly better precision (84.30% vs 81.93%), better recall (84.20% vs 81.13%) and better f1-measure (84.20% vs 81.24%).

The compiled corpus can be downloaded at the following URL[3]. However, according to the Twitter Guidelines[4], only the IDs are available (see *Redistribution of Twitter content* in the Twitter Guidelines). The IDs are ordered by class. The first 1000 tweets were classified as *positive* or *very-positive*, the next 1000 tweets were classified as *neutral* and the last 1000 tweets were classified as *negative* or *very negative*.

We will continue compiling more tweets for the corpus. Our idea is to compare the machine-learning classifier with tweets compiled from different time-intervals and different dialects of Spanish, such as the Castilian. Furthermore, we will explore the reliability of using linguistic models instead statistical ones. In concrete, we will use the Spanish version of LIWC [26] to obtain the frequencies of linguistic physiological relevant features. In addition, as some of the bigrams and trigrams retrieved contained propositions or articles we will test our NLP pipeline (1) by removing stop-words, and (2) by applying stemming to observe if the accuracy improves.

Acknowledgements. This work has been supported by the Spanish National Research Agency (AEI) and the European Regional Development Fund (FEDER/ERDF) through project KBS4FIA (TIN2016-76323-R).

References

1. Apolinardo-Arzube, Ó., García-Díaz, J.A., Medina-Moreira, J., Luna-Aveiga, H., Valencia-García, R.: Evaluating information-retrieval models and machine-learning classifiers for measuring the social perception towards infectious diseases. Appl. Sci. **9**(14), 2858 (2019)
2. Apolinario-Arzube, Ó., Medina-Moreira, J.A., Lagos-Ortiz, K., Luna-Aveiga, H., García-Díaz, J.A., Valencia-García, R.: Tecnologías inteligentes para la autogestión de la salud. Procesamiento del Lenguaje Natural **61**, 159–162 (2018)
3. Araujo, M., Reis, J., Pereira, A., Benevenuto, F.: An evaluation of machine translation for multilingual sentence-level sentiment analysis. In: Proceedings of the 31st Annual ACM Symposium on Applied Computing, pp. 1140–1145. ACM (2016)

---

[3] https://semantics.inf.um.es/joseagd/diabetes-and-obesity-positive-neutral-negative.rar.

[4] https://developer.twitter.com/en/developer-terms/more-on-restricted-use-cases.

4. Baccianella, S., Esuli, A., Sebastiani, F.: Sentiwordnet 3.0: an enhanced lexical resource for sentiment analysis and opinion mining. In: Lrec, vol. 10, pp. 2200–2204 (2010)

5. Barbieri, F., Ronzano, F., Saggion, H.: Is this tweet satirical? a computational approach for satire detection in spanish. Procesamiento del Lenguaje Natural **55**, 135–142 (2015)

6. Cho, N., et al.: Idf diabetes atlas: Global estimates of diabetes prevalence for 2017 and projections for 2045. Diabetes Res. Clin. Pract. **138**, 271–281 (2018)

7. Fan, R.E., Chang, K.W., Hsieh, C.J., Wang, X.R., Lin, C.J.: Liblinear: a library for large linear classification. J. Mach. Learn. Res. **9**, 1871–1874 (2008)

8. García-Sánchez, F., Paredes-Valverde, M., Valencia-García, R., Alcaraz-Mármol, G., Almela, Á.: Kbs4fia: leveraging advanced knowledge-based systems for financial information analysis. Procesamiento del Lenguaje Nat. **59**, 145–148 (2017)

9. Go, A., Bhayani, R., Huang, L.: Twitter sentiment classification using distant supervision. CS224N Project Report, Stanford 1(12), 2009 (2009)

10. Hall, M., Frank, E., Holmes, G., Pfahringer, B., Reutemann, P., Witten, I.H.: The weka data mining software: an update. ACM SIGKDD Explor. Newsl. **11**(1), 10–18 (2009)

11. Hsu, C.W., Chang, C.C., Lin, C.J., et al.: A practical guide to support vector classification (2003)

12. Huang, M., ElTayeby, O., Zolnoori, M., Yao, L.: Public opinions toward diseases: infodemiological study on news media data. J. Med. Internet Res **20**(5), e10047 (2018)

13. Ishijima, H., Kazumi, T., Maeda, A.: Sentiment analysis for the japanese stock market. Global Bus. Econ. Rev. **17**(3), 237–255 (2015)

14. Jianqiang, Z., Xiaolin, G.: Comparison research on text pre-processing methods on twitter sentiment analysis. IEEE Access **5**, 2870–2879 (2017)

15. Koppel, M., Schler, J.: The importance of neutral examples for learning sentiment. Comput. Intell. **22**(2), 100–109 (2006)

16. Martínez-Cámara, E., Martín-Valdivia, M.T., Urena-López, L.A., Montejo-Ráez, A.R.: Sentiment analysis in twitter. Nat. Lang. Eng. **20**(1), 1–28 (2014)

17. Medina-Moreira, J., Lagos-Ortiz, K., Luna-Aveiga, H., Paredes, R., Valencia-García, R.: Usage of diabetes self-management mobile technology: options for ecuador. In: Valencia-García, R., Lagos-Ortiz, K., Alcaraz-Mármol, G., del Cioppo, J., Vera-Lucio, N. (eds.) CITI 2016. CCIS, vol. 658, pp. 79–89. Springer, Cham (2016). https://doi.org/10.1007/978-3-319-48024-4_7

18. Miller, G.A.: Wordnet: a lexical database for english. Commun. ACM **38**(11), 39–41 (1995)

19. Moghaddam, S.: Beyond sentiment analysis: mining defects and improvements from customer feedback. In: Hanbury, A., Kazai, G., Rauber, A., Fuhr, N. (eds.) ECIR 2015. LNCS, vol. 9022, pp. 400–410. Springer, Cham (2015). https://doi.org/10.1007/978-3-319-16354-3_44

20. Moraes, R., Valiati, J.F., Neto, W.P.G.: Document-level sentiment classification: an empirical comparison between svm and ann. Expert Syst. Appl. **40**(2), 621–633 (2013)

21. Ochoa, J.L., Valencia-García, R., Perez-Soltero, A., Barceló-Valenzuela, M.: A semantic role labelling-based framework for learning ontologies from spanish documents. Expert Syst. Appl. **40**(6), 2058–2068 (2013)

22. Orces, C.H., Lorenzo, C.: Prevalence of prediabetes and diabetes among older adults in ecuador: analysis of the sabe survey. Diab. Metab. Syndr. Clin. Res. Rev. **12**(2), 147–153 (2018)

23. Pang, B., Lee, L., et al.: Opinion mining and sentiment analysis. Found. Trends® Inf. Retrieval **2**(1–2), 1–135 (2008)
24. Peñalver-Martinez, I., et al.: Feature-based opinion mining through ontologies. Expert Syst. Appl. **41**(13), 5995–6008 (2014)
25. Powers, M.A., et al.: Diabetes self-management education and support in type 2 diabetes: a joint position statement of the american diabetes association, the american association of diabetes educators, and the academy of nutrition and dietetics. Diabetes Educ. **43**(1), 40–53 (2017)
26. Ramírez-Esparza, N., Pennebaker, J.W., García, F.A., Suriá, R.: La psicología del uso de las palabras: Un programa de computadora que analiza textos en español. Rev. Mex. Psicología **24**(1), 85–99 (2007)
27. Salas-Zárate, M.P., Medina-Moreira, J., Lagos-Ortiz, K., Luna-Aveiga, H., Rodriguez-Garcia, M.A., Valencia-Garcia, R.: Sentiment analysis on tweets about diabetes: an aspect-level approach. Comput. math. methods med. **2017**, 9 (2017)
28. Salas-Zárate, M.P., Paredes-Valverde, M.A., Rodriguez-García, M.Á., Valencia-García, R., Alor-Hernández, G.: Automatic detection of satire in twitter: a psycholinguistic-based approach. Knowl.-Based Syst. **128**, 20–33 (2017)
29. Salas-Zárate, M.P., Valencia-García, R., Ruiz-Martínez, A., Colomo-Palacios, R.: Feature-based opinion mining in financial news: an ontology-driven approach. J. Inf. Sci. **43**(4), 458–479 (2017)
30. Schouten, K., Frasincar, F.: Survey on aspect-level sentiment analysis. IEEE Trans. Knowl. Data Eng. **28**(3), 813–830 (2015)
31. Shaw Jr., G., Karami, A.: Computational content analysis of negative tweets for obesity, diet, diabetes, and exercise. Proc. Assoc. Inf. Sci. Technol. **54**(1), 357–365 (2017)
32. Suttles, J., Ide, N.: Distant supervision for emotion classification with discrete binary values. In: Gelbukh, A. (ed.) CICLing 2013. LNCS, vol. 7817, pp. 121–136. Springer, Heidelberg (2013). https://doi.org/10.1007/978-3-642-37256-8_11
33. Wilson, T., Raaijmakers, S.: Comparing word, character, and phoneme n-grams for subjective utterance recognition. In: Ninth Annual Conference of the International Speech Communication Association (2008)

Automatic Spelling Detection and Correction in the Medical Domain: A Systematic Literature Review

Jésica López-Hernández[1](✉), Ángela Almela[2],
and Rafael Valencia-García[1]

[1] Facultad de Informática, Universidad de Murcia, Murcia, Spain
{jesica.lopez,valencia}@um.es
[2] Facultad de Letras, Universidad de Murcia, Murcia, Spain
angelalm@um.es

Abstract. Automatic spelling correction is one of the most important problems in natural language processing. Its difficulty increases in medical corpora, due to the intrinsic particularities that have these texts. These features include the use of specific terminology, abbreviations, acronyms and the presence of writing errors. In this article we present a systematic review of the literature on automatic spelling detection and correction for the medical domain. There are many works on detection and automatic correction, but there is no review delving into the process of automatic correction in the medical domain. Therefore, we intend to synthesize all the existing information on this research topic and the types of studies that have been carried out to date. We present the main techniques and resources, and finally also the limitations and specific challenges. The results reflect the importance of compiling an exhaustive dictionary. In addition, the results show the ordinary use of distance algorithms of spelling and phonetic similarity, as well as with statistical techniques. The improvement of performance in recent years is especially relevant because of the use of context-based methods, such as linguistic models or neural embeddings.

Keywords: Literature review · Automatic spelling detection ·
Automatic spelling correction · Medical domain · Spelling errors · Misspellings

1 Introduction

Automatic medical text processing is an emerging topic in natural language processing. There are many works on disambiguation of medical text, recognition of named entities and extraction of medical information [1]. Automatic spelling detection and correction is extremely important for the correct processing of the data, hence its presence in many automatic clinical processing tasks.

However, in medical domain texts, due to their terminological complexity and linguistic particularities, the usual spellcheckers are ineffective [2] and automatic processing is a challenge on many occasions. Conventional methods of correcting spelling errors are often based on the use of dictionaries and the minimum edit distance between a spelling error and its correction candidates. Over the years these methods

© Springer Nature Switzerland AG 2019
R. Valencia-García et al. (Eds.): CITI 2019, CCIS 1124, pp. 95–108, 2019.
https://doi.org/10.1007/978-3-030-34989-9_8

have added new techniques, such as those based on phonetic similarity [3], probabilistic techniques, such as n-gram analysis [4], rule-based and heuristic techniques [5], techniques based on noisy channel models [6], language models, or the most current, based on machine learning and deep learning [7].

Accordingly, this work presents a piece of research based on the analysis and review of the literature on detection and automatic spelling correction in the medical domain. A systematic literature review allows retrieving, studying and evaluating all the research that is relevant in a given field of research. It is necessary to highlight the need to carry out a systematic review of studies conducted in this area because, although there are current works that present reviews on automatic spelling correction, there is not a systematic literature review on the medical domain. There are several studies that have investigated the process of automatic correction, but the literature on automatic spelling correction in the medical domain is scarce and is not presented systematically. Hence the need to gather methods, resources and techniques, to identify limitations and help in future research seeking to get into this topic. Besides, a systematic review of the literature is a crucial step to delve into the state of the art of the subject and find all the relevant and useful information for our own research. It is worth noting that the present revision procedure is based on the method proposed by Kitchenham [8] for systematic reviews, with some adaptations. Therefore, the present authors attempted to carry out the compilation, analysis and evaluation of all available research regarding their starting question.

The study is structured as follows: Sect. 2 shows the development of the systematic review and the methodology used; in Sect. 3, the results obtained are presented and the data extracted are analyzed; and in Sect. 4 some relevant conclusions are drawn.

2   Methodology

This systematic review was undertaken following a series of steps that are detailed below. First, the need to carry out this research was assessed taking into account previous studies. In the absence of previous work that collected information on this problem, it was decided that its performance was relevant. Multiple works on detection and automatic spelling correction were found, but they are extremely diverging and with very different characteristics, so it was considered useful to establish a filter to know the current challenges that automatic correction presents in medical language specifically. Accordingly, a series of studies that have the criteria established previously, the relevant data were extracted, an analysis was carried out, and finally an evaluation of the quality of the study and the results was made.

As stated above, this review has several objectives. The first, and most important, aim is to identify the techniques and methods used in automatic detection and correction in the medical domain. The second aim is to collect resources, corpus and data sources that may be useful for researchers attempting to begin in this field of research. The third aim is to know what limitations and problems are to be faced by researchers in this area. All things considered, the ultimate aim is to provide answers to the first questions posed by researchers when he begins to work in this domain, in order to speed up and facilitate the search work.

2.1 Research Questions

Considering the objectives of this review, the three research questions posed are as follows:

RQ1: What kinds of studies have been done on automatic correction in the medical domain and what characteristics do they usually have?

RQ2: What techniques are most widely used in automatic detection and correction in the medical domain?

RQ3: What are the limitations or problems in this area?

2.2 Digital Libraries

Table 1 shows the databases and digital libraries that were consulted for the review process. The present authors had access to public and restricted electronic journals, conference proceedings and books. These search sources were used because they contain most of the studies on the selected topic.

Table 1. Databases and digital libraries.

Google Scholar
ACM Digital Library
Research Gate
Web of Science (WOS)
Medline
SciELO Citation Index
Current Contents Connect (CCC)
Derwent Innovations Index (DIIDW)
KCI - Korean Journal Database (KJD)
InCites
Biosis Citation Index
Russian Science Citation Index (RSCI)
Chinese Science Citation Index
Elsevier

2.3 Search Strategy

The search strategy entailed using keywords to find the articles which are particularly pertinent to the research questions. The terms that were to be searched and their combinations were defined. For this purpose, the words that usually appear in this kind of study and are relevant to the research questions were identified. Then, they were combined with each other through the Boolean operators "AND" and "OR". Synonyms and words with related meanings were considered as well. The strings used were the following:

- (spell* OR check*) AND (clinical OR medical) AND correction
- (spell* OR check*) AND (clinical OR medical) AND correction AND/OR (errors OR error OR mispellings).

2.4   Study Selection Criteria

In this phase of the process, the review rules and criteria for inclusion and exclusion of results were established. Accordingly, the studies meeting a series of requirements for time period, relevance, issue and quality were selected. The search was narrowed to publications of the last ten years (2009–2019), so that the most relevant and updated works appeared. The search language chosen was English.

The works were obtained through advanced search in digital libraries. In the databases, searches of the previously defined strings were made with the option "topic", which included the title, summary and keywords of articles. To register the information properly the Mendeley©[1] reference manager has been used.

We obtained a total of 114 results, but it was necessary to filter these results manually, as many of the pieces of research were not directly related to the study objectives and did not answer the research questions posed. To decide which studies to discard, we carried out a manual review in which we analyzed the abstract of the articles and some sections of the methodology. An example was the study with P300 Speller software. This software is used to recognize misinterpreted commands in brain-computer interface (BCI) systems [9]. Consequently, those works that were not directly related to our research topic were discarded, as well as duplicate works and those not written in English. Table 2 shows the form used to record the information collected from the various works.

Table 2. Data collection form

Study identifier	S
Title	
Authors	
Type	Journal article/Book section/Conference proceedings/Thesis
Journal/Conference	
Year	2009–2019
Research question	RQ1, RQ2, RQ3
Method	
Limitation	

3   Systematic Review

At this stage, all the studies found that could potentially be included in the review have been analyzed. Table 3 includes a brief description about the 14 selected studies, with title, journals in which they were published, and year of publication. Table 4 shows information about the corpora used in each study. Finally, in Table 5 the different methods and resources used in each work are listed.

---

[1] Official website: https://www.mendeley.com/.

Table 3. Description of relevant studies.

Study identifier	Title	Conference/Journal	Year
S1 [10]	Misspellings in drug information system queries: Characteristics of drug name spelling errors and strategies for their prevention	International Journal of Medical Informatics	2010
S2 [2]	Spelling correction in clinical notes with emphasis on first suggestion accuracy	2nd Workshop on Building and Evaluating Resources for Biomedical Text Mining	2010
S3 [11]	Statistical semantic and clinician confidence analysis for correcting abbreviations and spelling errors in clinical progress notes	Artificial Intelligence in Medicine	2011
S4 [12]	Improved chemical text mining of patents with infinite dictionaries and automatic spelling correction	Journal of Chemical Information and Modeling	2012
S5 [13]	Context-aware correction of spelling errors in Hungarian medical documents	Computer Speech & Language	2014
S6 [14]	An ensemble method for spelling correction in consumer health questions	AMIA Annual Symposium Proceedings	2015
S7 [15]	Automated misspelling detection and correction in clinical free-text records	Journal of Biomedical Informatics	2015
S8 [16]	Context-Sensitive Spelling Correction of Consumer-Generated Content on Health Care	JMIR Medical Informatics	2015
S9 [17]	Customised OCR Correction for Historical Medical Text	Digital Heritage	2015
S10 [18]	Identification and Correction of Misspelled Drugs' Names in Electronic Medical Records (EMR)	Proceedings of the 18th International Conference on Enterprise Information Systems (ICEIS 2016)	2016
S11 [19]	Unsupervised Context-Sensitive Spelling Correction of Clinical Free-Text with Word and Character N-Gram Embeddings	Proceedings of the BioNLP 2017 Workshop	2017
S12 [20]	Improving Terminology Mapping in Clinical Text with Context-Sensitive Spelling Correction	Studies in health technology and informatics	2017
S13 [21]	Improving Spelling Correction with Consumer Health Terminology	AMIA Clinical Informatics Conference	2018
S14 [22]	An efficient prototype method to identify and correct misspellings in clinical text	BMC Research Notes	2019

Table 4. Corpus information.

Study identifier	Corpus
S1 [10]	Electronic drug information systems queries. More than 95,000 brand names and more than 10,000 active ingredients. 221,437 users at the University Hospital of Heidelberg queried the DIS 575,142 times
S2 [2]	Corpus of clinical records of the Emergency Department at the Concord Hospital, Sydney. 57,523 unique words/7,442 misspellings (training data). 164,302 unique words/65,429 misspellings (test data)
S3 [11]	Clinical progress notes. Test set of 30 samples from a corpus of 2,433 actual progress notes. 961 words, each note with an average of 32 words
S4 [12]	Chemical text mining of IBM's text database of around 12 million United States, European, and World patents
S5 [13]	Anonymized clinical documents from various departments of a Hungarian hospital. Gold standard: 50,394 tokens. The size of the test set was 3,722 tokens. The test set has 89 different misspelled words 2000 sentences (17,243 tokens/6,234 types) randomly selected from the whole clinical corpus from various departments
S6 [14]	Consumer health questions. 372 questions for training and 100 questions for testing
S7 [15]	Clinical free-text records. Training set of 275 notes, 106,668 words, 475 misspelled, and a test set of 40 notes, with 15,247 words and 78 misspellings. Second data set was constructed from randomly selected free-text allergy entries. Allergy Repository (PEAR). 6,460 words and 307 misspellings in training set. The testing set made up of 442 entries with 1,380 words and 55 misspellings. Third data set was comprised of randomly selected free-text medication orders entered by clinicians through Partners' ambulatory EHR system. 402 misspellings, 5,069 words formed the training set, while 392 entries (872 words and 59 misspellings) formed the test set
S8 [16]	Consumer-generated content, such as posts on social networking websites. 150 postings (21,358 words) from MedHelp's bulletin board system (BBS). This set of postings is related to a drug named Zoloft and contains consumers' descriptions of their symptoms and suggestions from others
S9 [17]	Historical Medical Texts. Character recognition (OCR) in scanned page images. Collection of 24 hand-corrected documents, consisting of three documents taken from each of the following decades: 1840s, 1860s, 1880s, 1900s, 1920s, 1940s, 1960s and 1980s
S10 [18]	Electronic medical record (EMR). 250 electronic medical records
S11 [19]	Clinical free-text. MIMIC-III database (physician-generated progress notes, nursing notes, etc.). 873 contextually different instances of 357 unique error types
S12 [20]	Unstructured clinical text. Swedish medical text. Controlled evaluation with medical literature text with induced errors. Partial evaluation on clinical notes
S13 [21]	Consumer health questions. Consumer health data. 39,042 words
S14 [22]	Two different corpora: surgical pathology reports, and emergency department progress and visit notes, extracted from Veterans Health Administration resources. 76,786 clinical notes

Table 5. Methods used to develop spell checker.

Study identifier	Methods	Resources
S1 [10]	Dictionary look-up Edit distance Friedman's test Similarity key Frequency-based approach	Aspell Metaphone and DoubleMetaphone encoding Needleman-Wunsch algorithm
S2 [2]	Dictionary look-up Edit distance Edit distance-based rules Rule-based suggestion generation system Context-sensitive classification algorithm Statistical language model - Trigram model	Aspell CMU-Cambridge Statistical Language Modelling Toolkit Snomed CT
S3 [11]	Dictionary look-up Edit distance Hamming distance 1 search Statistical semantic analysis based on Web data	Aspell The Yahoo! spelling suggestion service
S4 [12]	Dictionary look-up Edit distance Text mining Chemical Entity Name Classification Infinite Dictionaries (Grammars) input for name-to-structure software Hamming distance 1 search Regular expressions	Aspell CaffeineFix Finite State Machine Dictionaries
S5 [13]	Dictionary look-up Edit distance Statistical Machine Translation (SMT) decoder Language Modeling	Aspell Moses, statistical machine translation (SMT) toolkit
S6 [14]	Dictionary look-up Edit distance Contextual method based on similarities Frequency-based approach Phonetic and edit distance-based spelling suggestions	Word2vec toolkit ESpell DoubleMetaphone
S7 [15]	Dictionary look-up Edit distance Shannon's noisy channel model Named entity recognition Regular expressions Rule-based system Similarity key Parts-of-Speech tagging Suffix and prefix based suggestion list	Aspell Stanford NER UMLS Simplified version of the Double Metaphone algorithm

(continued)

Table 5. (*continued*)

Study identifier	Methods	Resources
S8 [16]	Dictionary look-up Edit distance Ontologies Parts-of-Speech tagging	Google Spell Checker MedHelp Snomed CT RxNorm National Center for Biomedical Ontology (NCBO) Annotator
S9 [17]	Dictionary look-up Edit distance Optical Character Recognition Rule-based correction of regular errors Frequency-based approach	Hunspell's dictionary OpenMedSpel dictionary
S10 [18]	Dictionary look-up Edit distance Parts-of-Speech tagging Stemming Lemmatization Regular Expressions Term frequency (TF) calculation Cosine similarity Information retrieval Frequency-based approach	Aspell Gspell Brown corpus's Parts Of Speech Tagging (POST)
S11 [19]	Dictionary look-up Edit distance Damerau-Levenshtein edit distance of 2 from a reference lexicon Neural embeddings Tokenization Similarity key	Aspell FastText skipgram model SPECIALIST Lexicon Pattern tokenizer Dictionary from Jazzy, a Java open source spell checker Double Metaphone algorithm
S12 [20]	Dictionary look-up Edit distance Ontologies Trigram frequencies	Aspell Snomed CT
S13 [21]	Dictionary look-up Edit distance Frequency-based approach N-gram analysis	CSpell dictionary SPECIALIST Lexicon UMLS Metathesaurus and MEDLINE
S14 [22]	Dictionary look-up Edit distance Corpus term frequencies Neural embeddings	Word2Vec SPECIALIST Lexicon

4 Results and Discussion

This section answered the research questions previously put.

4.1 RQ1. What Kinds of Studies Have Been Done on Automatic Correction in the Medical Domain and What Characteristics Do They Usually Have?

As has been seen, the number of works is limited and works are heterogeneous, since they have been applied to different environments, languages and problems. However, most of the contributions have been made in medical reports that have a structured format: clinical records of emergency department [2], progress notes [11] and electronic health records [13, 15, 18, 19, 22]. Likewise, there are also studies on error analysis in consultations carried out by patients or consumers to improve search systems [10, 14], and with patents of pharmaceutical interest [12] to improve the data mining process.

Health professionals often suffer from work overload and have little time to write these documents, which include complex terminology and do not usually have a subsequent review. Due to these circumstances, the number of errors in clinical documents is usually high. According to Siklósi, Novák, and Prószéky [13] the most frequent types of errors are: mistyping, lack or improper use of punctuation marks, grammatical errors, domain-specific and often ad hoc abbreviations and Latin medical terminology, among others.

Most of the automatic spelling correction works for the medical domain have been carried out for English. However, research for Swedish [20] and Hungarian [13] is remarkable as well.

As regards automatic correction of errors in the medical domain, different specialties are involved, and this circumstance influences the type of method chosen. In many cases, the correction process is part of major investigations that include other techniques. For example, Wong and Glance [11] work with disambiguation techniques, and in Sayle et al. [12] the main task is chemical text mining.

Almost all the studies focus on non-word errors and typographical errors, whereas cognitive and grammatical errors [18] are barely addressed.

4.2 RQ2. What Techniques Are Most Widely Used in Automatic Detection and Correction?

The techniques used in automatic detection and correction processes in this domain are diverse. Nevertheless, there are techniques that are used in all the works analyzed. A trend is detected, as we move towards more recent studies, the use of techniques based on context increased.

The starting point is usually the dictionary look-up, which is used in all the reviewed works. The procedure is straightforward, if a word or character set does not appear in the dictionary search it is likely to be a misspelled word. In addition to general dictionaries, contained in Aspell, Hunspell or Google Spell Checker, it is necessary to incorporate domain-specific terminology for them to be effective. Specific lexicons are created from the combination of different sources and they usually include lists of abbreviations and acronyms, gazetteers, lists of diseases, medications, symptoms, active ingredients and other medical terms. There are several resources and dictionaries mentioned throughout the review: The Unified Medical Language System (UMLS) [23], Systematized Nomenclature of Medicine-Clinical Terms (SNOMED-CT) [24], The Moby Lexicon [25], MedlinePlus [26], PubMed [27] or The SPECIALIST Lexicon [28].

The method based on the minimum edit distance also has a high presence in the poll of works. Levenshtein's edit distance [29] refers to the minimum number of operations required to transform one string of characters into another. Damerau [30] established that more than 80% of spelling errors are usually at distance 1 from the correct word. Therefore, through the minimum editing distance, suggestions are generated and classified.

In the same way that there are methods based on the similarity between words or editing distance, some techniques working with phonetic similarity can be found, especially useful in those cases with words whose pronunciation is similar but their spelling is different. It consists of mapping a key to each character string. In this method we should point out the Soundex system and systems such as Metaphone and Double-Metaphone [2, 14, 19]. Aspell includes the Metaphone and Double-Metaphone algorithm.

Rule-based systems [2, 17, 18] are also used, such as those that use regular expressions. In these cases, searches in dictionaries can be adapted according to previously defined rules to eliminate abbreviations. The automatic correction of cases that are clearly defined is also possible, or of words that are usually misspelled and their correction has no ambiguities. Likewise, there are many studies that incorporate statistical methods [11], such as frequency data on the appearance of words in corpus for the ordering and election of candidates.

An error model can be applied in the technique known as the noisy channel model [31]. This technique starts from the theory of communication [32]; in this theory a sender sends a sequence of symbols to a receiver. However, during the transfer, certain symbols of the transmitted sequence are confused due to the deficiencies of the transmission channel. The objective of the receiver is to reconstruct the original sequence using the knowledge of the source and the properties of the transmission channel. Lai et al. [14] use this technique in their study and achieve a correction accuracy of around 80% in a set of clinical notes.

In those cases where words cannot be corrected in isolation, other techniques such as the use of statistical language models [2], the analysis of n-grams (usually of bigrams or trigrams) and/or machine learning techniques are necessary. In all these cases it is intended to add contextual information to the system. It is relevant to mention the use of ontologies [16, 20], such as Wordnet [33], RxNorm [34] or SNOMED-CT [24], which can help identify the semantic distance of a word with respect to adjacent words.

Context-dependent error methods are essential in cases where the correctly written word is replaced by another existing word, making identification very difficult. In these cases, the issue is no longer at the word level, but at the phrase or text level, as grammatical and semantic issues. Patrick et al. [2] design a system that includes rule-based techniques, frequency of occurrence and a context-based classification algorithm composed of a trigrams language model.

In recent years, new techniques and approaches based on vector models have emerged, such as the use of neural embeddings [19] that can be successfully exploited in those cases where context is required. This method measures the similarity between word vectors and represents the contexts in which a word appears.

4.3   RQ3. What Are the Limitations or Problems in This Area?

All of the studies in the final poll coincide in pointing out the important number of errors presented by these texts and the complexity of the treatment of clinical records, both because of the large number of abbreviations contained, as well as the complex terminology, the lack of standardization of forms and of subsequent review [2, 13, 15]. The noise presented by these texts in many cases is high, hence the difficulty in their processing.

Although there have been many advances in recent years, there are still limitations, many of the techniques can have a complex configuration, and spellcheckers are not yet completely successful. It is extremely important to have exhaustive dictionaries, and it is not always easy to compile these dictionaries. Neologisms are constantly created to refer to new realities that are emerging. Similarly, a measure that increases the size of the dictionary, the number of errors that are included in it may involuntarily increase.

Most works measure the precision and accuracy of their spell checking methods only in cases of non-real words, due to the complexity involved in cases of real words, impossible to detect in isolation. Another limitation is that the degree of success in correcting misspelled words is measured, but it is also worth measuring the rate of false positives, in which words that were correct are incorrectly corrected.

The major challenges appear in grammatical and semantic errors [14]. Very few are the studies address this problem. This requires a further development of techniques that involve semantic aspects and context. A greater degree of universality of the solutions developed would also be convenient.

In case of neural embeddings, very large volumes of text are necessary so that they can be trained and the technique is effective. In smaller corpus the effectiveness is reduced, and it is one of the main problems of this type of contextual methods. The shorter the text, the less information can be extracted from the context, which may lead to a wrong choice of the candidate for the correction. In addition, texts usually contain errors and abbreviations that can distort the results and minimize accuracy.

5   Conclusion and Future Work

In this piece of research, a systematic review of the literature on detection and correction spelling errors in the medical domain has been undertaken. The most appropriate studies were selected basing on a set of significant criteria. At the beginning of this review, many works that were not relevant to our objectives were retrieved, hence the careful selection of those that were directly related. A detailed description of the systematic review process was described, and an analysis of the results was conducted. In this way, a starting point is provided for those researchers interested in this topic.

The results reflect that an adequate selection or combination of methods is essential to achieve effectiveness in the correction process. It is also essential to have a dictionary as exhaustive and complete as possible, a task that is not always easy due to the characteristics of the domain and the constant creation of neologisms by health professionals. The techniques studied are diverse, the starting point being the search in dictionaries, followed by the distance of spelling and phonetic editing, the statistical methods and the approaches that consider the context, such as language modeling or neural embeddings. The results of the research indicate that there is still work to be done to improve precision and recall measures; further development and universality of resources is necessary to promote knowledge sharing.

In the future, we aim to develop a deeper analysis of the techniques and algorithms, as well as obtain further quantitative data on error rates. Finally, we want to delve into the generation of candidates, to know what resources are used in that phase to choose the best candidate in the decision architecture. This work is also the first step in the development of an implementation of our own that combines several techniques for medical reports written in Spanish. Therefore, there is much ground to explore and there is potential for future research.

Acknowledgments. This research was funded by the Spanish National Research Agency (AEI) and the European Regional Development Fund (FEDER/ERDF) through project KBS4FIA (TIN2016-76323-R). This research is also funded by the Ministry of Education of Spain through the National Program for University Teacher Training (FPU/Ayudas para la formación de profesorado universitario).

References

1. Ruch, P., Baud, R., Geissbühler, A.: Using lexical disambiguation and named-entity recognition to improve spelling correction in the electronic patient record. Artif. Intell. Med. **29**(1), 169–184 (2003)
2. Patrick, J., Sabbagh, M., Jain, S., Zheng, H.: Spelling correction in clinical notes with emphasis on first suggestion accuracy. In: 2nd Workshop on Building and Evaluating Resources for Biomedical Text Mining, pp. 1–8 (2010)
3. Pollock, J.J., Zamora, A.: Collection and characterization of spelling errors in scientific and scholarly text. J. Am. Soc. Inf. Sci. **34**(1), 51–58 (1983)
4. Verberne, S.: Context-sensitive spell checking based on trigram probabilities. Master's thesis, University of Nijmegen (2002)
5. Kukich, K.: Techniques for automatically correcting words in text. ACM Comput. Surv. **24**(4), 377–439 (1992)
6. Brill, E., Moore, R.C.: An improved error model for noisy channel spelling correction. In: Proceedings of the 38th Annual Meeting of the Association for Computational Linguistics – ACL, Hong Kong, pp. 286–293 (2000)
7. Pande, H.: Effective search space reduction for spell correction using character neural embeddings. In: Proceedings 15th Conference of the European Chapter of the Association for Computational Linguistics–EACL 2017, Valencia, pp. 170–174 (2017)

8. Kitchenham, B., Pearl Brereton, O., Budgen, D., Turner, M., Bailey, J., Linkman, S.: Systematic literature reviews in software engineering - a systematic literature review. Inf. Softw. Technol. **51**(1), 7–15 (2009). https://doi.org/10.1016/j.infsof.2008.09.009
9. Takahashi, H., Yoshikawa, T., Furuhashi, T.: Reliability-based automatic repeat request with error potential-based error correction for improving P300 speller performance. In: Wong, K., Mendis, B., Bouzerdoum, A. (eds.) ICONIP 2010. LNCS, vol. 6444, pp. 50–57. Springer, Heidelberg (2010). https://doi.org/10.1007/978-3-642-17534-3_7
10. Senger, C., Kaltschmidt, J., Schmitt, S.P.W., Pruszydlo, M.G., Haefeli, W.E.: Misspellings in drug information system queries: characteristics of drug name spelling errors and strategies for their prevention. Int. J. Med. Inf. **79**, 832–839 (2010). https://doi.org/10.1016/j.ijmedinf.2010.09.005
11. Wong, W., Glance, D.: Statistical semantic and clinician confidence analysis for correcting abbreviations and spelling errors in clinical progress notes. Artif. Intell. Med. **53**(3), 171–180 (2011)
12. Sayle, R.A., Petrov, P., Winter, J., Muresan, S.: Improved chemical text mining of patents using infinite dictionaries, translation and automatic spelling correction. J. Chem. Inf. Model. **3**, 51–62 (2012). https://doi.org/10.1186/1758-2946-3-S1-O16
13. Siklósi, B., Novák, A., Prószéky, G.: Context-aware correction of spelling errors in Hungarian medical documents. Comput. Speech Lang. **35**, 219–233 (2014)
14. Kilicoglu, H., Fiszman, M., Roberts, K., Demner-Fushman, D.: An ensemble method for spelling correction in consumer health questions. In: AMIA Annual Symposium Proceedings, pp. 727–736 (2015)
15. Lai, K.H., Topaz, M., Goss, F.R., Zhou, L.: Automated misspelling detection and correction in clinical free-text records. J. Biomed. Inform. **55**, 188–195 (2015)
16. Zhou, X., et al.: Context-sensitive spelling correction of consumer-generated content on health care. JMIR Med. Inform. 31 **3**(3), 27 (2015). https://doi.org/10.2196/medinform.4211
17. Thompson, P.M., McNaught, J., Ananiadou, S.: Customised OCR correction for historical medical text. Digit. Herit. **1**, 35–42 (2015)
18. Hussain, F., Qamar, U.: Identification and correction of misspelled drugs' names in electronic medical records (EMR). In: Proceedings of the 18th International Conference on Enterprise Information Systems, vol. 2, pp. 333–338 (2016)
19. Fivez, P., Suster, S., Daelemans, W.: Unsupervised context sensitive spelling correction of clinical free-text with word and character N-Gram embeddings. In: Proceedings of the BioNLP 2017 Workshop, Vancouver, pp. 143–148. Association for Computational Linguistics (2016)
20. Dziadek, J., Henriksson, A., Duneld, M.: Improving terminology mapping in clinical text with context-sensitive spelling correction. In: Informatics for Health: Connected Citizen-Led Wellness and Population Health, vol. 235, pp. 241–245. IOS Press, Amsterdam (2017)
21. Lu, C.J., Demner-Fushman, D.: Improving spelling correction with consumer health terminology. In: AMIA 2018 Annual Symposium Proceedings, p. 2053. American Medical Informatics Association (2018)
22. Workman, T.E., Shao, Y., Divita, G., Zeng-Treitler, Q.: An efficient prototype method to identify and correct misspellings in clinical text. BMC Res. Notes **12**(1), 42 (2019). https://doi.org/10.1186/s13104-019-4073-y
23. Unified Medical Language System (UMLS). https://www.nlm.nih.gov/research/umls/index.html. Accessed 20 Aug 2019
24. International Health Terminology Standards Development Organisation, SNOMED CT. http://www.ihtsdo.org/snomed-ct/. Accessed 20 Aug 2019
25. Moby Project. https://mobyproject.org. Accessed 20 Aug 2019
26. Medline Plus. https://medlineplus.gov/. Accessed 20 Aug 2019

27. PubMed. https://www.ncbi.nlm.nih.gov/pubmed/. Accessed 20 Aug 2019
28. The SPECIALIST Lexicon. http://lexsrv3.nlm.nih.gov/Specialist/Summary/lexicon.html. Accessed 20 Aug 2019
29. Levenshtein, V.I.: Binary codes capable of correcting deletions, insertions, and reversals. Sov. Phys. Dok-lady **10**, 707 (1966)
30. Damerau, F.J.: A technique for computer detection and correction of spelling errors. Commun. ACM **7**(3), 171–176 (1964)
31. Kernighan, M.D., Church, K.W., Gale, W.A.: A spelling correction program based on a noisy channel model. In: Proceedings of the 13th Conference on Computational Linguistics, vol. 2, pp. 205–210 (1990)
32. Shannon, C.E.: A mathematical theory of communication. Bell Syst. Tech. J. **27**, 379–423 (1948)
33. WordNet. A Lexical Database for English. https://wordnet.princeton.edu/. Accessed 20 Aug 2019
34. National Library of Medicine, RxNorm. http://www.nlm.nih.gov/research/umls/rxnorm/. Accessed 20 Aug 2019

CyberDect. A Novel Approach for Cyberbullying Detection on Twitter

Antonio López-Martínez, José Antonio García-Díaz,
Rafael Valencia-García, and Antonio Ruiz-Martínez

Facultad de Informática, Universidad de Murcia, Campus de Espinardo,
30100 Murcia, Spain
{antonio.lopez41,joseantonio.garcia8,valencia,arm}@um.es

Abstract. Bullying is the deliberate physical and psychological abuse that a child receives from other children. The term cyberbullying has recently emerged to denote a new type of bullying that takes place over digital platforms, where the stalkers can perform their crimes on the vulnerable victims. In severe cases, the harassment has lead the victims to the extreme causing irreparable damage or leading them to suicide. In order to stop cyberbullying, the scientific community is developing effective tools capable of detecting the harassment as soon as possible; however, these detection systems are still in an early stage and must be improved. Our contribution is *CyberDect*, an online-tool that seeks on Social Networks indications of harassment. In a nutshell, our proposal combines Open Source Intelligence tools with Natural Language Processing techniques to analyse posts seeking for abusive language towards the victim. The evaluation of our proposal has been performed with a case-study that consisted in monitor two real high school accounts from Spain.

Keywords: Cyberbullying · Natural Language Processing · Open Source Intelligence · Twitter

1 Introduction

Bullying is the deliberate and continuous abuse that a child receives from other children [39]. Bullying can be physical, psychological, or both. Regardless of the type of harm, continuous harassment can lead to permanent harm to the victims. In severe cases, bullying has lead to children traumatised for life, or to commit suicide [13]. Moreover, the difficulty of bullying detection arises when victims do not report their abuse, or when teachers or parents do not overhear or see bullying taking place downplaying the situation [20].

It is clear that the Internet has changed the way people learn, exchange information and communicate which each other. However, the Internet can be used for the wrong reasons, such as bullying or scams. Cyberbullying is a new type of bullying that consists in the use of electronic communication devices

© Springer Nature Switzerland AG 2019
R. Valencia-García et al. (Eds.): CITI 2019, CCIS 1124, pp. 109–121, 2019.
https://doi.org/10.1007/978-3-030-34989-9_9

to bully a person, typically by sending messages to the victims of an intimidating or threatening nature. The key differences between traditional bullying and cyberbullying (sometimes refereed as online bullying) have been identified in [29]. First, online bullying is more likely experienced outside of school. Second, cyberbullies are more likely to harass again because their crime remains unpunished most of the time. Third, whereas traditional bullying occurs mainly in young students, online bullying is more frequently during the last years of the school or during the high school. Fourth, children who have experienced cyberbullying are less able to easily defend or escape from it, specially because the stalker has an infinite number of potential supporters.

Cyberbullying is a serious threat. In US, around the 34% of children have experimented online bullying at least once [14]. Moreover, it affects especially to discriminated groups. Three quarters of the victims are high school girls with a different skin colour. Almost half of LGBT youth have experienced online bullying, and more than a half female victims have feelings of powerlessness because of it[1]. In Spain, according to Save the Children, one in ten children has suffered cyberbullying [8].

Stalkers can harass the victims in several forms. He can disseminate false rumours, manipulate photographs, or post offensive comments with insults or cruel jokes towards the victim. Bullying can take place in public or private scenarios. In private scenarios, stalkers menace the victims with messages only for them by using SMS, emails or private messages. In public scenarios, stalkers intimidate the victims where other users can see it. The most common place for public cyberbullying are social networks, popular places on the Internet where people can talk freely about anything. Stalkers take advantage about the anonymity that Social Networks provides, so the identity of the stalker remains private.

As cyberbullying is a recent phenomena, as far as our knowledge there are not yet effective tools for preventing it. The scientific community is making serious efforts towards this field. However, the difficulty in this task is that the analysis of social behaviour is very cultural and context dependant. Therefore, it is necessary to analyse in-depth for a specific cultures and languages. Consequently, we propose *CyberDect*, a novel tool capable of detect cyberbullying from post in social networks in Spanish.

The remainder of the paper is structured as follows: In Sect. 2, background information and related work about automatic tools for cyberbullying detection are discussed. Section 3 contains an explanation of our proposal and its architecture. Section 4 describes the experiments conducted in order to verify the accuracy of our proposal. Finally, Sect. 5 summarises the paper and suggests further work lines.

2   Related Work

This section contains background information about automatic tools for cyberbullying detection (see Sect. 2.1), and some background information concerning

---

[1] https://techjury.net/stats-about/cyberbullying/.

(1) Natural Language Processing, and (2) Open Source Intelligence (see Sect. 2.2), as they are the base of our proposal.

2.1 Automatic Cyberbullying Detection

With the aim of preventing cyberbullying, some researches have explored the reliability of using image detection techniques in order to extract features from media files that could harm the victim. For example, Putjol et al. [27] proposed a tool for cyberbullying detection through image processing. They developed an algorithm to create a profile of stalkers based on gender and age.

Other researches have explored the reliability of performing linguistic analysis on the posts in Social Networks. In [30], the authors explore the reliability of using deep learning techniques for cyberbullying detection. Motivated by the success in other fields, they test with three neural networks: a simple CNN, a hybrid CNN-LSTM and a mixed CNN-LSTM-DNN. The texts they used to test were represented by the word2vec model and extracted from Google-News, Twitter or Formspring. In [42], the authors propose a linguistic model based on word embeddings from pre-defined insulting words, a Bag-of-Words, and semantic features. The final representation of bullying features was used with a linear SVM classifier.

Additionally, it is possible to find in the bibliography frameworks that mix both techniques [19]. Other researches have argued that including personal traits from the stalkers and from the victims can help to improve cyberbullying detection [40]. These researches have focused in different social networks. Therefore, it is possible to find research that has focused in (1) Instagram, a photo and video-sharing social network [17]; (2) Facebook, the world's most popular social network [2]; and (3) Twitter, a micro-blogging social networks where users can post texts no longer than 280 characters [15,22,40] among other social networks. Similar to our proposal, Choong Hon and Dewi Varathan, from the University of Malaya, performed a Cyberbullying Detection System on Twitter [15]. This system relies on the presence of a lexicon of negative keywords, such as insults or degrading words. Once a hazardous tweet was detect, the system emits an alert. However, this solution is focused on the English language. As far as our knowledge, there are no specific research towards the Spanish language. Fore more information concerning cyberbullying detection, the reader can go to [31], and [36].

2.2 Natural Language Processing and Open Source Intelligence

Natural Language Processing. To a great extent, cyberbullying is performed by textual messages, such as emails, or posts in social networks. Therefore, it is necessary to use methods capable of understanding natural language. Natural Language Processing (NLP) is the research field responsible for handling the communication between humans and machines. However, it is very difficult for a machine to perfectly understand the natural language. The main reason of this complexity is that the human language is ambiguous and context-dependant.

Moreover, there are linguistic devices that can vary and change the literal meaning of an utterance, such as irony, tone, idiomatic expressions, or negation clauses among others. Despite these difficulties, NLP has demonstrated to be useful in several scenarios, such as chat-bots, or speech recognition.

Opinion Mining (OM) is the task of NLP and Information Retrieval (IR) that consists in the extraction the subjective opinion of the society towards a specific topic. SA has proven to be useful in several domains, such as marketing [9], the stock-market [24, 35] or public-health [18, 32, 34] just to name a few.

There are, basically, two main approaches for conducting Opinion Mining experiments: (1) Semantic Orientation (SO), and (2) Machine Learning. On the one hand, the SO approach makes use of a set of lexicons which have labelled an score of its polarity: positive, neutral or negative [1]. On the other hand, the Machine Learning approach makes use of statistical algorithms in order to learn the patterns for detecting the polarity from a set of labelled examples. Machine-learning requires that the texts are encoded in a way computers can handle it. In this sense, there statistical methods, such as the Bag of Words (BoW) [3] that represents the texts as the frequency of the words in the text, or linguistic approaches, that represents texts as the frequency of the terms that appear in some psychologically relevant linguistic categories [33].

Opinion Mining techniques can also be classified according to the specificity of the analysis. First, Opinion Mining can extract the subjective polarity of the texts as a whole, labelling them as positive, neutral, or negative. However, there are situations where a more fine-grained analysis is needed. For long documents, some researches have decided to divide the documents in paragraphs and sentences and they have extracted their polarity individually; however, due to the complexity and ambiguity of the natural language, this approach has proven to be insufficient. A more complex approach consists in the classification of the documents by subtopics. In this sense, the usage of ontologies have proven to represent the knowledge of the topic [26, 38].

Open Source Intelligence. Open Source Intelligence (OSINT) consists in the extraction of the public information from open-sources [6]. OSINT sources are several, such as print newspapers, blogs, social networks, public government reports, or professional and academic publications [28]. To exploit effectively OSINT, there are available different tools that ease to query different search engines and social networks simultaneously. For example, for Twitter we can mention *AllMyTweets* to gather all the tweets from a account, *Bioischanged* to determine when some user has changed its biography, or *Sentiment140* [11], a tool capable of guess if an specific tweet is positive, neutral, or negative.

3   CyberDect: A System for the Detection of Cyberbullying Based on NLP and OSINT

CyberDect is a novel approach that allows simultaneously monitoring several Twitter accounts for cyberbullying detection. In this section the reader will find an overview of *CyberDect* and its architecture followed by an detailed explanation of each module.

CyberDect combines OSINT and NLP technologies. In a nutshell, *CyberDect* uses OSINT to compile information from the victim's Twitter account and from all its followers. Then, tweets from every follower is analysed by means of NLP techniques. Finally, the results of the analysis are displayed on a dashboard with information about possible cyberbullying cases. The results obtained can be visualised from two profiles. From the stalker profile, with all tweets posted by a specific stalker, and from the victim profile, with all tweets which mentioned him and the users which performed the bully.

The system architecture of *CyberDect* composed by two main layers: (1) the back-end layer, and (2) the front-end layer. The back-end layer is responsible for retrieving and processing the information, whereas the front-end layer is a web interface with a dashboard where the users can visualise the results. An overview of the architecture is shown in Fig. 1.

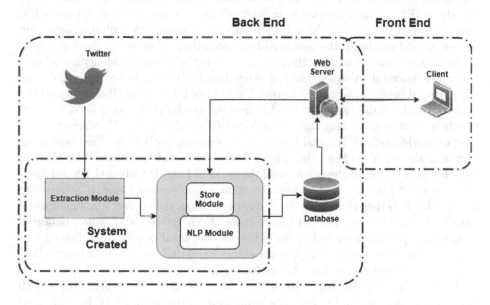

Fig. 1. Architecture of CyberDect

The Back-End Layer. This layer is divided into three modules: (1) the extraction module, (2) the store module, and (3) the NLP module.

First, the **extraction module** is responsible for extracting the tweets from the victim's Twitter account and from their followers. This module filters non-important tweets as re-tweets, because bullying occurs only with direct mentions. In the first version of the prototype, Maltego[2] was the tool selected to compile

---

[2] https://www.maltego.com/.

the information about the followers of the target account. The reason of using Maltego is because this tool obtains a graph that represents the relationship among the followers. This relationship can be useful to detect if the stalkers are supporting or coordinating each others. However, the free version free version of Maltego limits the maximum results to 15. In order to solve this concern, we used *Twitter4J* to collect the tweets. *Twitter4J* [41] is an unofficial Java library that integrates Twitter API with the Java platform.

Next, the **store module** makes use of MongoDB [5] to store the tweets and the social structure of the followers and the victims. A non-relational database system was selected prior a relational database system due to its scalability, as a Twitter accounts may contains thousands of followers and tweets.

Last, the **NLP module** is responsible for the NLP tasks. In order to select which NLP framework use for the *processing module*, we performed a benchmark between Stanford CoreNLP Natural Language Processing Toolkit [21] and Apache OpenNLP [16]. Due to the serious consequences of bullying, we measured our proposal with two specific metrics: False Positives (FP), and False Negatives (FN). These metrics were selected because we are more interested in knowing when our system fails, because an ideal automatic bullying detection system should minimise the number of classification errors as much as possible, specially the number of FN, that occurs when the classifier identifies as not-harmful a harmful message. On the other hand, FP stands for the number of non-harmful tweets classified as harmful, a kind of false alarm. We measured the accuracy and reliability for both NLP frameworks by selecting a subset of 200 tweets extracted from accounts suspicious of cyberbullying. We observed that the Stanford CoreNLP Natural Language Processing Toolkit obtained best accuracy and also required less time. Figure 2 shows the results obtained by the two tools for each subset of the corpus and the total of False Positives (FP) and False Negatives (FN) detected. However, the comparison revealed that it is easier to mismatch FP rather than FN. We can observe that the correct classification of harmful is complex because our classifier has been trained with a non-balanced corpus with predominance of harmful tweets over legal tweets. Unbalanced corpus decreases the accuracy of the classifier; nevertheless, we can observe that almost all harmful tweets have been classified.

We use the *Ibereval 2018* [10] which contains 3307 tweets in Spanish with harmful and not harmful texts. It is important to remark that we have divided the *Ibereval 2018* into three subsets, namely, (1) negligible, (2) dominant, and (3) sexual and stereotyped. In addition, we have included a model composed by insults and offensive language.

The Front-End Layer. This layer provides a dashboard where users can (1) design new studies, (2) evaluate existing studies, and (3) list the accounts which mentioned the victim account. A screen-capture of the graphical user interface is shown in Fig. 3, where we can see the first page of the front-end layer.

To search for cyberbullying, it is need to introduce in *CyberDect* the Twitter account of a possible victim. Then, the *NLP module* compiles the information

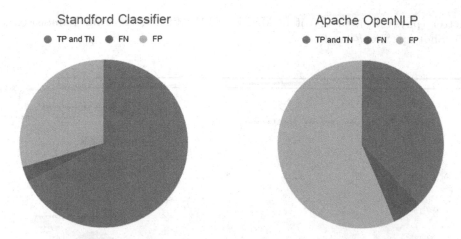

Fig. 2. Comparison between Standford Classifier and Apache NLP framework according to the number of True Positives (TP), True Negatives (TN), False Positives (FP) and False Negatives (FN)

App to perform cyberbullying detection studies on Twitter.

Indicates a Twitter user to perform a new study.		Start

User	Study for stalker	Study for harassed
IesCiudadJaen	Inspect	Inspect
IESLaFlorida	Inspect	Inspect
SanjeMARES	Inspect	Inspect

Fig. 3. Screen capture of the application with a list of the cyberbullying monitoring experiments

about the user and their followers and it is stored by the *Store Module*. Once the information is obtained, the user can choose between two different profiles: the stalker profile, and the victim profile.

From the victim profile, the dashboard consists in a list with all tweets what have mentions to the target account, and their respective authors. This view allows to the users to view if the target account is receiving some type of harassment.

From the stalker profile we can observe the positive's number of each model and the ratio of suspicious tweets to the ratio of normal tweets. Figure 4 shows the dashboard from a stalker profile. In Fig. 4 appears some tweets from a specific user. A possible translation would be: (1) Mario uploads Volta[3], (2) You are

---

[3] Possibly: EA Sports Volta Football.

better (physically), (3) Do it in Madrid, motherfucker, (4) Your Pambisitos[4], (5) Shut up, *"torch-head"*.

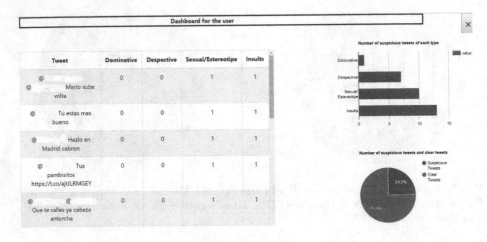

Fig. 4. Dashboard

4   Evaluation and Results

In order to measure the accuracy of *CyberDect* and the NLP engine, we conducted a case-study consisted in monitoring two Twitter accounts from two different high school students. After the *Extract module* and the *Processing module*, a total of 1348 tweets were collected from both accounts: 729 tweets for the first Twitter account, and 619 for the second Twitter account. Figure 5 contains an example of the corpus that contains insults and derogatory language. The text can be translated as: *"Let's see if you laugh so much now, piece of sh*t. Sentence of La Manada, live: 15 years in prison for sexual assault"*. This tweet was used as example of a FP because, although it contains foul language, can be understood more in the context of a discussion rather than a bullying situation.

Figure 6 shows the result obtained for the two case-studies performed. In the first experiment, 229 tweets were marked as suspicious, but after a manual revision of the tweets, 65 resulted to be FP. In this second experiment, from the 619 collected tweets, 174 were labelled as suspicious but 56 resulted to be FP. An in-depth analysis reveals that the majority of FP occurs by the *negligible model* because it is the model with large number of examples and, consequently, produces more coincidences. As the number of FN is minimum, the NLP engine directly discards FN. Therefore, the classifier does not save all tweets, only those that have tested positive on one of the models.

---

[4] Slang, stupid or retarded.

A ver si ahora te ríes tanto, pedazo de mierda.

Sentencia de la Manada, en directo: 15 años de cárcel por agresión sexual

El Confidencial

Reacciones al fallo de la Manada, en directo: el guardia civil será expulsado del c...
Además de 15 años de cárcel para cada uno de los integrantes y de dos más para
Antonio Manuel Guerrero por robar el móvil de la víctima, el fallo prohíbe ...
🔗 elconfidencial.com

3:02 p. m. · 21 jun. 2019 · Twitter for Android

Fig. 5. An example of a tweet of the corpus.

The experimentation stage revealed that our proposal successfully performs well in the task of cyberbullying identification. We can observe that in both experiments the results performed similarly and the system is able to detect texts with bullying statements (TP), and texts without bullying (TN). In addition, we observed an percentage of FP of 8.90% and 9.04% for the first and second test-case respectively.

In addition, we conducted a manual revision of the results by selecting randomly some followers from both accounts to manually analyse their tweets. This manual revision of the tweets indicated that the system decreases its accuracy when

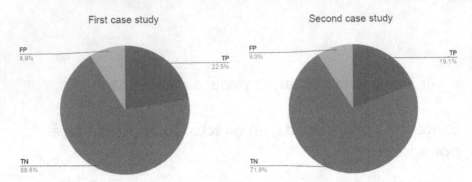

Fig. 6. Results of the two case-studies comparing the number of True Positives (TP), True Negatives (TN), False Positives (FP) and False Negatives (FN)

the tweets contain hyperlinks, emoticons, or non-Spanish words. We assume that the error rating achieved is affordable. However, we think that human supervision is always needed in cyberbullying detection. To help in the manual supervision, we are planning to including an alert system to send alerts via emails or text-messages to the supervisors when suspicious tweets are detected.

We found that, as we introduce more examples to the NLP framework, the accuracy improves. Therefore, we are searching for different corpus to include in the training stage. As the task of searching manually for corpus is time-consuming, we will explore the reliability of using distant-supervision to obtain new examples [37].

5   Conclusions

In this work, *CyberDect*, a novel approach for automatic cyberbullying detection on Twitter based on OSINT and NLP has been described. The validation of this tool was focused in discover the number of FP and FN in two real test-cases from high school students from Spain. During the first test-case, our tool successfully detected the 8.9% suspicious tweets, whereas in the second test-case a total of 28.38% suspicious tweets. The error rating was 9.04% and 32.18% for the first test-case and the second test-case, respectively. These results show that *CyberDect* has been capable of classifying correctly the harmful tweets.

During the experimentation stage two concerns were identified. First, we observed that the accuracy decreases when the tweets have hyperlinks, emojis, uppercase words, or words that are not Spanish. Second, the free version of *Maltego* limited to only fifteen results. On the one hand, concerning the loss of accuracy, we will explore the reliability of (1) extracting specific linguistic features from Spanish [33], (2) applying general-purpose information retrieval techniques, such as word2vec [12] to train a CNN, and (3) the usage of ontologies for modelling cyberbullying for an aspect-level classification [7,25]. On the other hand, concerning *Maltego*, we will explore alternatives to extract the information of the network composed by the victim and its followers [23]. In addition, we are planning to include meta information of the tweets, such as the publication date, or the number of previous tweets with mentions to the target account. With this extra information, we expect to improve the accuracy of our model and to reduce FN.

Concerning the interface, we will (1) include an alert system to the back-end layer capable of emitting alerts by different transport methods, such as emails, or SMS, and (2) provide methods where schoolmates can report anonymously cases of those who have witnessed. In this sense, we will develop an mobile-app similar to [4] but oriented to the cyberbullying domain.

Acknowledgements. This work has been supported by the Spanish National Research Agency (AEI) and the European Regional Development Fund (FEDER/ERDF) through project KBS4FIA (TIN2016-76323-R).

References

1. Agarwal, B., Mittal, N.: Semantic orientation-based approach for sentiment analysis. In: Agarwal, B., Mittal, N. (eds.) Prominent Feature Extraction for Sentiment Analysis. SC, pp. 77–88. Springer, Cham (2016). https://doi.org/10.1007/978-3-319-25343-5_6
2. Anderson, J., Bresnahan, M., Musatics, C.: Combating weight-based cyberbullying on facebook with the dissenter effect. Cyberpsychol. Behav. Soc. Netw. **17**(5), 281–286 (2014)
3. Apolinardo-Arzube, O., García-Díaz, J.A., Medina-Moreira, J., Luna-Aveiga, H., Valencia-García, R.: Evaluating information-retrieval models and machine-learning classifiers for measuring the social perception towards infectious diseases. Appl. Sci. **9**(14), 2858 (2019)
4. Apolinario, Ó., Medina-Moreira, J., Luna-Aveiga, H., García-Díaz, J.A., Valencia-García, R., Estrade-Cabrera, J.I.: Prevención de enfermedades infecciosas basada en el análisis inteligente en RRSS y participación ciudadana. Proces. del Leng. Nat. **63**, 163–166 (2019)
5. Banker, K.: MongoDB in Action. Manning Publications Co., New York (2011)
6. Bazzell, M.: Open Source Intelligence Techniques: Resources for Searching and Analyzing Online Information. CreateSpace Independent Publishing Platform, Scotts Valley (2016)
7. Beydoun, G., Low, G., García-Sánchez, F., Valencia-García, R., Martínez-Béjar, R.: Identification of ontologies to support information systems development. Inf. Syst. **46**, 45–60 (2014)
8. Calmaestra, J.: Yo a eso no juego: bullying y Ciberbullying en la infancia. Save the Children (2016)
9. Fang, X., Zhan, J.: Sentiment analysis using product review data. J. Big Data **2**(1), 5 (2015)
10. Fersini, E., Rosso, P., Anzovino, M.: Overview of the task on automatic misogyny identification at IberEval 2018. In: IberEval@ SEPLN, pp. 214–228 (2018)
11. Go, A., Bhayani, R., Huang, L.: Twitter sentiment classification using distant supervision. CS224N Project Report, Stanford, vol. 1, no. 12 (2009)
12. Goldberg, Y., Levy, O.: Word2vec explained: deriving Mikolov et al.'s negative-sampling word-embedding method. arXiv preprint arXiv:1402.3722 (2014)

13. Hinduja, S., Patchin, J.W.: Bullying, cyberbullying, and suicide. Arch. Suicide Res. **14**(3), 206–221 (2010)
14. Hinduja, S., Patchin, J.W.: Cyberbullying fact sheet: identification, prevention, and response. Cyberbullying Research Center (2010). Accessed 30 Jan 2011
15. Hon, L., Varathan, K.: Cyberbullying detection system on twitter. IJABM **1**(1), 1–11 (2015)
16. Hornik, K.: OpenNLP: apache OpenNLP tools interface. R package version 0.2-5 (2015)
17. Hosseinmardi, H., Mattson, S.A., Rafiq, R.I., Han, R., Lv, Q., Mishra, S.: Detection of cyberbullying incidents on the instagram social network. arXiv preprint arXiv:1503.03909 (2015)
18. Jung, H., Park, H.A., Song, T.M.: Ontology-based approach to social data sentiment analysis: detection of adolescent depression signals. J. Med. Internet Res. **19**(7), e259 (2017)
19. Kansara, K.B., Shekokar, N.M.: A framework for cyberbullying detection in social network. Int. J. Curr. Eng. Technol. **5**(1), 494–498 (2015)
20. Larrañaga, E., Yubero, S., Ovejero, A., Navarro, R.: Loneliness, parent-child communication and cyberbullying victimization among Spanish youths. Comput. Hum. Behav. **65**, 1–8 (2016)
21. Manning, C., Surdeanu, M., Bauer, J., Finkel, J., Bethard, S., McClosky, D.: The Stanford CoreNLP natural language processing toolkit. In: Proceedings of 52nd Annual Meeting of the Association for Computational Linguistics: System Demonstrations, pp. 55–60 (2014)
22. Mouheb, D., Abushamleh, M.H., Abushamleh, M.H., Al Aghbari, Z., Kamel, I.: Real-time detection of cyberbullying in arabic twitter streams. In: 2019 10th IFIP International Conference on New Technologies, Mobility and Security (NTMS), pp. 1–5. IEEE (2019)
23. Myers, S.A., Sharma, A., Gupta, P., Lin, J.: Information network or social network? The structure of the twitter follow graph. In: Proceedings of the 23rd International Conference on World Wide Web, pp. 493–498. ACM (2014)
24. Pagolu, V.S., Reddy, K.N., Panda, G., Majhi, B.: Sentiment analysis of twitter data for predicting stock market movements. In: 2016 International Conference on Signal Processing, Communication, Power and Embedded System (SCOPES), pp. 1345–1350. IEEE (2016)
25. Penalver-Martinez, I., et al.: Feature-based opinion mining through ontologies. Expert Syst. Appl. **41**(13), 5995–6008 (2014)
26. Pontiki, M., et al.: SemEval-2016 task 5: aspect based sentiment analysis. In: Proceedings of the 10th International Workshop on Semantic Evaluation (SemEval-2016), pp. 19–30 (2016)
27. Pujol, F.A., et al.: Detección automática de ciberbullying a través del procesamiento digital de imágenes. In: VIII International Congress of Physiology and Education (2016)
28. Richelson, J.T.: The US Intelligence Community. Routledge, New York (2018)
29. Robinson, E., et al.: Parental involvement in preventing and responding to cyberbullying. Fam. Matters **92**(92), 68 (2013)
30. Rosa, H., Matos, D., Ribeiro, R., Coheur, L., Carvalho, J.P.: A "deeper" look at detecting cyberbullying in social networks. In: 2018 International Joint Conference on Neural Networks (IJCNN), pp. 1–8. IEEE (2018)
31. Rosa, H., et al.: Automatic cyberbullying detection: a systematic review. Comput. Hum. Behav. **93**, 333–345 (2019)

32. Rosa, R.L., Rodríguez, D.Z., Schwartz, G.M., de Campos Ribeiro, I., Bressan, G.: Monitoring system for potential users with depression using sentiment analysis. In: 2016 IEEE International Conference on Consumer Electronics (ICCE), pp. 381–382. IEEE (2016)

33. Salas-Zárate, M.P., López-López, E., Valencia-García, R., Aussenac-Gilles, N., Almela, Á., Alor-Hernández, G.: A study on LIWC categories for opinion mining in Spanish reviews. J. Inf. Sci. **40**(6), 749–760 (2014)

34. Salas-Zárate, M.P., Medina-Moreira, J., Lagos-Ortiz, K., Luna-Aveiga, H., Rodriguez-Garcia, M.A., Valencia-Garcia, R.: Sentiment analysis on tweets about diabetes: an aspect-level approach. Comput. Math. Methods Med. **2017**, 1–9 (2017)

35. Salas-Zárate, M.P., Valencia-García, R., Ruiz-Martínez, A., Colomo-Palacios, R.: Feature-based opinion mining in financial news: an ontology-driven approach. J. Inf. Sci. **43**(4), 458–479 (2017)

36. Salawu, S., He, Y., Lumsden, J.: Approaches to automated detection of cyberbullying: a survey. IEEE Trans. Affect. Comput. **99**, 1 (2017)

37. Sanchez, H., Kumar, S.: Twitter bullying detection. Ser. NSDI **12**(2011), 15 (2011)

38. Schouten, K., Frasincar, F.: Survey on aspect-level sentiment analysis. IEEE Trans. Knowl. Data Eng. **28**(3), 813–830 (2015)

39. Slonje, R., Smith, P.K.: Cyberbullying: another main type of bullying? Scand. J. Psychol. **49**(2), 147–154 (2008)

40. Tahmasbi, N., Rastegari, E.: A socio-contextual approach in automated detection of cyberbullying. In: Hawaii International Conference on System Sciences (HICSS), pp. 2151–2160 (2018)

41. Yamamoto, Y.: Twitter4J Java library (2017)

42. Zhao, R., Zhou, A., Mao, K.: Automatic detection of cyberbullying on social networks based on bullying features. In: Proceedings of the 17th International Conference on Distributed Computing and Networking, p. 43. ACM (2016)

A Byte Pattern Based Method for File Compression

José Luis Hernández-Hernández[1]([✉])[iD], Mario Hernández-Hernández[2][iD],
Sajad Sabzi[3][iD], Mario Andrés Paredes-Valverde[4][iD],
and Alejandro Fuentes Penna[5][iD]

[1] TecNM/Technological Institute of Chilpancingo, Chilpancingo, Mexico
joseluis.hernandez@itchilpancingo.edu.mx
[2] Autonomous University of Guerrero, Chilpancingo, Mexico
mhernandezh@uagro.mx
[3] University of Mohaghegh Ardabili, Ardabil, Iran
sajadsabzi2@gmail.com
[4] University of Murcia, Murcia, Spain
marioandres.paredes@um.es
[5] TecNM/CIIDET, Querétaro, Mexico
afuentes@ciidet.edu.mx

Abstract. This research presents a method to allows the data compression from a file containing any type of information by combining the pattern theory with the theory of data compression. This proposal can reduce the storage space of a file data from any kind of computer, platform or operating system installed on that computer. According to the fundamentals of patterns, a pattern is a regularity of bytes contained within a file with self-similarity characteristics; if this concept applies to data files, we find certain amounts of auto-similar or patterns repeated several times throughout the file; with a store data representation and being referenced, at a certain point data can be recovered from the original file without losing a single data, and consequently saving space on the hard disk.

In the search for various ways to compress data, led me to analyze and implement the proposed methodology in a beta mode compression software for Windows 10, which presents very compromising results.

Keywords: Patterns · Data compression · Tiles · Mathematical pattern

1 Introduction

This research proposes a file compression method that allows reducing file size so that it takes up less space on the computer's hard drive. This method does not affect the content or structure of the file, it simply reduces the space it occupies [9].

In computer science, the purpose of compressing a data file is to use an algorithm and apply it to the data so that it has a transformation and takes

© Springer Nature Switzerland AG 2019
R. Valencia-García et al. (Eds.): CITI 2019, CCIS 1124, pp. 122–134, 2019.
https://doi.org/10.1007/978-3-030-34989-9_10

up less storage space. Depending on the data types contained in the file, the implemented algorithm may be more or less effective. Aiming to perform the file compressing process, a well-crafted algorithm, a large memory capacity, and a processor with good processing speed are needed [14,17].

Data compression typically applies when a file needs to be sent over the Internet because email and messaging applications put limits on the size of the files that can be sent. Therefore, the file is usually compressed to be sent over the network. Data compression, which involves transforming data into a given format, helps to reduce storage and communication costs [8,11,12,21].

The file compression method proposed in this work uses the fundamentals of patterns approach for data compression purposes. A pattern in an image is the minimum unit of the image that bears a resemblance in colour and size and that is repeated several times in an image or group of images [23].

The most basic patterns of images are commonly called tiles based on repetition and recurrence. A single template, tile or cell, is combined by unchanged duplicates or modifications [1].

The fractals are another kind of pattern, that are geometric objects whose basic structure, fragmented or seemingly irregular, is repeated at different scales [20]. The term was proposed by mathematician Bernot Mandelbrot in 1975 and derives from Latin fractus, meaning broken or fractured. Many natural structures are fractal type as it says [3]. The key mathematical property of a genuinely fractal object is that its fractal metric dimension is a rational number and is not an integer [4].

The type of pattern that can be used in flat files are adjacent bytes, which form syllables, word fragments, words, or similar fragments [15]. In a data file that contains any type of information (image, video, text, etc.), the bytes that are stored one after the other correspond to the ASCII code. This group of elements can be letters, numbers, special characters, or characters of control; so that each byte has a value between the range 0 to 255 according to ASCII code. In this way, a block of bytes can be simplified and represented by a single integer [19].

The form of self-similarity representation has much to do with the fractal concept established by Bernot Mendelbrot. This property allows to recognize elements that have the characteristics of the whole, from which it is extracted and it allows that to replicate that whole can be regenerated. Figure 1 shows the 4 types of patterns described above.

Data compression is useful because it helps to reduce the use of expensive resources, such as disk space or the bandwidth to transmit data [7]. On the negative side, compressed data must be decompressed to be seen and this additional process may be detrimental to some applications. For instance, a compression scheme for video may require expensive hardware, so that the video is decompressed fast enough as to be seen while decompressing (there is the option to decompress the video completely before seeing it, but this is inconvenient and storage space required to see the decompressed video). Thus, the design of data compression schemes implies compensation among several factors such as

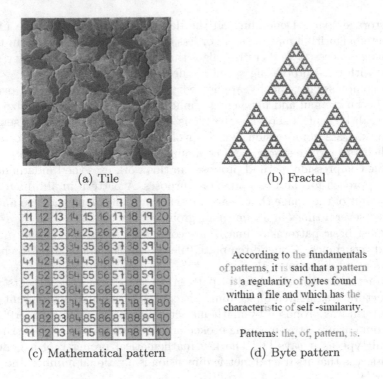

(a) Tile

(b) Fractal

According to the fundamentals of patterns, it is said that a pattern is a regularity of bytes found within a file and which has the characteristic of self-similarity.

Patterns: the, of, pattern, is.

(c) Mathematical pattern

(d) Byte pattern

Fig. 1. Diversity of patterns that can be used.

number of bytes in the file, degree of compression, the compression algorithm used and necessary computing resources to compress/decompress the data [2,18].

Nowadays, a file compressor application is installed on many computers. This application allows grouping multiple files and/or folders into a single package to reduce the space you occupy on the storage medium.

The two most used file compressors are: WinZip © and WinRar ©. The most important characteristics of these tools are described below:

- WinZip © is a commercial file compressor developed by WinZip Computing (formerly known as Nico Mak Computing) that works on Microsoft Windows. It can handle several additional file formats. (WinZip © is a registered trademark of Microsoft Corporation ®) [22].
- WinRar © is a useful application that allows creating, managing and controlling directories. It is the most widely used solution for decompression and compression of information, helping to reduce the size and improve response time when sending content or creating a backup. It is compatible with any type of document or application and provides a RAR and UnRAR file decompressor for multiple platforms. (WinRar © is a registered trademark of RAR-BAL ®) [13].

WinZip © and WinRar ©, compress any type of data contained in a file and can subsequently decompress it without data loss. It performs data compression using byte patterns and strings that repeat throughout the file and perform exactly the same function.

2   Materials and Methods

To perform data compression, is considered of the fact that groups of elements exist that have the basic properties of self-similarity and through which it is possible to reproduce all and each of the combinations that can be found in ASCII code.

The first step of the file compression process consists in representing 2 adjacent bytes as a pattern of its original elements. The result of this task is a representation of each pair of adjacent bytes of a defined block of bytes. This process is repeated with the new patterns found in order to create patterns of 2, 4, 8, 16, 32, ..., n byte groups.

Thanks to this process, the data storage is very efficient since instead of storing the entire block of bytes, only its pattern-based representation is stored.

The file compression and decompression processes require a master pattern file that has the format shown in Table 1.

Table 1. Data structure of the master pattern file.

Pattern number	Left byte	Right byte
Any integer from 256	Any integer value with its respective sign	Any integer value with its respective sign

Where:

a. Pattern number. It is a positive integer that is generated with values ranging from 0 to 255 because they are taken directly from the ASCII code to represent each of the respective characters (some not printable and other control).
b. Left byte. It is a positive or negative number, which corresponds to the first byte of the pair of bytes that you want to handle as a pattern.
c. Right byte. It is a positive or negative number, which corresponds to the second byte of the pair of bytes that you want to handle as a pattern.

The data structure above presented corresponds to each pattern stored in a file known as Pattern Master File. Once file compression using integer patterns is performed, a file composed of the next two parts is obtained:

a. Header. It contains data that identifies it as a patterns file, file size, as well as the name of the original file (original unit, path, file name, and your extension), as shown in Table 2.
b. Data area. It contains only integer numbers that correspond to patterns consisting of a group of three integer values.

Table 2. Structure of the pattern file header.

Identifier	Size in bytes	File name
This field is composed of 2 bytes as follows: ASCII code: 80 letter 'P'; ASCII code: 97 letter 'a'	This field stores in an integer value, the amount in bytes occupied by the file name	This field contains: storage unit, path, file name and your extension (original)

2.1 Compressor Architecture

Regarding the man-machine interface, the project includes tools that allow users to build the form look & feel of user interfaces [16], to configure the screen layout. These features allow users to configure the information displayed on the screen in terms of information density and attributes of deployment such as colours, types of lines, filling patterns of the figures, sizes, titles, resolution, etc. Figure 2 depicts the architecture of the file compression application proposed in this work.

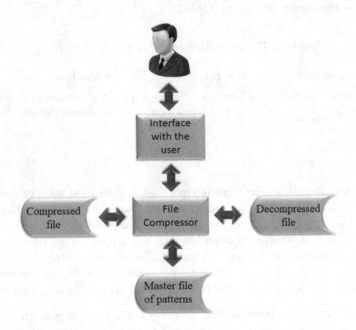

Fig. 2. Basic scheme of the file compressor.

It also uses context-sensitive support to assist the user in the operation of the interface and of interaction techniques and dialogues. The reliability and acceptance of the system involve some considerations that must be taken into account in all aspects of design and development to minimise the possibility of data failures.

2.2 Compression Process

For developing the file compression application here proposed, it is required to analyse all the file to be compressed and search for repetitive patterns which will be considered as similar auto entities. Then, these patterns are represented as a unique integer numeric value and are stored in a pattern file that will be used by the decompression process. This file is also known as data dictionary.

The new patterns that are generated are stored in a file, however, any known pattern is no longer stored; it is simply used for compression and the decompression of a file.

At the time of finding new patterns is always verified the pattern obtained, against those that already exist and if it exists takes its entire numerical value to represent it in the file being compressed.

Unfortunately, the patterns are generated in a static form and are defined as the data necessary to represent the pattern [5, 6, 10, 17]. These data are represented by the structure shown in Table 3.

Table 3. Structure to store the patterns that are obtained.

Pattern	Left element	Right element
One number	One number	One number

The structure of Table 3 will be used and stored in a file called MASTER. CFP (Compressed file with patterns) and will be found in the unit C in the folder C:\WINDOWS of the computer in use and with this form of compression, stored patterns are simply used. A drawback is that each time a new pattern is generated, it is stored in the master file of patterns that will continue growing. The Algorithm 1 used to compress the data of a file using patterns is shown below.

A training process consisting of testing about 100 files with different content is performed. This process aims to store the most amount of patterns that may be required for the decompression operation in the master file of fractals.

When installing the software, it will copy the master file of fractals to the root level on the computer in use.

When performing the compression process, the master file of fractals will grow a little and at that time the new patterns will be updated in a copy that will be in the cloud. Such a copy of the cloud updates the fractal master file in real-time installed on any computer.

2.3 Decompression Process

The decompression process starts by opening a file that has been compressed with the compression project software. In the file opening dialog box, the application only shows those files that have extension CFP.

Algorithm 1. Algorithm to compress a file using patterns.

1: Open file to compress (source)
2: Open file where the compressed data will be (output)
3: **while** (not end of file) **do**
4:    Read 50 bytes from the source file
5:    Take numerical value according to the ASCII code of each character
6:    Take pairs of bytes to create patterns
7:    Check if the pattern exists in the pattern master
8:    If the pattern does not exist, store it in the master pattern file
9:    Rebuild pattern repeatedly
10:    Write the pattern to the output file
11: **end while**
12: Close files

Once a file with the specified extension is opened, the application verifies that the characters "P" and "a" exist in the first 2 bytes. If the file does not have this identifier, it means that the file is damaged and/or was not created with this application.

In this process, a string of characters containing information such as unit, the path, file name, and the extension with which the file will be created is used to determine where it will be decompressed. Then, integer values or patterns are read, one by one until you reach the end of the file to decompress.

The decompression process is performed for each integer value or pattern identified. The Algorithm 2 used to decompress data from a file using patterns is shown below.

Algorithm 2. Algorithm to decompress a file using patterns.

1: Open file to decompress
2: Open the output file
3: Read the header of the file to be decompressed
4: Verify that the first 2 bytes have the characters "Pa"
5: **while** (not end of file) **do**
6:    Read an integer (pattern)
7:    Search for the pattern in the pattern master file
8:    Take the 2 numerical values
9:    Find each numerical value in the master pattern file
10: **end while** (values are in the range of 0-255)
11: Write all the patterns found in the output file
12: Close files

2.4   Case Study of Compression/Decompression with Patterns

The operation we are going to perform is to compress the "Pattern" text. The first step consists of taking the ASCII code from each of the characters. The result of this step is: 80, 97, 116, 116, 101, 114, 110 and 115.

Next, pairs are taken of which only the corresponding value of the ASCII code is considered and each pair is assigned a consecutive number from 256 (it should be noted that the values of 0 al 255 correspond to the character set values of the ASCII code) as shown in Fig. 3.

P	a	t	t	e	r	n	s
80	97	116	116	101	114	110	115
256		257		258		259	

Fig. 3. Patterns generated from pairs of integer values.

The values obtained are taken, the same procedure as shown above is applied and we get what is shown in Fig. 4.

256	257
260	

258	259
261	

260	261
262	

Fig. 4. Other patterns generated from pairs of integer values.

Once the previous operations were performed, an integer number, which is equivalent to the corresponding couple, is obtained for each pair. The obtained numbers are stored in the pattern master file with their corresponding values as shown in Table 4.

Table 4. Patterns that are stored in the master pattern file.

Pattern	Left	Right
256	80	97
257	116	116
258	101	114
259	110	115
260	256	257
261	258	259
262	260	261

Finally, an integer equivalent to the pattern of the chain is obtained. This result is shown in Fig. 5.

Instead of the string, the number 262, which occupies only 2 bytes, is stored thus obtaining a compression rate of 96% of the original file size to be compressed i.e., the text uses 2 bytes of storage.

String	Corresponds to	Pattern
"Pattern"	⟶	262

Fig. 5. Text string with its respective pattern.

It should be noted that the master patterns file grows each time the compression process is performed because of this file stores all unknown combinations of byte pairs (also called patterns). Figure 6 depicts how the patterns were formed from top to bottom.

P	a	t	t	e	r	n	s
80	97	116	116	101	114	110	115
256		257		258		259	
260				261			
262							

Fig. 6. Creating patterns from top to bottom.

The second operation that is performed is decompressing the pattern 262. The decompression process, which consists of performing the opposite compression process, is applied to each pattern identified.

To clarify this process, let's take the example of compression: Be the pattern 262.

The pattern is taken and is searched in the pattern master file. This pattern is equivalent to the following values: 260 and 261. Once we have such values, the same previous process is done for each number thus obtaining the following values: 256, 257, 258 and 259.

The four numbers obtained previously are searched into the master pattern file thus obtaining the following values: 80, 97, 116, 116, 101, 114, 110 and 115.

Finally, the string obtained in the uncompressed file is written. In this way, the size of the resulting file is 2 bytes instead of 8 bytes as shown in Fig. 7.

Figure 7 depicts the complexity pyramid to decompose the patterns until recovering the original data from the file.

262							
260				261			
256		257		258		259	
80	97	116	116	101	114	110	115
P	a	t	t	e	r	n	s

Fig. 7. Pyramid of complexity of the decompression process.

3   Results and Discussion

In the investigation that was done about file compressors that exist commercially or well as shareware, can be counted by hundreds and of very different forms of operation, in various environments.

We compare the compressor operation using patterns, WinZip © and WinRar ©; in order to have comparison parameters.

They took 6 Word files that have extension. docx, they were compressed with the proposed file compressor, the WinZip © [22] and WinRar © [13]. The results and percentages obtained are shown in Table 5.

Table 5. Word files (documents) compressed with the 3 compressors.

File name	Size in bytes	Pattern compression		WinZip ©		WinRar ©	
		Size	Percentage	Size	Percentage	Size	Percentage
Pattern_Basics.docx	5,471	253	4.62%	1,696	31.00%	1,624	29.68%
Fractal.docx	9,142	397	4.34%	3,760	41.13%	3,720	40.69%
My_story.docx	12,921	549	4.25%	4,922	38.09%	4,916	38.05%
Collaboration.docx	10,567	455	4.31%	1,075	38.56%	4,033	38.17%
References.docx	9,666	419	4.33%	3,598	37.22%	4,555	47.12%
Prologo.docx	8,021	355	4.43%	3,165	39.46%	3,120	38.90%

Based on the data presented in Table 5, a comparative graph of united points was generated, obtaining the results shown in Fig. 8.

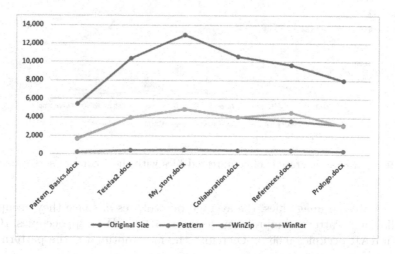

Fig. 8. Comparative graphic of compressed files with the 3 compressors.

In compressed text files, the average percentages of space they occupy are the following: Pattern compression has 4.36%, WinZip has 32.58% and WinRAR has 38.75%. Therefore the most optimal is the Pattern compression.

Another 6 image files (.BMP) were compressed with the 3 compressors that are being evaluated. The resulting percentages are shown in Table 6.

Table 6. Image files compressed with the 3 compressors.

File name	Size in bytes	Pattern compression		WinZip ©		WinRar ©	
		Size	Percentage	Size	Percentage	Size	Percentage
Circle.bmp	7,422	335	4.5%	521	7.0%	457	6.2%
Fig410.bmp	8,702	387	4.5%	1,296	14.9%	1,161	13.3%
Arrow.bmp	7,322	331	4.5%	618	8.4%	513	7.0%
Duck.bmp	18,678	783	4.2%	1,313	7.0%	1,213	6.5%
Jlhh1.bmp	8,062	360	4.5%	819	10.2%	752	9.3%
Curve.bmp	5,862	272	4.6%	788	13.4%	708	12.1%

Based on the data presented in Table 6, a comparative graph of united points was generated, obtaining the results shown in Fig. 9.

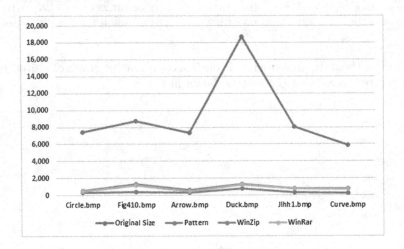

Fig. 9. Comparative graphic of compressed files with the 3 compressors (images).

In compressed image files, the average percentages of space they occupy are the following: Pattern compression occupies 4.46%, WinZip occupies 10.15% and WinRAR occupies 9.06%. Therefore the most optimal is the pattern compression.

The disadvantages of pattern compression are the following:

- A complete file folder cannot be compressed/decompressed. It is working so that in the next version, you can compress several files that are inside a folder.
- It is not compatible with WinZip and WinRAR.

4   Conclusions

In today's times, data storage devices have made dizzying progress, but also the software is becoming more complex and data files require more and more space.

In the case of executable files and any file that stores an image, sound or video, they require a large amount of space in bytes to be able to fully store the information of the same.

For many years, computer users have discussed the benefits and limitations of video cards, audio cards, memory or hard drives. However, all these components called hardware would have taken many more years to evolve without there being the need to break existing physical boundaries when handling information. It's then that it's about data compression.

As for the benefit you can use the compressor made with a certainty of 99.8%. It was used personally to compress approximately 50 files and worked correctly 100% in both their compression and decompression.

Through the development and implementation of this file compressor, new approaches, extensions, and improvements have emerged to it.

File compression and decompression may no longer be as popular today due to improvements in storage capacities, both on email accounts, hard drives, and Internet speed; in addition to the decrease of direct downloads and the growth of the torrent download (small file that contains all the information about other content that we want to download), but anyway it is still a very useful tool.

As a research project has its limitations and scopes, further work can be proposed to improve it.

Acknowledgments. Authors are grateful to TecNM/Technological Institute of Chilpancingo, Autonomous University of Guerrero (UAGro), University of Mohaghegh Ardabili, University of Murcia and TecNM/CIIDET for supporting this work.

References

1. Akiyama, J.: Tile-makers and semi-tile-makers. Am. Math. Mon. **114**(7), 602–609 (2007)
2. Bachu, S., Chari, K.M.: A review on motion estimation in video compression. In: 2015 International Conference on Signal Processing and Communication Engineering Systems, pp. 250–256. IEEE (2015)
3. Belchor, P.M., et al.: Use of fractals channels to improve a proton exchange membrane fuel cell performance. J. Energy Power Eng. **9**, 727–730 (2015)
4. Bellomo, N., Bellouquid, A., Tao, Y., Winkler, M.: Toward a mathematical theory of Keller-Segel models of pattern formation in biological tissues. Math. Models Meth. Appl. Sci. **25**(09), 1663–1763 (2015)
5. Bentley, J., McIlroy, D.: Data compression using long common strings. In: Proceedings DCC 1999 Data Compression Conference (Cat. No. PR00096), pp. 287–295. IEEE (1999)
6. Bentley, J., McIlroy, D.: Data compression with long repeated strings. Inf. Sci. **135**(1–2), 1–11 (2001)

7. Kuhn, M., Kunkel, J.M., Ludwig, T.: Data compression for climate data. Supercomput. Front. Innov. **3**(1), 75–94 (2016)
8. Larsson, N.J.: Structures of String Matching and Data Compression. Lund University, Sweden (1999)
9. Lippert, L., Gross, M.H., Kurmann, C.: Compression domain volume rendering for distributed environments. Comput. Graph. Forum **16**, C95–C107 (1997)
10. Long, P.M., Natsev, A.I., Vitter, J.S.: Text compression via alphabet re-representation. Neural Netw. **12**(4–5), 755–765 (1999)
11. Makkar, A., Singh, G., Narula, R.: Improving LZW compression 1 (2012)
12. Müldner, T., Leighton, G., Diamond, J.: Using XML compression for WWW communication. In: Proceedings of the IADIS WWW/Internet 2005 Conference (2005)
13. RarLab, WinRar: software system for compress files (2019). http://www.win-rar.com/rarproducts.html. Accessed 08 Aug 2019
14. Reghbati, H.K.: Special feature an overview of data compression techniques. Computer **14**(4), 71–75 (1981)
15. Reghizzi, S.C., Pradella, M.: Tile rewriting grammars and picture languages. Theor. Comput. Sci. **340**(2), 257–272 (2005)
16. Santaolaya, S.R.: Ambiente de Desarrollo para la Programación Visual de Interfaces de Usuario para Monitoreo de Procesos en Línea. Ph.D. thesis, Centro Nacional de Investigación y Desarrollo Tecnológico (CENIDET) (1995)
17. Sayood, K.: Introduction to Data Compression. Morgan Kaufmann, Burlington (2017)
18. Sikora, T.: MPEG digital video coding standards. In: Compressed Video over Networks, pp. 45–88. CRC Press (2018)
19. Soria, F.G., et al.: Sistemas evolutivos. Boletín de Política Informática. México (1986)
20. Stamps, A.E.: Fractals, skylines, nature and beauty. Landsc. Urban Plan. **60**(3), 163–184 (2002)
21. SubhamastanRao, T., Soujanya, M., Hemalatha, T., Revathi, T.: Simultaneous data compression and encryption. Int. J. Comput. Sci. Inf. Technol. **2**(5), 2369–2374 (2011)
22. WinZip: Program of compression for windows (2019). http://www.winzip.com/ru/prodpagewz.htm. Accessed 08 Aug 2019
23. Wu, H., Chen, Q., Yachida, M.: Face detection from color images using a fuzzy pattern matching method. IEEE Trans. Pattern Anal. Mach. Intell. **21**(6), 557–563 (1999)

Internet of Things and Computer Architecture

PESSHIoT: Smart Platform for Monitoring and Controlling Smart Home Devices and Sensors

Isaac Machorro-Cano[1]([⊠]) [iD], Mario Andrés Paredes-Valverde[1] [iD],
Giner Alor-Hernandez[1] [iD], María del Pilar Salas-Zárate[1] [iD],
Mónica Guadalupe Segura-Ozuna[2] [iD],
and José Luis Sánchez-Cervantes[3] [iD]

[1] Tecnológico Nacional de México/I. T. Orizaba, Av. Oriente 9, 852. Col.
Emiliano Zapata, 94320 Orizaba, Veracruz, Mexico
imachorro@gmail.com,
{mparedesv,galor,msalasz}@ito-depi.edu.mx
[2] Universidad del Papaloapan (UNPA), Circuito Central #200. Col. Parque
Industrial, 68301 Tuxtepec, Oaxaca, Mexico
msegura@unpa.edu.mx
[3] CONACYT-Tecnológico Nacional de México/I. T. Orizaba, Av. Oriente 9,
852. Col. Emiliano Zapata, 94320 Orizaba, Veracruz, Mexico
jlsanchez@conacyt.mx

Abstract. The Internet of Things (IoT) allows for the development of a wide
range of products, useful in everyday life in contexts such as education, health,
trade, tourism, agriculture, environment, and home, among others. In the home
context, domotics emerged as a set of smart home automation systems controlling nearly everything in a house – e.g. lights, appliances, electrical outlets,
cooling systems. To this end, domotic systems collect information through
sensors and execute a series of tasks accordingly. Domotic systems have
numerous advantages, including safety, comfort, and efficient energy consumption, among others. Nowadays, many applications can control smart home
devices, yet in technology monitoring, applications giving comfort and energy
saving recommendations based on user behavior patterns have not yet been
developed. To address this gap, we propose a technological platform for monitoring and controlling smart home devices and sensors. The platform can
provide users automatic recommendations for increased comfort at home and
efficient energy consumption. Finally, this platform combines different
approaches and technologies such as semantic Web, collaborative filtering, and
web/mobile application development.

Keywords: IoT · Recommender systems · Sensors

R. Valencia-García et al. (Eds.): CITI 2019, CCIS 1124, pp. 137–150, 2019.
https://doi.org/10.1007/978-3-030-34989-9_11

1 Introduction

The Internet of Things (IoT) allows for the development of a wide range of products, useful in everyday life in contexts such as education, health, trade, tourism, agriculture, environment, and home, among others. In the household context, the concept of domotics – also known as home automation – emerged following the IoT trend. The Collins English Dictionary defines home automation as "the control of domestic appliances by electronically controlled systems;" that is, domotics involves smart homes that know the needs of their dwellers and seek to meet those needs. To this end, home automation systems collect information through sensors and then execute a series of tasks accordingly. Some of the main advantages of the IoT technologies applied in households include safety through alarm systems and surveillance cameras, home incident (e.g. water/gas leaks) management and notification, comfort management (particularly useful for persons with disabilities), energy use control (e.g. automatic on/off light switch), lighting management in general (e.g. smart shades can lower or raise depending on the amount of natural light entering the room where they are installed), water consumption management, and room temperature management.

Nowadays, many applications can control smart home devices, yet in technology monitoring, applications giving comfort and energy saving recommendations based on user behavior patterns have not yet been developed. Consequently, the gap must be addressed with home applications that both promote energy saving and seek to improve user life style, which has an ultimate positive impact on user quality of life and utility bills.

Recommender systems use the opinions of a community of users to help individuals in that community more effectively identify content of interest from a potentially overwhelming set of choices [1]. Recommender systems can be mainly categorized as either content-based filtering (CBF) systems or collaborative filtering (CF) systems [2]; however, some recommender systems are known to be hybrid, thus combining CBF and CF characteristics. Some popular applications relying on recommender systems include Pandora Radio, Netflix, and the Amazon web – the latter recommends customers products that have been previously purchased by other customers with similar preferences [3].

This work proposes PESSHIoT, a smart platform for monitoring and controlling home sensors and smart devices. PESSHIoT seeks to develop its own IoT-based technologies and offer its users automatic recommendations for efficient energy consumption and increased comfort at home. Additionally, PESSHIoT recommendations use CF and data mining techniques to identify user behavior patterns. The remainder of this work is structured as follows: Sect. 2 discusses a set of works related to IoT-based architecture design and development in the context of home automation. Section 3 introduces the architecture of PESSHIoT and describes its outstanding modules. Section 4 discusses a usability test conducted on the mobile application of PESSHIoT. Finally, in Sect. 5 we present our conclusions.

2 Related Work

This section discusses relevant literature on domotic proposals. For instance, in [4] the authors proposed a set of architectural designs for smart homes that use hierarchical wireless multimedia management systems. In the architecture, all the home network components are controlled by a home gateway acting as a service provider for users. From a similar perspective, in [5], the authors proposed a smart home architecture based on an optimization protocol for wireless sensor networks (WSNs). The architecture is divided in two main environments, indoor and outdoor, which are interconnected via an access point. Researchers in [6] developed a web-of-object service architecture for the home service environment. The architecture is composed of three main layers – the presentation layer, the management layer, and the information layer. In [7], the authors proposed a smart home management system architecture whose goals are to ensure home safety and efficient energy use and control smart home devices. In this architecture, the WSN connects safety sensors, such as smoke, gas, temperature, or motion sensors. In [8], the researchers presented a cloud-based and ontology-based multilayered architecture for IoT-based smart homes. From a similar perspective, authors in [9] proposed an interoperable IoT platform for smart homes that relies on a cloud architecture and the Web-of-objects technology. The architecture allows users to control home appliances from anywhere, provides smart home data for a wide range of application services and analysis, and seeks to improve resource utilization. Finally, in [10], the authors introduced the architectural design of a Web-of-Things (WoT) system for smart home device management. The system architecture seeks to comply with standardized business and quality requirements of the smart home domain.

Even though the aforementioned works provide domotic solutions, none of them can provide recommendations for increased comfort at home and efficient energy consumption based on user behavior patterns and lifestyle. To address this limitation, we propose an IoT-based platform, called PESSHIoT, for monitoring and controlling smart home devices and sensors. PESSHIoT can provide users automatic recommendations for increased comfort at home and efficient energy consumption. This platform combines different approaches and technologies such as semantic Web, collaborative filtering, and web/mobile application development. The following section describes the main details of this platform.

3 PESSHIoT: Architecture and Functionality

3.1 Architecture

Figure 1 depicts the overall design of our architecture that monitors and controls smart home sensors. As can be observed, the architecture comprises seven main layers – presentation, IoT services, security, management, communication, data, and devices. To ensure scalability in the platform, the different modules of each layer execute their corresponding tasks independently.

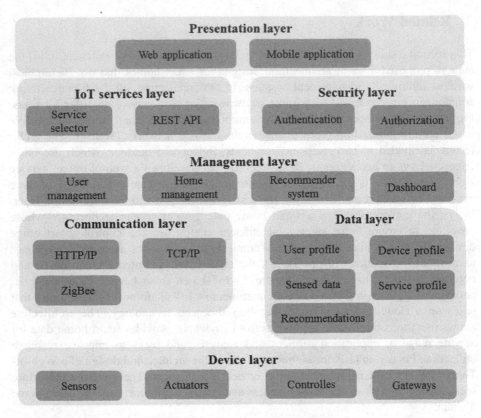

Fig. 1. Architecture of PESSHIoT.

The following section describes the architecture of PESSHIoT, our smart platform, including its main modules. We begin by describing the lower layers and end by discussing the upper layers, to which final users have direct access.

- **Device layer.** Provides interfaces to connect and receive information from multiple domotic devices. Moreover, the device layer provides interfaces through which home devices and actuators can be controlled. Some examples of the devices available can be listed as follows:
  - **Sensors.** These are devices gathering information on multiple parameters of the centralized control system, such as ambient temperature, water/gas leaks, and break-ins, among others.
  - **Actuators.** They are used by the centralized control system to modify the status of some equipment or installation. For instance, actuators allow the centralized control system to increase or decrease the temperature of the heater/air conditioner, interrupt the water/gas supply system, and send an alarm to the security system, among others. Like sensors, actuators can be of different kinds and installed in an entire building.

- **Controllers.** They control domotic devices according to the actuation parameters set up by users. The centralized control system gathers information from all the sensors in the building or house, processes this information using an algorithm introduced in its memory, and generates the necessary orders to execute the actuators. Moreover, the system provides operators information on its status and allows them to intervene or take over the process. Operators can program and control all the sensors and actuators in the building/house using the centralized control system. Programming and controlling tasks can be performed using the device's keyboard and screen, push buttons and controllers, and speech interfaces, among others.
- **Gateways.** Residential gateways are objects that interconnect multiple home/building automation devices, and thus work as a common interface for all these devices toward external networks. Consequently, gateways make it possible to control all the devices either locally or remotely. In other words, residential gateways are border devices that provide network access between the local and external networks of a building. Since the multiple devices installed in a house or building can connect to the Internet or other networks, residential gateways manage the only access point common between said networks.
- **Data layer.** Manages all the data generated in the device layer. Namely, in the PESSHIoT platform, the data layer manages the following information:
  - **User profile.** This module manages user information, such as name, last name, and age, among others.
  - **Device profile.** This module manages profile data of smart home devices, such as location and status, among others.
  - **Sensed data.** This module manages data coming from the device layer. Examples of sensed data include room temperature and water/gas/power usage.
  - **Service profile.** This module manages data on the services provided by the platform.
  - **Recommendations.** This module manages wellbeing recommendations based on user behavior patterns.
- **Communication layer.** Comprises HTTP and TCP/IP components, mobile communication (e.g. 4G), and a sensor framework to allocate device-specific communication protocols. The communication layer enables the interaction between other layers with domotic devices available in the house or building. Examples of protocols used by the communication layer are listed as follows:
  - **HTTP/IP.** The HTTP (i.e. HyperText Transfer Protocol) was developed by the Internet Engineering Task Force (IETF) and the World Wide Web Consortium (W3C). It is used in all kinds of internet transactions. It can help easily define the syntax and semantics used by the different types of web software – including clients, servers, and proxy – to interact among them. The HTTP is a request-response-client-server protocol, where an HTTP client sends a request to an HTTP server, and in turn, the server returns a response message. Client requests have to do with files, execution programs, database consultations, and translations, among others. All the information running on the Web through the HTTP is identified with a uniform resource locator (URL) or an HTTP address.

- **TCP/IP.** The TCP/IP (i.e. Transmission Control Protocol/Internet Protocol) was initially developed by the US Department of Defense with the aim of interconnecting computers having different operating systems, including PCs, minicomputers, and central computers working on local-area network (LAN) and wide area network (WAN). More than a single protocol, the TCP/IP is a set of protocols defining a series of rules and premises for heterogeneous machines to exchange information through LAN, WAN, and public telephone networks. The Internet itself is designed on the TCP/IP.
- **ZigBee.** This protocol was developed by ZigBee Alliance following the IEEE802.15.4 low-rate wireless network standard. It is a high-level, low-cost protocol used to create personal area networks with small, low-power digital radios that transmit data in larger areas. Additionally, ZigBee is used in applications requiring short-range and low-rate wireless data transfer, longer battery life, and secure network devices. The ZigBee protocol can handle different kinds of topologies, such as star, mesh, and tree topologies.

- **Security layer.** Includes security components (e.g. authentication and authorization) to ensure data confidentiality and secured data collection from both the device layer and final users. Two of the most important components of the security layer are the following:
  - **Authentication.** This is the process of determining or confirming that an object or user is real by checking user-provided evidence. Object authentication may imply confirming its precedence, whereas user authentication usually implies confirming their identity. In PESSHIoT, authentication implies demonstrating that the user trying to interact with the platform is really who they claim to be. Then, PESSHIoT allows said user to access and perform the actions permitted in the platform.
  - **Authorization.** This is a part of the system responsible for protecting user data and preventing unidentified users to access particular information or perform particular tasks. Authorization is not the same as authentication, since it refers to either actions that users can execute or data that these users can access once they validated their identity. Authorization can be applied either to each element individually or to a group of elements. In smart home management, each element refers to an action to be performed.

- **IoT services layer.** This layer offers a set of REST-based web services, through which it communicates with both the management layer and the application layer, thus allowing users to perform each one of the functionalities offered by the platform. The two main components of the IoT services layer can be listed as follows:
  - **Service selector.** This module selects the requested services and validates the parameters sent by the presentation layer. The service selector module can either grant or deny the services, according to the parameters received and the authentication credentials used.
  - **REST API.** REST is a cross-system interface that uses the HTTP to collect data or perform operations on such data in all the available formats, such as XML and JSON. REST is a popular alternative if compared to other standard data exchange protocols, such as SOAP (i.e. Simple Object Access Protocol), which have great capacity but are also particularly complex.

- **Management layer.** This layer manages and performs all the necessary tasks to meet user requests, made through the application layer. Communication between the management layer and the presentation layer is possible thanks to the IoT layer, specifically the REST API. The tasks performed by the management layer can be divided into four groups:
  - **User management.** Includes user registration, user removal, password reset, and user profile editing, among others.
  - **Home management.** Includes home device management, data editing, and data removal, to name but a few.
  - **Recommender system.** Involves tasks such as providing recommendations on wellbeing and energy saving according to user behavior patterns, among others.
  - **Dashboard.** Involves making a graphical representation of the main home indicators (e.g. water/gas/electricity consumption) and user habits.
- **Presentation layer.** This layer provides the graphical user interfaces (GUIs) and tools that users need to control and manage the home devices. Namely, PESSHIoT offers the following alternatives:
  - Web application. This is a fully responsive web application allowing users to easily control home devices from any device.
  - Mobile application. It is an Android mobile application offering a range of options for users to control and manage home devices. PESSHIoT provides an Android-based mobile application that allows users to monitor rooms and domotic devices, register a house's room, add a domotic device to a specific room, obtain the energy consumption and the energy-saving recommendations. The mobile application provides a set of charts for visualizing energy consumption information where the users can adjust and optimize the use of domotic devices to reduce costs. Additionally, the mobile application provides energy saving recommendations for helping convince users to change their energy consumption patterns.

3.2 Ontology of Home Automation Resources

Multiple research efforts propose modeling ontologies for home automation. For instance, the literature reports a Service-Oriented Context-Aware Middleware (SOCAM) architecture [11] for building context-aware services. Similarly, Kim and Choi [12] proposed an ontology-based model for ubiquitous computing that can describe context information in the home domain and process both context metadata and context information. On the other hand, DogOnt [13] is introduced as an ontology for modeling smart domotic environments. DogOnt fits the characteristics of real-world domotic systems and supports interoperability between currently available and future system characteristics. In their work, Xu et al. [14] proposed a set of modeling ontologies for four specific domains within smart homes: devices, functions, environment, and policies. The literature also reports both OntoDomo [15] and OBAR [16]; the former can represent domotic system elements, whereas the latter is an ontology-based activity recognition system for describing context-aware infrastructure through concepts of objects and places found within the house. The SSN (i.e. Semantic Sensor Network) [17] ontology can describe sensors in terms of their capabilities, measurement processes, observations, and deployment. On the other hand, the SHO (i.e. Smart Home Ontology) [18] is able to describe sensor networks for SSN-based smart homes. In turn, ODAR [19] is introduced as an ontology for home automation which can describe the necessary concepts to provide better services to users by taking into account their needs. Finally, the literature reports SmartHome [20], an ontology for assisting in sensor-based environments.

After a thorough review of the state of the art, we decided to use OWL-DL to develop our domotic ontology. OWL-DL is a sub-version of the Web Ontology Language (OWL) and is based on the SHI2 description logic. Similarly, it has richer vocabulary and is more expressive than RDFS. Figure 2 introduces an extract of our ontology, which describes the main concepts of the domotics domain, such as activity, devices, rooms, and preferences, among others.

Fig. 2. Extract of the domotic ontology.

We used Methontology to develop our domotic ontology [21]. Namely, we performed a series of tasks, each one of them being focused on a particular aspect of the conceptual model of knowledge: terms, taxonomy, relationships, axioms, rules, and – depending on the authors – mathematical approximations of elements.

3.3 Module for Comfort and Energy Saving Recommendations

PESSHIoT's module for comfort and energy saving recommendations adopts a CF-based approach to issue appropriate recommendations, because the CBF recommendations depends on users former choices and CBF algorithms try to recommend items based on similarity count [22]. On the other hand, CF approach uses a large amount of data collected from user behavior in the past and predicts which items users will like. It does not need to analyze the content of the items. Instead, it relies on the relationship between users and items, which are typically encoded in a rating feedback matrix with each element representing a specific user rating on a specific item [23]. The CF-based recommendation approach has two main tasks: generating semantic neighborhoods and predicting ratings based on neighbor users. These processes are briefly described as follows:

1. **Generate semantic neighborhoods.** The CF-based recommendation method assumes that active users have neighbor users with whom they share similarities. The correlation between user ratings assigned to recommendation is used to estimate similarity between two users.
2. **Predict user rating from neighbor users.** The CF-based recommendation method estimates the rating that an active user will assign to a recommendation by adding the ratings from said user's neighbors. The neighborhood of an active user is formed by a number of users with whom the active user shares similarities. However, if a prospect neighbor user does not rate an item whose rating is already being predicted, the system will not add this prospect user to the active user's neighborhood, even if their correlation is high. The neighborhood of an active user, thus, comprises an η number of users that both share similarities with the active user and have previously rated the item being predicted by the system. Figure 3 depicts the mobile application interface where PESSHIoT issues a set of energy saving recommendations according to user behavior patterns.

PESSHIoT's module for comfort and energy saving recommendations use CF and semantic Web to analyze data collected by the domotic devices and to detect energy consumption patterns. These patterns allow generating energy-saving recommendations. The technologies used have an important role in energy saving decisions because users can visualize energy consumption and behavior patterns by a set of charts. In this manner, users know their energy consumption and they can optimize their consumption through recommendations provided by this module.

The data collected by PESSHIoT's module for comfort and energy saving recommendations are categorized based by the room's temperature, power consumption per day, power consumption per domotic devices; domotic devices use patterns, and user's presence patterns.

The functional requirements of this module are the energy consumption analysis, room ambient conditions and user behavior patterns analysis. PESSHIoT's module for comfort and energy saving recommendations allows users to monitor and to control the energy consumption of domotic devices. The control of domotic devices is achieved through a set of energy-saving recommendations, which considers the user's behavior patterns.

Fig. 3. Energy saving recommendations issued by the mobile application.

4   Evaluation

Web or mobile applications achieve their goals to the extent to which end-users feel satisfied with them. Quality factors or attributes having a strong impact on user satisfaction include content quality and content usefulness, service quality and assistance, and application design quality. In this research, we tested the mobile application version of PESSHIoT in terms of design quality from a user satisfaction perspective. We used the System Usability Scale (SUS) for evaluating the usability metric of the mobile application. The SUS is a well-researched and widely used questionnaire for assessing the usability of mostly Web-based applications [24, 25]. The design of an application is crucial, since it defines how users interact with the application; hence, application design makes it possible, or not, for users to reach their goals (e.g. find information, make a purchase, learn).

4.1   Sample

In order to assess the satisfaction of users with PESSHIoT, we designed a survey questionnaire. The survey was administered to a set of 23 participants who interacted with the application for 30 days. The set of participants is comprised by 11 men and 12 women, ranging from 22 to 58 years old. The following section briefly describes the structure of the survey and discusses the results of its administration.

4.2 Survey Design

Table 1 introduces the design of the survey, which was developed to assess the navigability and design of PESSHIoT's mobile application.

Table 1. Survey to measure user satisfaction with the mobile application.

1	How would you define the application's interface in terms of structure, distribution, and organization?				
	Very good	Good	Fair	Bad	Very bad
2	How would you consider the application's interface design in terms of navigability, usage, and accessibility?				
	Very good	Good	Fair	Bad	Very bad
3	What's the most convenient rating for the organizational structure of the sections?				
	Very good	Good	Fair	Bad	Very bad
4	Can you see all the content the application covers?				
	Yes	No			
5	Are the terms used to describe functions, sections, and links clear?				
	Yes	No			
6	Can you access interesting content with a few gestures?				
	Yes	No			
7	Can you rapidly access information, even if the Internet connection is slow?				
	Yes	No			
8	Do you think the application handles information overload?				
	Yes	No			
9	Does the application use clear and concise language?				
	Yes	No			
10	Does the application use appropriate font style and font size?				
	Yes	No			
11	How good can the application control domotic devices?				
	Very good	Good	Fair	Bad	Very bad
12	Was any section lacking information? Which one?				
13	What improvements would you suggest we make on the application?				

4.3 Survey Results

We assessed our recommender platform through its mobile application version and from a user satisfaction perspective. A sample of users rated the PESSHIoT application through a survey questionnaire after using it in their homes to both control their own domotic devices and receive recommendations for increasing comfort and decreasing utility costs (e.g. water, gas, and electricity). The survey results demonstrated a high degree of user acceptance. However, according to the participants' comments, the application might need to overcome usability problems, such as font size and style, information overload, and language clarity, among others. The survey results do not indicate the usability of the application, but rather the satisfaction of the surveyed users. Generally, when user satisfaction is low, usability must be improved. Fortunately, our results demonstrate high user satisfaction, yet we will take into account each comment from the survey participants to eventually enhance our application's design. In consequence, user satisfaction can be higher, thus contributing to the success of PESSHIoT.

5 Conclusions

The IoT technologies allows for the development of a wide range of products, useful in every-day life in contexts such home, where the concept of domotics – also known as home automation – emerged following the IoT trend. The domotic solutions revised in the literature does not used user's behavior patterns to generate energy-saving recommendations and offer increased comfort at home. This work proposes a smart platform for monitoring and controlling home devices and sensors. As its main advantage, the platform takes into account user behavior patterns to issue recommendations for increased comfort at home and energy saving. Moreover, the platform use technologies, such as CF, the semantic Web, and mobile and web application development. The mobile application version of our platform was assessed in terms of usability, namely navigability and design. The assessment results revealed the application's high acceptance among target users; that is, people willing to rely on a domotic device control system to increase comfort at home and energy saving. According to the evaluation results, we believe that our platform can adequately monitor and control domotic devices. On the one hand, users can monitor in real time the status of the domotic resources, including variables such as ambient temperature and humidity. On the other hand, the same users can receive recommendations on increased comfort at home and energy saving, according to their behavioral patterns. All these capabilities are achieved thanks to the integration of emerging technologies, such as the semantic Web, multi-device applications, data mining, and user profile characterization based on behavioral patterns.

As future work, we will perform a comparative analysis of big data analytics technologies and machine learning used in the smart home context. Then, we will seek to integrate such technologies into PESSHIoT for home energy-saving purposes. Finally, we plan assess PESSHIoT's performance in a residential housing complex of at least 10 units.

Acknowledgments. This work was supported by Tecnológico Nacional de México (TecNM) and sponsored by the National Council of Science and Technology (CONACYT), the Secretariat of Public Education (SEP) through PRODEP (Programa para el Desarrollo Profesional Docente) and the Sistema de Universidades Estatales de Oaxaca (SUNEO).

References

1. Resnick, P., Varian, H.R.: Recommender systems. Commun. ACM. **40**, 56–58 (1997)
2. Herrera-Viedma, E., Herrera, F., Martínez, L., Herrera, J.C., López, A.G.: Incorporating filtering techniques in a fuzzy linguistic multi-agent model for information gathering on the web. Fuzzy Sets Syst. **148**, 61–83 (2004). https://doi.org/10.1016/j.fss.2004.03.006
3. Anil, R., Owen, S., Dunning, T., Friedman, E.: Mahout in Action. Manning Publications Co., Shelter Island (2011)
4. Lee, S., Caytiles, R.D., Lee, S.: A study of the architectural design of smart homes based on hierarchical wireless multimedia management systems. Int. J. Control Autom. **6**(6), 261–266 (2013). https://doi.org/10.14257/ijca.2013.6.6.25
5. Adiono, T., Putra, R.V.W., Fathany, M.Y., Wibisono, M.A., Adijarto, W.: Smart home platform based on optimized wireless sensor network protocol and scalable architecture. In: 2015 9th International Conference on Telecommunication Systems Services and Applications (TSSA), pp. 1–5 (2015). https://doi.org/10.1109/tssa.2015.7440441
6. Lee, N., Lee, H., Lee, H., Ryu, W.: Implementation of smart home service over web of object architecture. In: 2015 International Conference on Information and Communication Technology Convergence (ICTC), pp. 1215–1219 (2015). https://doi.org/10.1109/ictc.2015.7354778
7. Zhou, C., Huang, W., Zhao, X.: Study on architecture of smart home management system and key devices. In: 2013 3rd International Conference on Computer Science and Network Technology (ICCSNT), pp. 1255–1258 (2013). https://doi.org/10.1109/iccsnt.2013.6967330
8. Tao, M., Zuo, J., Liu, Z., Castiglione, A., Palmieri, F.: Multi-layer cloud architectural model and ontology-based security service framework for IoT-based smart homes. Futur. Gener. Comput. Syst. **78**, 1040–1051 (2018). https://doi.org/10.1016/j.future.2016.11.011
9. Iqbal, A., et al.: Interoperable internet-of-things platform for smart home system using web-of-objects and cloud. Sustain. Cities Soc. **38**, 636–646 (2018). https://doi.org/10.1016/j.scs.2018.01.044
10. Chauhan, M.A., Babar, M.A.: Using reference architectures for design and evaluation of web of things systems: a case of smart homes domain. In: Managing the Web of Things, pp. 205–228. Elsevier (2017). https://doi.org/10.1016/B978-0-12-809764-9.00009-3
11. Gu, T., Wang, X.H., Pung, H.K., Zhang, D.Q.: An ontology-based context model in intelligent environments. In: Proceedings of Communication Networks and Distributed Systems Modeling and Simulation Conference, pp. 270–275 (2004)
12. Kim, E., Choi, J.: An ontology-based context model in a smart home. In: Gavrilova, M.L., et al. (eds.) ICCSA 2006. LNCS, vol. 3983, pp. 11–20. Springer, Heidelberg (2006). https://doi.org/10.1007/11751632_2
13. Bonino, D., Corno, F.: Dogont - ontology modeling for intelligent domotic environments. In: Sheth, A., et al. (eds.) ISWC 2008. LNCS, vol. 5318, pp. 790–803. Springer, Heidelberg (2008). https://doi.org/10.1007/978-3-540-88564-1_51
14. Xu, J., et al.: Ontology-based smart home solution and service composition. In: 2009 International Conference on Embedded Software and Systems, pp. 297–304. IEEE (2009). https://doi.org/10.1109/icess.2009.60

15. Valiente-Rocha, P.A., Lozano-Tello, A.: Ontology-based expert system for home automation controlling. In: García-Pedrajas, N., Herrera, F., Fyfe, C., Benítez, J.M., Ali, M. (eds.) IEA/AIE 2010. LNCS (LNAI), vol. 6096, pp. 661–670. Springer, Heidelberg (2010). https://doi.org/10.1007/978-3-642-13022-9_66

16. Wongpatikaseree, K., Ikeda, M., Buranarach, M., Supnithi, T., Lim, A.O., Tan, Y.: Activity recognition using context-aware infrastructure ontology in smart home domain. In: 2012 Seventh International Conference on Knowledge, Information and Creativity Support Systems, pp. 50–57. IEEE (2012). https://doi.org/10.1109/kicss.2012.26

17. Compton, M., et al.: The SSN ontology of the W3C semantic sensor network incubator group. Web Semant. Sci. Serv. Agents World Wide Web 17, 25–32 (2012). https://doi.org/10.1016/j.websem.2012.05.003

18. Berat Sezer, O., Can, S.Z., Dogdu, E.: Development of a smart home ontology and the implementation of a semantic sensor network simulator: an internet of things approach. In: 2015 International Conference on Collaboration Technologies and Systems (CTS), pp. 12–18. IEEE (2015). https://doi.org/10.1109/cts.2015.7210389

19. Lyazidi, A., Mouline, S.: ONDAR: an ontology for home automation. In: 2015 15th International Conference on Intelligent Systems Design and Applications (ISDA), pp. 260–265. IEEE (2015). https://doi.org/10.1109/isda.2015.7489235

20. Alirezaie, M., et al.: An ontology-based context-aware system for smart homes: e-care@home. Sensors 17, 1586 (2017). https://doi.org/10.3390/s17071586

21. Fernández-López, M., Gómez-Pérez, A., Juristo, N.: Methontology: from ontological art towards ontological engineering. In: Proceedings of the Ontological Engineering AAAI-97 Spring Symposium Series, March 1997, pp. 24–26. Stanford University, EEUU (1997)

22. Thorat, P.B., Goudar, R.M., Barve, S.: Survey on collaborative filtering, content-based filtering and hybrid recommendation system. Int. J. Comput. Appl. 110(4), 31–36 (2015)

23. Wei, J., He, J., Chen, K., Zhou, Y., Tang, Z.: Collaborative filtering and deep learning based recommendation system for cold start items. Expert Syst. Appl. 69, 29–39 (2017). https://doi.org/10.1016/j.eswa.2016.09.040

24. Harrati, N., Bouchrika, I., Tari, A., Ladjailia, A.: Exploring user satisfaction for e-learning systems via usage based metrics and system usability scale analysis. Comput. Hum. Behav. 61, 463–471 (2016). https://doi.org/10.1016/j.chb.2016.03.051

25. Kaya, A., Ozturk, R., Altin Gumussoy, C.: Usability measurement of mobile applications with system usability scale (SUS). In: Calisir, F., Cevikcan, E., Camgoz Akdag, H. (eds.) Industrial Engineering in the Big Data Era. LNMIE, pp. 389–400. Springer, Cham (2019). https://doi.org/10.1007/978-3-030-03317-0_32

Modern Code Applied in Stencil in Edge Detection of an Image for Architecture Intel Xeon Phi KNL

Mario Hernández-Hernández[1]($\boxtimes$) ⓘ, José Luis Hernández-Hernández[2] ⓘ,
Edilia Rodríguez Maldonado[1], and Israel Herrera Miranda[3] ⓘ

[1] Engineering Faculty, Autonomous University of Guerrero,
Chilpancingo, México
mhernandezh@uagro.mx, edy_r_m@hotmail.com
[2] TecNM/Technological Institute of Chilpancingo, Chilpancingo, Mexico
joseluis.hernandez@itchilpancingo.edu.mx
[3] Government and Public Management Faculty, Autonomous University of Guerrero,
Chilpancingo, México
israel_hm@hotmail.com

Abstract. Modern, high-performance computers are built with a combination of heterogeneous resources, including multi-core and many cores processors, large cache, fast memory, mesh communication between large processes bandwidth, as well as high support for Input/Output capabilities. In order to achieve the best hardware results it is necessary to design highly-performance parallel software with faster modern code that could take full advantage of the vast amount of resources of today's modern machines. Code modernization encompasses a wide range of activities that aim to improve the performance of highly parallel software. Code modernization is an issue that is being discussed more and more in the field of parallel software development.

In this context, the experimentation with Stencil codes through a series of strategies for reorganizing code and algorithms, has shown to increase thread parallelism, vector/SIMD operations and compute intensity in modern architectures.

For example, with the use of Stencil codes we have achieved a better performance in image edge detection by a factor of three faster than we could achieved with a standard processor.

Keywords: Modern code · Stencil · Edge detection · KNL · Image processing

1 Introduction

The rise of research fields based on simulation and modeling, are challenging the computing capabilities of high-performance architectures. Research fields such as quantum mechanics, predictability of physical phenomena, climate research, DNA analysis, etc., add to the challenges of the services sector (web and databases) that needs to face the steady increase in the computing requirements of data centers.

© Springer Nature Switzerland AG 2019
R. Valencia-García et al. (Eds.): CITI 2019, CCIS 1124, pp. 151–163, 2019.
https://doi.org/10.1007/978-3-030-34989-9_12

Modern computers for high-performance computing (HPC) are built with a combination of heterogeneous resources and therefore high-performance software must be designed to make the most of this wealth of resources [21].

Creating parallel versions of software can allow applications to run a set of data in less time, or run large-scale datasets that are prohibitive with software that is not optimized. The success of parallelization is typically quantified by measuring the acceleration of the parallel version with respect to the serial version. However, in addition to this comparison, it is also useful to compare that acceleration against the upper limit of the potential acceleration [9, 20].

Good code design takes into account several levels of parallelism: (i) Vector parallelism (within a core) where identical computational instructions are performed on large pieces of data; (ii) thread parallelism, is characterized by a series of cooperating threads of a single process, communicating through shared memory and cooperating collectively in a given task; (iii) distributed memory range parallelism.

The development of code that uses all three levels of parallelism effectively, efficiently and with high performance is a fundamental factor for code modernization.

2   Background and Related Work

2.1   Knights Landing Overview

Knights Landing (KNL) is a multi-core processor that offers massive parallelism of threads and data with a high memory bandwidth [10, 27]. It was designed to offer high performance in parallel workloads. KNL provides many improvements and innovations with respect to Intel Xeon Phi Knights Corner (KNC) coprocessor. KNL presents a more modern and efficient core in the use of energy that triples (3x) scalar and vectorial performance compared to KNC. KNL offers over three TFLOP/s of double precision and six TFLOP/s of single precision peak floating point performance. It introduces a new memory architecture that uses two types of memory (MCDRAM and DDR) to provide both high memory bandwidth and large memory capacity [24].

Other Key Features of KNL Architecture: 2D Mesh Architecture; Out-of-Order Cores; 3X Single-Thread vs. KNC; Intel AVX-512 Instructions; Scatter/Gather Engine; Integrated Fabric - OPA.

2.2   Stencil

A stencil is a map in which each output depends on a "neighborhood" of inputs specified using a set of fixed offsets relative to the output position. Stencils are important in many applications such as image processing, include photography, satellite images, medical images and seismic reconstruction [5, 8, 11, 18, 25, 26].

To estimate a derivative of an image represented by a discrete set of pixels, we need to resort to an approximation. Derivatives are rather naturally approximated by finite differences.

Stencil operators take an input image and combine it with the Stencil kernel to produce the output image [14]. Template operators are used in fluid dynamics, where they are used to solve partial differential equations of fluid movement. Templates are also found in image processing and this will be the case of study in our experimental tests. We will use a nine-point template that performs edge detection. See Eq. 1.

$$
\begin{aligned}
Q_{x,y} = {} & C_{00}P_{x-1,y-1} + C_{01}P_{x,y-1} + C_{02}P_{x+1,y-1} \\
& + C_{10}P_{x-1,y} + C_{11}P_{x,y} + C_{12}P_{x+1,y} \\
& + C_{20}P_{x-1,y+1} + C_{21}P_{x,y+1} + C_{22}P_{x+1,y+1}
\end{aligned}
\tag{1}
$$

The input image will be a large 36 megapixel image. And the result of this template is that if you have a uniform area in the input image, you will have a dark area in the output image. And if it had a defined limit, it will have a bright line in the output image. Then perform edge detection. At the same time, the mathematics of this operation are similar to the mathematics used, for example, in fluid dynamics. In the basic implementation, we will keep our input and output images as arrays of floating point numbers. To apply the template, we configure two matrices that cross all the pixels of the image and for each pixel we take the pixel and its eight neighbors, we multiply them by the weights in the template matrix, we add them, and this produces the value of the output image For the task of image processing, we must verify if this value is within the limits of our depth of intensity. Specifically, this brightness must be between 0 and 255 for an 8-bit grayscale image. The initial implementation performs the task correctly but is not optimal in terms of performance. Then, in the following sections, we will see what it takes to optimize this code to get the best performance [1].

The Algorithm 1 shows the Stencil edge detection core of an image.

Algorithm 1. Generic *Stencil kernel solution. width, height* are the dimensions of the data set.

```
1:  const int width = img_in.width;
2:  const int height = img_in.height;
3:  P * in = img_in.pixel;
4:  P * out = img_out.pixel;
5:  for (int i = 1; i < height − 1; i + +) do
6:      for (int j = 1; j < width − 1; j + +) do
7:          Stencil_solver_kernel();
8:          val = (val < 0 ? 0 : val);
9:          val = (val > 255 ? 255 : val);
10:         out[i * width + j] = val;
11:     end for
12: end for
```

2.3 Related Work

To performance of stencil computations some work focused on using optimizations to improve the data locality and parallelism on multicore and many-core processors [12,19,24]. Kamil et al. proposed a performance model to study the performance of stencil computations on modern processors [11]. Can be found in a review by Datta et al. [5] an overview about the state of the art in stencil optimizations. In paper CODE MODERNIZATION STRATEGIES TO 3-D STENCIL-BASED APPLICATIONS ON INTEL XEON PHI: KNC AND KNL [2], The authors implemented scalar optimization's, code vectorization, parallelization and optimizing memory access. In Technical Report KNL UTILIZATION GUIDELINES [22], the authors presents a set of recommendations for running effectively on Intel's second-generation Xeon Phi Knights Landing (KNL) processors. Finally, there are several books that show the computing capabilities of the Xeon Phi processor [20]. Also, we emphasize that "Code modernization" is a new paradigm that aims to provide both code and performance portability [17].

3 Code Modernization

Modern high-performance computers are built with a combination of resources, including multi-core and manycore processors, large caches, high speed memory, high-bandwidth, inter-processor communications fabric, and broad support for I/O capabilities. High-performance software needs to be designed to take full advantage of this wealth of resources.

Code modernization is a form of writing scalable code that uses multi-layered parallelism to take all the performance benefits of modern hardware capabilities.

Code modernization is reorganizing the code, and perhaps changing algorithms, to increase the amount of thread parallelism, vector/SIMD operations, and compute intensity to optimize performance on modern architectures [6,7]. Thread parallelism, vector/SIMD operations, and an emphasis on temporal data reuse are all critical for high-performance programming. Many existing applications were written before these elements were required for performance, and therefore, such codes are not yet optimized for modern computers.

The future for many-core processors is bright. Neo-heterogeneous programming is already enabling code modernization for parallelism, while trending to get easier in each generation of Intel Xeon Phi devices.

3.1 Vectorization

A key ingredient for good parallel performance on modern hardware is to take full advantage of vector instructions, also known as Single Instruction Multiple Data (SIMD) instruction sets [23]. We optimize scalar and serial operations by maintaining the proper precision, type constants, and using appropriate functions and precision flags.

One of the key design features of the Xeon Phi architecture is the use of wide SIMD registers and vector functional units to improve performance.

The MIC Knights Landing (KNL) architecture implements a subset of the AVX512 instruction set that operates over 512-bit wide registers. It is crucial to make use of SIMD features in order to get the best performance out of this architecture.

There are several issues that need to be addressed to achieve the automatic vectorization of the code. The first one is data alignment. Data accesses must start with an address aligned to 64 bytes.

3.2 Multithreading and Multinode (Cluster)

By increasing the number of active threads in the code, is taken advantage of all of the available cores on modern hardware [16].

The option of partitioning data set between threads/processes, we were use it for image processing. We use a computing-oriented framework for shared-memory programming. Open Multi-Processing (OpenMP) [3,4,13]. The OpenMP library distribute the iterations of the loop following the #pragma omp parallel for across threads. See Algorithm 2.

Algorithm 2. Multithreading.

1: **#pragma omp parallel for**
2: **for** (int $i = 1; i < height - 1; i + +$) **do**
3:    **#pragma omp simd**
4:    **for** (int $j = 1; j < width - 1; j + +$) **do**
5:        out[i*width + j] =;
6:        -in[(i-1)*width + j-1] - in[(i-1)*width + j] - in[(i-1)*width + j+1]
7:        -in[(i)*width + j-1] + 8*in[(i)*width + j] - in[(i)*width + j+1]
8:        -in[(i+1)*width + j-1] - in[(i+1)*width + j] - in[(i+1)*width + j+1];
9:    **end for**
10: **end for**

The cluster architecture can achieve high levels of parallel performance that can be scaled with the algorithm. We apply to using the message passing interface (MPI) and the distributed memory model to design our applications [15].

3.3 Memory Optimization and Non-uniform Memory Access (NUMA)

On all systems-from laptops to supercomputers-the cores can only operate at a full compute capacity if they are provided with data at the maximum rate at which they can process it. Therefore, for HPC and regular applications, performance will be higher if the majority of memory requests hit nearby caches. If that is not the case, vectorizing and parallelizing the code can be ineffective.

We need the computing power of multicore Intel Xeon processors, but the system's DIMMs are no match for the needs of the many-vector processing units, therefore our program stalls. We apply to change our application's data access characteristics so the L1 and L2 caches provide the needed 10,000+ GB/s.

As the trend continues to improve system performance by bringing memory closer to processor cores, NUMA plays an increasingly important role in system performance. Modern processors such as Intel Xeon Phi KNL have multiple memory ports, and memory access latency varies even depending on the position of the core in the die relative to the controller.

4   Materials and Methods

4.1   Platform and Tools

A high-performance computing (HPC) cluster helps solve the most challenging intensive computing tasks faced by business, educational, and scientific communities; by integrating the latest advances into industry-standard servers, high-speed interconnects, and leading open source and commercial software.

The cluster used in this job has powerful compute nodes with multicore processors, vector instruction support, NUMA architecture, hierarchical caches, high-bandwidth memory (MCDRAM on Intel family processors Xeon Phi 7200) and coprocessors (such as Intel family coprocessors Xeon Phi 7100).

The compiler used was Intel C++. Also the editors Emacs, Gedit and Nano (the easiest to use). Code snippets were created, compiled, and run for experimental testing by one of these editors.

In order to compile and run test codes, we connect to the cluster using the Secure Shell (SSH) protocol. To run the codes, you go through a queue and there is a resource manager who takes care of the queue (The qsub utility is used to send work to the queue) See Fig. 1.

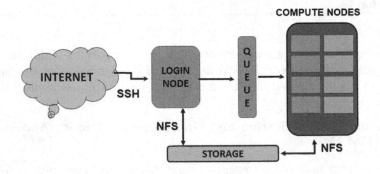

Fig. 1. Access to the cluster

4.2 Base Code (The Stencil's Edge Detection of an Image)

The basic implementation of our code from which we start is shown in The Algorithm 3, which consists of the Stencil's edge detection kernel of an image.

Algorithm 3. Sample of a Test *Stencil base code. width, height* are the dimensions of the data set.

```
1:  const int width = img_in.width;
2:  const int height = img_in.height;
3:  P * in = img_in.pixel;
4:  P * out = img_out.pixel;
5:  for (int i = 1; i < height − 1; i + +) do
6:     for (int j = 1; j < width − 1; j + +) do
7:        P val = -in[(i-1)*width + j-1] - in[(i-1)*width + j];
8:        - in[(i-1)*width + j+1] -in[(i )*width + j-1];
9:        + 8*in[(i )*width + j] - in[(i )*width + j+1]
10:       -in[(i+1)*width + j-1] - in[(i+1)*width + j]
11:       - in[(i+1)*width + j+1];
12:       val = (val < 0 ? 0 : val);
13:       val = (val > 255 ? 255 : val);
14:       out[i * width + j] = val;
15:    end for
16: end for
```

---

5 Results and Discussion

5.1 Results

This section shows the result of practical experimentation that has allowed us to develop new skills in the field of high-performance computing (HPC). A cluster of computing designed for this purpose was used, in addition to a set of codes with which it was possible to experiment. The computer cluster is equipped with industry-leading technology, such as Intel Xeon Phi 64-core processors. Compute nodes in the cluster are based on Intel Xeon Phi x200 (formerly KNL) processors.

This hands-on experimentation shows how optimization and parallel programming methods work on frontline computers.

It experimented with 7 versions of code with different optimization strategies. Such strategies are listed below:

1. SIMD.
2. THREADS.
3. MCDRAM.
4. MEMKIND.
5. NONTEMPORAL.
6. PNGBYTE.
7. MPI.

In our first version (SIMD) of experimental tests, we proceeded to vectorize our base code. We will flip over all pixels in the input image. Applying the Stencil matrix to the input image and write the result in the output. At first the compiler assumed dependence on the vector and did not vectorize, we annul said assumption using the compiler directives #pragma omp simd. This pragma allows us to vectorize the internal cycle of our main kernel. When compiling we use the -xMIC-AVX512 directive, this tells the compiler to point to the AVX 512 instruction set. We start with a performance of about two gigahertz per second and after vectorization we improve the performance by about 17 GHz per second.

We compile our code with the directives:

```
icpc -c -qopt-report=5 -xMIC-AVX512 v1stencil.cc
```

In the second version (THREADS), we proceeded to parallelize our vectorized code across multiple threads. We use the #pragma omp simd in the innermost loop, but we try to parallelize across threads the outer loop. So the pragma omp parallel created threads, and then joined them to process different values of i. The only change we had to make with this code it was to insert the pragma: #pragma omp parallel for.

We compile our code with the directives:

```
icpc -c -qopenmp -qopt-report=5 -xMIC-AVX512 v2stencil.cc
```

The third version uses MCDRAM memory, achieving considerable performance, as shown in the Sect. 5.2.

In the fourth version (MEMKIND), we didn't improve our performance over version 3, so the performance achieved is maintained.

Optimized the calculation of the Stencil by putting the entire application in high bandwidth memory. This was possible because we needed less than 16 gigabytes of RAM. We allocate memory buffers to store image data, using the high bandwidth allocator, hpw posix memalign. When we try to compile, we receive a build error, this is because at the time of the link we are not telling the linker to look for the memkind library. After the compilation and linking were successful, and we sent the work for its execution. In the results we achieved almost 220 GB/s of bandwidth. Which meant that our buffers were successfully to high-bandwidth memory.

If we cache the data and reuse it later, the data will be accessed faster. But there's also a case where it makes sense to avoid caching data and saving it directly to memory. Stencil operators are a notable example of streaming store users. Another reason for doing that is that Intel Architecture, specifically Xeon Phi, supports a special kind of stores that works on a line data. It is designed for streaming and it works better than a general purpose store. We have a loop you can make the compiler implement streaming stores in that loop using the directive #pragma vector nontemporal.

This code is a great candidate for streaming stores for two reasons. Streaming stores allow us to exploit the aligned nature of outbound memory access. And the second reason is that by making stores streaming we avoid cache pollution and keep more of the cache for data reuse in the input data.

In the fifth version (NONTEMPORAL), we added the pragma #pragma vector nontemporal in the internal cycle of our main kernel. And then recompile and rerun. Instructs the compiler to use non-temporary stores (that is, streaming).

The performance was a lot better. What we saw were 699 gigaflops per second, corresponding to 311 GB per second of memory than width.

So far, our Stencil calculation was using images containing floating point numbers. We also know that our performance is limited by the memory bandwidth. So, can we further optimize this code, so that we use memory less, and do more math. Taking advantage of the fact that we are really working with an image, since the image contains pixels with an intensity depth of eight bits. We can potentially save on memory traffic by storing our images as images or type png_bytes. This is an eight bit data type. What we see now is that the amount of time did drop quite a bit from 0.9 ms to 0.6 ms. We are using less memory benefit then we needed before, but the number of operations that we are performing. Now, they are not fully on point operations, but rather integer operations have nearly doubled. We went from 699 operations per second to 1,032 billion operations per second. In the sixth version (PNGBYTE) we managed to increase the performance considerably.

Finally, in the seventh version we used the MPI library. It is important to note that before we compiled our MPI program, we set the appropriate environment settings for the compiler and for the Intel MPI library.

Our Stencil code can run in a cluster. We take advantage of parallelism in the form of vectorization and multiple threading and have optimized the pattern of memory access. The next logical step was to try to parallelize this code further, to run on multiple independent computers in a cluster. We divide the work among several independent computers. Each computer was responsible for processing only its own part of the image with a template operator. So this was the process 0, 1, 2, 3, and each process produced its own part of the output. In MPI, applications are generally designed in such a way that each processor executes the same code, but will have different numerical IDs, ranges. Using the range, you can calculate the first row and the last row that I am the processor, and responsible for it. When compiled, the MPI container is used around the Intel C++ compiler, and this allows the code to be linked to the MPI library. And when the calculation is queued for execution, four nodes are requested and these four nodes will be requested, and their host names will be placed in the special node file, produced by our resource manager. As you can see, we are achieving 3.2 billion operations per second, which is a factor of three faster than we could do with a processor. Then, four processors accelerate us by a factor of three.

We have taken the template code very far from where we started. We start at 2.3 billion operations per second, and we end up with three billion operations per second through vectorization, multiple threading, improvements in memory access and clustering. This is how parallelism allows you to unlock the performance potential of a modern computer system.

5.2 Discussion

As can be seen from the results presented in this section, we have achieved great performance by applying the different strategies for our Intel Xeon Phi KNL processor architecture.

The Table 1 shows the results of the average performance evaluation of seven versions of the Stencil code. For these results, ten runs were performed for each code version, and the average of the ten runs was calculated, the same as shown in the Table 1. The image size for testing was 6000 × 6000 pixels for the edge detection of our 3 × 3 Stencil.

Table 1. Seven-version performance evaluation of Stencil code on Intel Xeon Phi KNL

Code	Time, ms	GB/s	GFLOP/s
simd	40.4	7.1	16.0
Threads	7.4	38.8	87.4
mcdram	1.3	224.9	506.0
memkind	1.3	228.3	513.7
nontemporal	0.9	311.0	699.7
pngbyte	0.6	114.7	1032.2
mpi	0.4	168.4	1516.0

The results of our different versions can be seen in the graph shown in the Fig. 2, expressing the performance in GFLOPS, as well as the acceleration achieved.

6   Conclusions

This research work has allowed us to experiment in the area of high-performance computing (HPC) using the Intel Xeon Phi KNL architecture.

We test through seven versions of code (Stencil kernel of image edge detection) the performance of the architecture, if you have a uniform color background, it becomes black and the images clear or sharp are shown white, so that work, the brightness was placed in a range of 0 to 255.

Once experimented with Intel Xeon Phi, we concluded that Intel Xeon Phi KNL offers clear benefits for this kernel, from the point of view of runtime acceleration. The results demonstrate the capabilities of the latest generation new technologies (Intel Xeon Phi KNL).

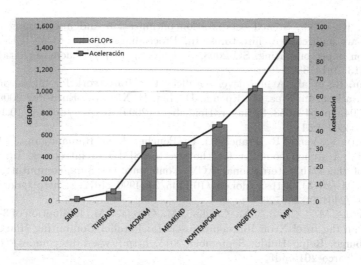

Fig. 2. Performance (Gflop/s) and acceleration for different versions of our code.

Finally, as a future job, we could work with other codes that involve a lot of computing to modernize or migrate to these new architectures. It would be very interesting to test Intel Xeon Phi architecture with other patterns that are not memory-constrained.

Acknowledgments. Authors are grateful to Autonomous University of Guerrero (UAGro) and TecNM/Technological Institute of Chilpancingo for supporting this work.

References

1. Andreolli, C., Thierry, P., Borges, L., Skinner, G., Yount, C.: Characterization and optimization methodology applied to stencil computations. In: Reinders, J., Jeffers, J. (eds.) High Performance Parallelism Pearls: Multicore and Many-Core Programming Approaches, vol. 1, pp. 377–396. Morgan Kaufmann, Boston, MA, USA (2015). https://doi.org/10.1016/B978-0-12-802118-7.00023-6. http://www.sciencedirect.com/science/article/pii/B9780128021187000236
2. Cebrián, J.M., Cecilia, J.M., Hernández, M., García, J.M.: Code modernization strategies to 3-D stencil-based applications on Intel Xeon Phi: KNC and KNL. Comput. Math. Appl. **74**(10), 2557–2571 (2017)
3. Chandra, R.: Parallel Programming in OpenMP. Morgan Kaufmann, Burlington (2001)
4. Cramer, T., Schmidl, D., Klemm, M., an Mey, D.: OpenMP programming on Intel® Xeon Phi TM coprocessors: an early performance comparison. In: Proceedings Many Core Applications Research Community (MARC) Symposium, pp. 38–44 (2012)
5. Datta, K., Kamil, S., Williams, S., Oliker, L., Shalf, J., Yelick, K.: Optimization and performance modeling of stencil computations on modern microprocessors. SIAM Rev. **51**(1), 129–159 (2009). https://doi.org/10.1137/070693199. http://epubs.siam.org/doi/abs/10.1137/070693199

6. Datta, K., et al.: Stencil computation optimization and auto-tuning on state-of-the-art multicore architectures. In: Proceedings of the ACM/IEEE Conference on Supercomputing, SC 2008, p. 4 (2008). http://dl.acm.org/citation.cfm?id=1413370.1413375

7. Dursun, H., et al.: A multilevel parallelization framework for high-order stencil computations. In: Sips, H., Epema, D., Lin, H.-X. (eds.) Euro-Par 2009. LNCS, vol. 5704, pp. 642–653. Springer, Heidelberg (2009). https://doi.org/10.1007/978-3-642-03869-3_61

8. Henretty, T., Veras, R., Franchetti, F., Pouchet, L.N., Ramanujam, J., Sadayappan, P.: A stencil compiler for short-vector SIMD architectures. In: Proceedings of the 27th International ACM Conference on Supercomputing, pp. 13–24. ACM (2013). https://doi.org/10.1145/2464996.2467268. http://doi.acm.org/10.1145/2464996.2467268

9. Hernández, M., Cebrián, J.M., Cecilia, J.M., García, J.M.: Evaluation of 3-D stencil codes on the Intel Xeon Phi coprocessor. In: Parallel Computing (ParCo) 2015, Edimburgo, Reino Unido, September 2015. http://www.ditec.um.es/~jmgarcia/papers/parco-2015.pdf

10. Jeffers, J., Reinders, J.: Intel Xeon Phi Coprocessor High Performance Programming. Morgan Kaufmann Publishers Inc., Boston (2013)

11. Kamil, S., Datta, K., Williams, S., Oliker, L., Shalf, J., Yelick, K.: Implicit and explicit optimizations for stencil computations. In: Proceedings of the Workshop on Memory System Performance and Correctness, MSPC 2006, pp. 51–60. ACM, New York, USA (2006). https://doi.org/10.1145/1178597.1178605. http://doi.acm.org/10.1145/1178597.1178605

12. Kamil, S., Husbands, P., Oliker, L., Shalf, J., Yelick, K.: Impact of modern memory subsystems on cache optimizations for stencil computations. In: Proceedings of the 2005 Workshop on Memory System Performance, MSP 2005, pp. 36–43. ACM, New York, NY, USA (2005). https://doi.org/10.1145/1111583.1111589. http://doi.acm.org/10.1145/1111583.1111589

13. Krishnamoorthy, S., Baskaran, M., Bondhugula, U., Ramanujam, J., Rountev, A., Sadayappan, P.: Effective automatic parallelization of stencil computations. In: Proceedings of the ACM SIGPLAN Conference on Programming Language Design and Implementation, PLDI 2007, pp. 235–244. ACM, New York, USA (2007). https://doi.org/10.1145/1250734.1250761. http://doi.acm.org/10.1145/1250734.1250761

14. McCool, M., Robison, A.D., Reinders, J.: Stencil and recurrence. In: Structured Parallel Programming: Patterns for Efficient Computation, pp. 199–207. Morgan Kaufmann Publishers Inc., Boston, MA, USA (2012). https://doi.org/10.1016/B978-0-12-415993-8.00007-4. http://www.sciencedirect.com/science/article/pii/B9780124159938000074

15. MPI: The Message Passing Interface (MPI) standard, 23 May 2019. http://www.mcs.anl.gov/research/projects/mpi/

16. OpenMP: OpenMP Architecture Review Board: The OpenMP Specification, 23 May 2019. http://www.openmp.org/

17. Pearce, M.: What is code modernization? (2015). https://software.intel.com/en-us/articles/what-is-code-modernization

18. Rahman, R.: Intel Xeon Phi Coprocessor Architecture and Tools: The Guide for Application Developers, 1st edn. Apress, Berkely (2013)

19. Rahman, S.M.F., Yi, Q., Qasem, A.: Understanding stencil code performance on multicore architectures. In: Proceedings of the 8th ACM International Conference on Computing Frontiers, CF 2011, pp. 30:1–30:10. ACM, New York,

NY, USA (2011). https://doi.org/10.1145/2016604.2016641. http://doi.acm.org/10.1145/2016604.2016641

20. Reinders, J., Jeffers, J. (eds.): High Performance Parallelism Pearls: Multicore and Many-Core Programming Approaches, vol. 2, 1st edn. Morgan Kaufmann Publishers Inc., Boston (2015)

21. Reinders, J., Jeffers, J.: Characterization and auto-tuning of 3DFD. In: High Performance Parallelism Pearls, Multicore and Many-Core Programming Approaches, pp. 377–396. Morgan Kaufmann (2014)

22. Rosales, C., et al.: KNL utilization guidelines. Technical report, TR-16-03, Texas Advanced Computing Center, The University (2016)

23. Seaton, M., Mason, L., Matveev, Z.A., Blair-Chappell, S.: Vectorization advice. In: Reinders, J., Jeffers, J. (eds.) High Performance Parallelism Pearls Volume Two: Multicore and Many-Core Programming Approaches, vol. 2, pp. 441–462. Morgan Kaufmann, Boston, MA, USA (2015). https://doi.org/10.1016/B978-0-12-803819-2.00015-X. http://www.sciencedirect.com/science/article/pii/B978012803819200015X

24. Strzodka, R., Shaheen, M., Pajak, D., Pomeranian, W.: Impact of system and cache bandwidth on stencil computations across multiple processor generations. In: Proceedings of the Workshop on Applications for Multi-and Many-Core Processors (A4MMC) at ISCA (2011)

25. Tang, Y., Chowdhury, R.A., Kuszmaul, B.C., Luk, C.K., Leiserson, C.E.: The pochoir stencil compiler. In: Proceedings of the Twenty-Third Annual ACM Symposium on Parallelism in Algorithms and Architectures, SPAA 2011, pp. 117–128. ACM, New York, NY, USA (2011). https://doi.org/10.1145/1989493.1989508. http://doi.acm.org/10.1145/1989493.1989508

26. Trottenberg, U., Oosterlee, C.W., Schuller, A.: Multigrid. Academic Press, Cambridge (2000)

27. Vladimirov, A., Asai, R., Karpusenko, V. (eds.): Parallel Programming and Optimization with Intel Xeon Phi Coprocessors, vol. 1, 2nd edn. Colfax International, CA, USA (2015)

OPTYFY: Industrial IoT-Based Performance and Production Optimization Based on Semantics

Álvaro Delgado-Clavero, Juan Miguel Gómez-Berbís[✉],
Antonio de Amescua-Seco, María-Isabel Sánchez-Segura,
and Fuensanta Medina-Domínguez

Department of Computer Science and Engineering,
Universidad Carlos III de Madrid, Madrid, Spain
{alvdelga, misanche, fmedina}@inf.uc3m.es,
{juanmiguel.gomez, antonio.amescua}@uc3m.es

Abstract. Industrial IoT-based Performance measuring and optimization is a critical and important challenge for Industry 4.0. Harnessing data integration across different industrial systems could optimize production and enable interoperability and seamless integration in a domain where proprietary and manufacturer-dependent protocols and data models has always prevailed. In this paper, we present OPTYFY, an IIOT Data Management platform which fosters semantics for monitoring Industrial IoT devices. OPTYFY gathers different IoT data under a particular formal semantics and visualizes in a dashboard several features. We also present a proof-of-concept which deals with features such as time, flow and rate of production to monitor and optimize the factory production process.

Keywords: IIoT · Industrial · Data management · Control platform

1 Introduction

Key parameters from the factory floor can be identified in Smart Factories, the cornerstone of the so-called upcoming new industrial breed codenamed "Industry 4.0". Now it is possible to monitor the performance of the factory floor at any place, in order to take action as soon as possible in case there are setbacks.

Industry 4.0 allows us to provide constant feedback from the performance of every IIoT device in the factory floor. In OPTYFY case scenario we are going to take advantage of the information provided by sensors and through the management of the relevant data in order to provide feedback from the performance in the factory. Systems or dynamically drawing inferences which are continually hampered by their reliance on ad-hoc, task specific frameworks.

In this paper, we present OPTYFY, an IIOT monitoring platform able to represent an improvement in Workflow Control and monitorization in Industrial Internet of Things. Firstly, we describe the motivating scenario and the research process we walked through the OPTIMUM research project to establish the proper requirements

© Springer Nature Switzerland AG 2019
R. Valencia-García et al. (Eds.): CITI 2019, CCIS 1124, pp. 164–177, 2019.
https://doi.org/10.1007/978-3-030-34989-9_13

for OPTYFY. Secondly, we made a survey on state of the art and literature related to these systems to identify a number of requirements for our solution.

This paper will provide a complete version of this project. Firstly, the paper examines the problem solved by the OPTYFY project, which consists of the difficulty of monitoring systems formed by an enormous quantity of nodes involved.

2 Motivating Scenario and Research Process

IoT systems and IoT platforms are still in the phase of rapid advancement and development and there are still many open and challenging points about technology, for example, in [1] they describe the difficulty involved in architecture, standardization, the fact that IoT systems have many heterogeneous devices, management and data transfer, in sections for and five we give our approach to overcome these issues.

As it is said in [2] the challenges described earlier become more complicated if we consider that we are talking about resource-constraint devices. Therefore, connectivity and memory in IoT devices are low, and in most of the cases, the connection is wireless, which is considerably less reliable and stable. Despite these difficulties, IoT devices have artificial intelligence and some degree of autonomy for taking decisions for themselves. IoT devices usually send, receive and process data periodically with extremely brief periods.

As a result, one of the greatest challenges that must be faced consists of developing smart and efficient platforms using resource-constrained hardware.

In addition to the previously mentioned constraints, the enormous size of IoT systems plays a significant role in designing such systems. IoT systems are usually composed of many more systems than regular networks, for this reason, certain features cannot be ignored to develop suitable systems.

Firstly, numerous smart nodes interconnected imply a vast number of events occurring at the same time which is crucial to handle appropriately. All the events must have a priority, in such a way, the full system will be intelligent.

Secondly, the network must be able to tolerate all the previously mentioned events without losing speed.

Finally, IoT networks must keep scalable despite their size. IoT systems are designed to increase continually. Not only to increase their size but also the type of devices and their functionalities.

Industrial IoT systems have two features that might make it difficult to generalize and evaluate the quality of their manufacture processes in their industrial applications. As stated in the previous paragraphs, these problematic properties are the number of connections in the network and the heterogeneity of the implied devices. On account of this fact, there is not a standardized approach to know the potential of the manufacturing system. OPTYFY aims to represent an improvement in this domain by building a platform capable of depicting the most relevant parameters in IIoT systems.

3 State of the Art and Literature Research

Internet of Things (IoT) emerged from the RFID community and was coined for the first time by British entrepreneur Kevin Ashton in 1999. Since then, with a greater interest in IoT, it has won multiple definitions with a broader understanding. They are some definitions.

First, in its special report on Internet of Things [3], IEEE described the phrase "Internet of Things" as: "A network of elements, each integrated with sensors, which are Connected to internet."

The W3C, which is an international community where member organizations, a full-time staff and the public work together to develop Web standards, addresses IoT as part of "Web of Things" and defines it as follows: "The Web of Things is essentially about the role of Web technologies to facilitate the development of applications and services for the Internet of Things, i.e., physical objects and their virtual representation. This includes sensors and actuators, as well as physical objects tagged with a bar code or NFC."

Another general definition of IoT is presented in [4] as "Interconnection of sensing and actuating devices providing the ability to share information across platforms through a unified framework, developing a common operating picture for enabling innovative applications. This is achieved by seamless large-scale sensing, data analytics and information representation using cutting edge ubiquitous sensing and cloud computing."

Along with these definitions, it is also worth to mention three visions of IoT elaborated in [4, 5], since they well capture the perspectives on IoT. These three visions are things-oriented vision, internet-oriented vision and semantic oriented vision. This paper considered the latter and it is explained by Singh et al. in [3] as following. The semantic-oriented vision "is powered by the fact that the number of sensors which will be available at our disposal will be huge and the data that they will collect will be massive in nature. Thus, we will have vast amount of information, possibly redundant, which needs to be processed meaningfully. The raw data needs to be managed, processed and churned out in an understandable manner for better representations and understanding."

After considering the IoT definition, it is necessary to define the IoT platform. Here are some definitions and discussions on IoT platforms.

In [6], an IoT platform is described as "cloud-based and on-premise software packages and related services that enable and support sophisticated IoT services. In some instances, IoT platforms enable application developers to streamline and automate common features that would otherwise require considerable additional time, effort and expense. In other instances, IoT platforms enable enterprises to manage thousands, millions, and even billions of devices and connections across multiple technologies and protocols. Finally, in some cases, IoT software enables developers to combine device and connection data with enterprise-specific customer and ERP data as well as data from third-party sources like social and weather data to create more valuable IoT applications" and in [7], IoT platform is presented using following description "Internet-of-Things (IoT) platform (often referred to as IoT middleware) is a software that enables connecting the machines and devices and then acquisition, processing, transformation, organization and storing machine and sensor data."

At this point of the paper reader should notice that OPTYFY will manage fundamentally IoT devices. We must not forget that OPTYFY ultimate objective is to manage the workflow of such devices. This involves the usage of certain technologies, protocols, methodologies and tools which will be described in the next paragraphs.

As said in [8] according to the literature there are basically two perspectives of workflow.

- Collaborative Workflow: In this case scenario devices communicate among them very often and process/receive data, OPTYFY clearly fits in this kind of workflow because it reports the current status of the tasks being realized in the manufacturing process.
- Production/administrative workflow: It analyzes scenarios where repetitive tasks are performed. It is a very common situation in manufacturing process because supply chains can be divided in a set of steps that are performed to fulfill a goal.

Additionally, there are three basic ways of cooperation between the elements of the supply chain depending on the necessity that a couple of elements have in order to work together.

The degrees of cooperation are the following:

- Compulsory collaboration: In this kind of collaboration agents are doing tasks which are dependent on one another. For this reason they are obliged to perform the same action simultaneously.
- Optional Collaboration: Only one of the agents is allowed to perform an action. However, there are many devices capable of performing it.
- Concurrent collaboration: Two or more elements can carry out different parts of one task following a concurrent fashion. This kind of collaboration reduces the time for performing an action due to the concurrency.

Modeling the workflow means to do a schema of the different workflow activities. For this reason, we might be able to say that a workflow use case is an instance of a workflow schema.

There are six fundamental patterns to model a workflow scenario, in Fig. 1 we can see a schema to help their understanding, the patterns are the following:

- **Serial.** The component needs to wait for the end of the action of the previous component in the supply chain to perform its action.
- **Iterative.** Certain action must be performed several times.
- **Parallel.** More than one action can be performed simultaneously.
- **Exclusive.** Several actions are ready to be performed. However, only one action can be executed at a time.
- **Alternative.** An action can work for other actions.
- **Reversible.** Two actions can perform, even if the sequential order is changed.

Internet of Things has been a revolutionary technology for automatization. However, to document all the details in the manufacturing process is vital to achieving

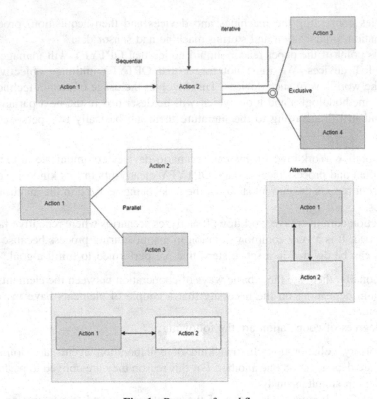

Fig. 1. Patterns of workflow

optimization. For this reason, certain technologies require a thorough analysis. They are the Manufacturing Execution Systems.

One of the most striking issues in the manufacturing process is the utilization of resources. Moreover, the economy of resources is so significant that it can be the reason for the success or failure of the whole output. In the following paragraphs, the necessity of Manufacturing Execution Systems will be developed in detail to help to understand the context of the OPTYFY platform.

As stated, several times in this text, IIoT systems are known for their vast number of components. IIoT systems can optimize their productivity through the usage of more accurate data and the elimination of non-value-added activities.

Given that manufacturing in IIoT systems are not strictly sequential, the order of the stages in the supply chain can play an important role in resource managing and efficiency. For this reason, Managing Execution Systems can reschedule activities in pursuit of a more efficient system.

We must not forget that a manufacturing process consists of a set of tasks performed by several agents, which can be humans or machines. It is necessary to be aware of what is the supposed behaviour of the manufacturing chain and ensure that the agents are fulfilling their tasks correctly. Furthermore, during the manufacturing process, some agents will rely on others to be capable of performing their duties. For this reason, reducing the time between tasks is vital for optimizing the manufacturing process. Manufacturing Execution Systems can decide when it is necessary to trigger the actuators in the systems to solve that problem.

Among the features of Managing Execution Systems described in [8], we must also resemble the capacity of managing the information about the processes. One of the most defining characteristics of IoT systems is their changing nature. With this in mind, stakeholders may be interested in holding a record of all the different stages and agents that the supply change has owned to have some guide to determine how to incorporate new components to the chain.

Another important functionality seen in Manufacturing Execution Systems is to check the performance of employees in order to track when an employee is performing as expected basing on qualification, cost, work patterns and business needs. Regarding the evidence, IoT might increase even more its presence in the factory floor. Not only will IoT devices enter for manufacturing purposes, but also, they will get there to track human labours in order to form employees or get the most efficient ones.

One of the most striking setbacks in the manufacturing process is the maintenance of the equipment in the factory floor, this functionality is very related to the functionality of the platform OPTYFY, if assets were working properly, they would have a minimum performance. In case the performance would not reach the minimum, the asset would be considered as broken.

Manufacturing Execution Systems commonly collect data from a specific job in progress. One of the essential functions of Manufacturing Execution Systems is giving some decision support to the stakeholders. Manufacturing Execution Systems have a central structure as described earlier in this document. The principal dilemmas which Managing Execution Systems must cope with are the specific characteristics of IIoT ecosystems.

As has been stated in this document, the heterogeneity of this kind of system denotes a prominent obstacle. Not only for the different devices that participate in Manufacturing processes, but also for the number of different sorts of manufacturing chain and actors involved in the processes. Furthermore, such different manufacturing processes are seldom totally sequential, and they must satisfy certain timing criteria, which will be carefully explained in Sect. 5. Nevertheless, timing standards can be satisfied by rescheduling the whole manufacturing system by parallelizing the most tasks possible. Finally, general interfaces must be implemented to represent extremely heterogeneous data.

Managing Execution systems have been designed to integrate with Enterprise Resource Planning (ERP) and cyber-physical systems (CPS) such integration has made it possible to create fully automated industrial environments, which is the definition of industry 4.0.

However, a single Management execution system may not be enough to fulfil the requirements of a distributed system, as in the case of OPTYFY.

For this reason, Manufacturing Execution Systems have to cooperate with the three following systems:

1. **ERP.** Enterprise Resources Planning is the platform that manages the resources. In other words, Managing Execution Systems should not be the component which

provides the final managing of resources, even though most of them have such task among their functionalities.

2. **Managing Execution Systems** process data from the manufacturing process and managing of resources is among such data. Nonetheless, Managing Execution Systems send this data to the ERP which is responsible for making decisions using this data.

3. **Operational Systems.** Managing Execution Systems must sort out, some essential information from the Enterprise Resource Planning and give the operational systems this information.

4. **Other MES.** As we are talking about a distributed platform, several Manufacturing Execution Systems are monitoring the actual performance of the supply chain. We must not have each distributed platform acting independently, in a distributed system a supply chain often uses other supply chain output as their input.

Figure 2 depicts the high-level relationship between the components of a distributed supply chain.

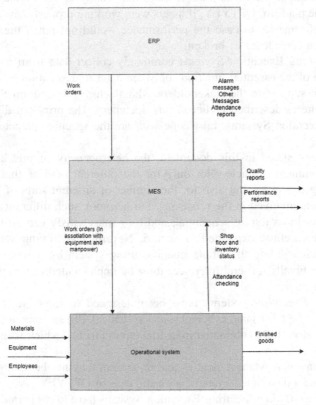

Fig. 2. Relationship between MES and other platforms in a distributed manufacturing environment

The organization of production system is susceptible to be modified even at run-time. For this reason, resources can be reallocated or as said in this section, it can be even rescheduled. Modern systems have too many devices and performance requirements are too demanding for manual approaches for optimization. The only feasible solution could be using knowledge-based software for optimization. The standard ISA-95 which is commonly accepted by the community is Automation ML. On the other hand, the bi-directional transformation of data is specified in the paper [9] by the AutomationML Association website.

4   OPTYFY Conceptual Model and Architecture

OPTYFY will make use of a four-layer architecture in a Service-oriented Architecture (SOA). OPTYFY will use a paradigm like such because it is the one which fits best with an IoT environment for the following reasons.

- Firstly, an IoT environment is made of a set of markedly different and distributed components. For this reason, as OPTYFY is an IIoT system an adequate approach would be that each component delegates in the rest of the components through a common interface.
- Secondly, as stated before it is necessary to integrate different components in the manufacturing chain as well as in the communication protocols among the different subsystems. Relying in services from other components is the best approach, so the best architecture is a loosely coupled architecture.
- Thirdly, OPTYFY roughly consist of the hardware placed on the devices in the factory floor as well as a set of communication protocols and a set of interfaces. As a result, we are talking about a dynamic system, whose components are open to change.
- Fourthly, each device and each system contained in OPTYFY has a specific outcome which can serve as a black box for consumers. For this reason, the less we use the internal code or data model of any of the subsystems the better. Of course, we might have to develop communication protocols in order to deal with dependencies. However, a service-oriented architecture is by far the most efficient manner to reduce them as much as we can.
- Fifthly, SOA provides a set of simple interfaces in which all the subsystems are interconnected because most of the work is provided for the services. This is a fundamental point in OPTYFY architecture because it does not matter which or how many IoT devices you have, they are all going to be shown in a simple interface with a simple message.
- Finally, each provider and consumer will have a clear contract that must be fulfilled in the endpoints. As stated in previous points this can make the components the most independent possible, making the system cheaper, more scalable and reusable through some standard based protocols.

OPTYFY architecture is a service-oriented architecture that follows a four-layer approach in the manner specified in Fig. 3.

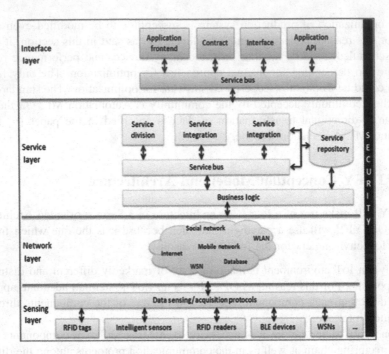

Fig. 3. SoA architecture for OPTYFY

Unlike classical four-tier architectures, tiers are ordered from the closest to the user to the closest from the IIoT devices, instead of ordering them from the closest to the user to the closest from the data.

In the following paragraphs layers of OPTYFY will be described and reasons for taking this approach will be thoroughly explained.

Layers are going to be explained from the top to the bottom taking a descending approach, we have to note that each layer makes abstraction from the previous layer, this means that we are going to move from the most elaborated data to the less.

1. **Interface Layer.** By the same token as typical four-layer architectures user will see information in a black-box approach, they are not interested neither in the details of how the services are performed nor in the data model of the specific IioT devices which are being monitored in the platform. The real concern in the user side is if contracts are being respected or not. Service layer will provide the user with all this information which is going to be shown in a set of message and interfaces shared by all the components in the application.

2. **Service Layer.** It is the layer where all the business logic is performed, it centralized the access to data and functions and it allows the version of the services. It has a repository where the information is stored with all the relevant data from the IoT devices, by categorizing and ordering the data. This layer is also the one which supports the integration of the different services which will be part of OPTYFY infrastructure. The service bus contains the set of rules needed for connecting the

devices to the platform and integrate their services on it. Service Layer is where most of the functionalities will be supported. Furthermore, service layer is where some non-functional requisites such as the security are fulfilled. In addition to the business logic and some other requisites the information flow and the data management are supported by the service layer.

3. **Network Layer.** This is the layer where the connection between IoT devices and the service Layer is performed. In a certain way, the role of this layer is to provide the service layer with the data obtained from the sensors and actuators. This layer applies a set of communication protocols with the IoT network which have been set in the factory floor. This layer is responsible for the addressing and routing tasks in order to integrate the devices in our system. This layer applies protocols such as TCP, UDP, HTTP and a set of IoT specific protocols which will play a major role in the system because the correct application of such protocols is the manner in which the whole system is connected.

4. **Sensing Layer.** The sensing layer is the layer which obtains the information directly from the factory floor, which actually is the unprocessed data which the service layer will interpret. Sensors and actuators are the main devices that collect the data from the factory floor and by the interpretation of the information collected by them is how we are going to be able to monitor the manufacturing chain and be able to evaluate how is the factory working for the latter taking of the decisions. Sensors are grouped according to their purpose and data types. Also, we need a gateway to collect the relevant information and communicate it to the network layer.

5 OPTYFY Architecture and Implementation

In this section we are going deeply in detail of how IoT infrastructure will communicate with the platform and we need to define which set of rules need to be followed in order to have a common view of the IoT devices which belongs to the platform (Fig. 4).

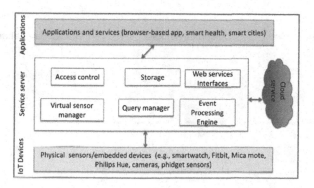

Fig. 4. Middleware based on IoT services.

As we can see in the figure, we use a middleware to standardize any kind of IoT device regarding the following aspects:

- **Access Control.** One of the most important concerns in order to incorporate a device to our system is to stablish a set of rules to identify a component as part of the network. Such devices need to be considered trustworthy, also it is necessary stablish when it should be connected to the server and provide data.
- **Virtual Sensor Manager.** Each IoT device collect the data by using sensors. As stated before IoT devices collect and process different kinds of information from different devices, this information will need to be taken following some standards in order to be readable.
- **Storage.** The way in which data is stored plays a major role in an IoT platform. Storage needs to be scalable to Big Data and it needs to be able to store structured and non-structured data.
- **Web Service Interfaces.** As services needs to be scalable and the factory floor will probably be under constant changes it is necessary to have a set of interfaces that, by using generic messages, they are going to be able to inform of the state of different services.
- **Query Manager.** OPTYFY will periodically ask for data to the IoT devices while the manufacturing chain is connected to the platform. As a result, queries will be triggered if the following two conditions are fulfilled:
  - The manufacturing chain is working and connected to OPTYFY.
  - Certain amount of time passed and we will ask the factory floor about the state of certain IoT device connected to it.
- The access to the service cloud where the data of the service will be needs to be in order and avoiding concurrence which is the duty of the query manager.
- **Event Processing Engine.** As well as information from the factory floor is read by the use of sensors it is necessary to activate or give some orders to other devices from the manufacturing chain, the service layer will notice that some event has occurred, and actuators will have to perform a determined action.

OPTYFY investigate the use case of a battery manufacturing, using some pressure sensors it will check in which stage of manufacturing is the battery, according to the three parameters showed in the Fig. 5.

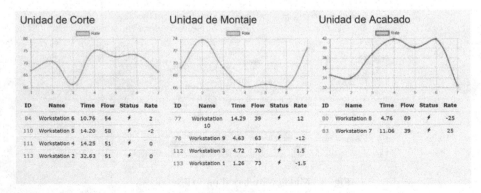

Fig. 5. Three stages of manufacturing process

The parameters which are going to be considered are time, which is the time that the manufactured product has been in the supply chain, rate which informs about the number of units processed in the last 10 min and flow which is the deviation from the average, this parameter is especially useful for detecting anomalies like in figure (Fig. 6).

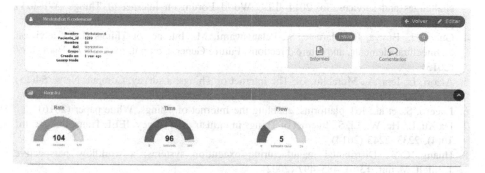

Fig. 6. Feedback about the parameters

6 Conclusions and Future Research

In this article, we have presented OPTYFY, a novel approach to improve industrial devices performance by monitoring the manufactured object by its weight and the information provided by sensors and actuators. Particularly, we have discussed how this strategy can enhance interoperability effectiveness in very concrete and well-defined domains.

In a larger context, the above-mentioned problem may be multiplied by thousands of data structures located in hundreds of incompatible databases and message formats. The problem is growing; the Industrial Internet of Things exponential growth, also empowered by the amount of user generated data from Smart Factories with applications which gather data constantly, reengineer intense and massive data techniques processes and integrate with more sources.

It is planned to include knowledge-based technologies such as ontologies to increase the intelligence of the system. Ontologies are the backbone technology for the Semantic Web and have been applied successfully to different domains such as finances [10, 11], tourism [12, 13], medicine [14, 15] or software engineering [16–18]

Finally, it would be interesting to include recommender system technologies based on ontologies such as the work presented in [19–21].

Acknowledgments. This work is supported by the ITEA3 CITISIM project and ITEA3 SCRATCH project, all of them funded by the Centro Tecnológico de Desarrollo Industrial (CDTI) and the ITEA3 EU funding program.

References

1. Ray, P.P.: A survey on Internet of Things architectures. J. King Saud Univ. Comput. Inf. Sci. **30**(3), 291–319 (2018)
2. Razzaque, M.A., Milojevic-Jevric, M., Palade, A., Clarke, S.: Middleware for Internet of Things: a survey. IEEE Internet Things J. **3**(1), 70–95 (2015)
3. Singh, D., Tripathi, G., Jara, A.J.: A survey of Internet-of-Things: future vision, architecture, challenges and services. In: 2014 IEEE World Forum on Internet of Things (WF-IoT), pp. 287–292. IEEE (2014)
4. Gubbi, J., Buyya, R., Marusic, S., Palaniswami, M.: Internet of Things (IoT): a vision, architectural elements, and future directions. Future Gener. Comput. Syst. **29**(7), 1645–1660 (2013)
5. Atzori, L., Iera, A., Morabito, G.: The Internet of Things: a survey. Comput. Netw. **54**(15), 2787–2805 (2010)
6. Lucero, S., et al.: IoT platforms: enabling the Internet of Things. White paper (2016)
7. Da Xu, L., He, W., Li, S.: Internet of Things in industries: a survey. IEEE Trans. Industr. Inf. **10**(4), 2233–2243 (2014)
8. Huang, C.Y.: Distributed manufacturing execution systems: a workflow perspective. J. Intell. Manuf. **13**(6), 485–497 (2002)
9. Wally, B.: Application recommendation provisioning for MES and ERP - support for IEC 62264 and B2MML. AutomationML e.V. c/o IAF, 7 November 2018. https://www.automationml.org/o.red/uploads/dateien/1542365399-AR_MES_ERP-1.1.0.zip
10. Salas-Zárate, M.d.P., Valencia-García, R., Ruiz-Martínez, A., Colomo-Palacios, R.: Feature-based opinion mining in financial news: an ontology-driven approach. J. Inf. Sci. **43**(4), 458–479 (2017)
11. Rodríguez-González, A., García-Crespo, Á., Colomo-Palacios, R., Iglesias, F.G., Gómez-Berbís, J.M.: CAST: using neural networks to improve trading systems based on technical analysis by means of the RSI Financial Indicator. Expert Syst. Appl. **38**(9), 11489–11500 (2011)
12. García-Crespo, A., Chamizo, J., Rivera, I., Mencke, M., Colomo-Palacios, R., Gómez-Berbís, J.M.: SPETA: social pervasive e-tourism advisor. Telematics Inform. **26**(3), 306–315 (2009)
13. Valencia-García, R., García-Sánchez, F., Castellanos-Nieves, D., et al.: OWLPath: an OWL ontology-guided query editor. IEEE Trans. Syst. Man Cybern. Part A Syst. Hum. **41**(1), 121–136 (2010)
14. Fuentes-Lorenzo, D., Morato, J., Gómez, J.M.: Knowledge management in biomedical libraries: a semantic web approach. Inf. Syst. Front. **11**(4), 471–480 (2009)
15. Rodríguez-González, A., Labra-Gayo, J.E., Colomo-Palacios, R., Mayer, M.A., Gómez-Berbís, J.M., García-Crespo, A.: SeDeLo: using semantics and description logics to support aided clinical diagnosis. J. Med. Syst. **36**(4), 2471–2481 (2012)
16. Paredes-Valverde, M.A., del Pilar Salas-Zárate, M., Colomo-Palacios, R., Gómez-Berbís, J. M., Valencia-García, R.: An ontology-based approach with which to assign human resources to software projects. Sci. Comput. Program. **156**, 90–103 (2018)
17. López-Lorca, A.A., Beydoun, G., Valencia-García, R., Martínez-Bejar, R.: Supporting agent-oriented requirement analysis with ontologies. Int. J. Hum. Comput. Stud. **87**, 20–37 (2016)
18. Colomo-Palacios, R., Gomez-Berbis, J.M., Garcia-Crespo, A., Puebla-Sanchez, I.: Social global repository: using semantics and social web in software projects. Int. J. Knowl. Learn. **4**(5), 452–464 (2008)

19. Colombo-Mendoza, L.O., Valencia-García, R., Rodríguez-González, A., Colomo-Palacios, R., Alor-Hernández, G.: Towards a knowledge-based probabilistic and context-aware social recommender system. J. Inf. Sci. **44**(4), 464–490 (2018)
20. Colombo-Mendoza, L.O., Valencia-García, R., Rodríguez González, A., Alor-Hernández, G., Samper Zapater, J.J.: RecomMetz: a context-aware knowledge-based mobile recommender system for movie showtimes. Expert Syst. Appl. **42**(3), 1202–1222 (2015)
21. García-Crespo, Á., Colomo-Palacios, R., Gómez-Berbís, J.M., García-Sánchez, F.: SOLAR: social link advanced recommendation system. Future Gener. Comput. Syst. **26**(3), 374–380 (2010)

SEDIT: Semantic Digital Twin Based on Industrial IoT Data Management and Knowledge Graphs

Juan Miguel Gómez-Berbís[✉] and Antonio de Amescua-Seco

Department of Computer Science and Engineering,
Universidad Carlos III de Madrid, Madrid, Spain
{juanmiguel.gomez, antonio.amescua}@uc3m.es

Abstract. A Digital Twin is a dynamic digital representation of a device, consumer or process and indicates an accurate current and predicted future status and components. Digital Twins are mainly based on sensor information collected from the real physical system, mostly from Internet of Things (IoT) Data. The Twin tries to predict and improve the system behavior and, for instance, the required maintenance actions during lifetime. Knowledge Graphs are a backbone of many information systems that require access to structured knowledge, be it domain-specific or domain- independent. Hence, Knowledge Graphs could be the perfect cornerstone for Digital Twins. In this paper, we present SEDIT, a first approach towards a Semantic Digital Twin based on IoT Data Management and Knowledge Graphs.

Keywords: IoT · Digital Twin · Data Management · Knowledge Graphs

1 Introduction

The term "Industry 4.0" describes the convergence of industrial production and digital communication technologies. Industry 4.0 enabling technologies cover cyber and physical systems, IoT, simulation and modelling, statistical methods, data analytics, machine learning and the, so-called, Digital Twins.

A Digital Twin, according to [1] since it was first introduced by [2] is a digital representative of the real world which can be used, for example, for monitoring and controlling the physical entity and to compare the virtual representation with the reality. The Twin itself can be based on data from sensors or data from physical based simulations or on both. Fundamentally, the Digital twin is a virtual copy of physical processes, systems, materials, products, assets and human individuals [3, 4]. It provides a (high-) fidelity representation and abstraction of their physical "twin" in the digital world.

Semantic technologies are crucial in recent researches and they have been applied in multiple domains such as finances [5, 6], tourism [7, 8], medicine [9, 10] or software engineering [11–13]. Some of these researches use ontologies as the knowledge base, but the manual construction of ontologies is a very time-consuming task [14]. For this

R. Valencia-García et al. (Eds.): CITI 2019, CCIS 1124, pp. 178–188, 2019.
https://doi.org/10.1007/978-3-030-34989-9_14

reason, currently other lightweight techniques such as Knowledge Graphs are being used.

Knowledge Graphs on the Web are a backbone of many information systems that require access to structured knowledge, be it domain-specific or domain-independent [15]. Those graphs are often constructed from semi-structured knowledge, such as Wikipedia, or harvested from the web with a combination of statistical and linguistic methods. The result are large-scale knowledge graphs that try to make a good trade-off between completeness and correctness.

In this paper, we argue the need of backing Digital Twins with Enterprise Knowledge Graphs (EKG) or, simply, Knowledge Graphs (KGs), since DT could be strengthened by using Semantic Technologies to provide a formal representation of the DT domain. The shift enabled by the use of machine understandable ontologies can outperform the current endeavors, that require finding data spread across Information Systems, or dynamically drawing inferences which are continually hampered by their reliance on ad-hoc, task specific frameworks.

In this paper, we present SEDIT, a first approach towards a Semantic Digital Twin based on IoT Data Management and Knowledge Graphs. Firstly, we describe the motivating scenario and the research challenge to establish the proper requirements for SEDIT. Secondly, we describe the state of the art and literature related to Digital Twins based on IoT Data and several definitions of Knowledge Graphs.

The remainder of the paper is organized as follows. In Sect. 4, we present the core of our research in a methodology based on 5 steps to build a Digital Twin based on IoT Data and Knowledge Graphs. Section 5 shows how to create a Digital Twin for Industrial Optimization based on two Digital Twins, one of them focused on production features and parameters and the other on data flow. Finally, Sect. 6 concludes the paper and outlines our future work.

2 Motivating Scenario and Research Challenge

The Digital Twin as a digital representation of a product or process becomes more and more accepted in Industry 4.0. Most of the Digital Twins are based on very complex systems like wind turbines of jet engines. In the future these Twins will also represent consumer products and they will therefore include device-human interaction.

Essentially, a Digital Twin (DT) is a dynamic digital representation of a particular real-world system and indicates an accurate current and predicted future status of the device/process, including their interaction. It enriches the existing high-quality user data with intelligence provided by the Digital Twin representation and is perfectly suited to provide deep human-device insights. In the following picture, we depict the Digital Twin lifecycle as we understand it (Fig. 1).

The challenge of this scenario is to be capable of improving and optimizing a particular industrial system through a Digital Twin. The Digital Twin evaluates/analyzes de the data for starters. Then, since it is a digital representation, it is capable of change the parameters and simulate the different features through a number of algorithms. The simulation will be evaluated, and a number of consequences inferred or enacted. Those consequences or results could then be applied to the real product/system.

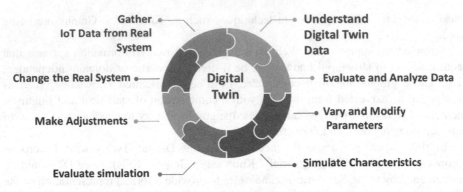

Fig. 1. Digital Twin lifecycle

3 State of the Art

Google coined the term Knowledge Graph in 2012[1] to build a model of the world. Meanwhile, it has become a hype term in product and service industry. The drive for Knowledge Graphs stems from the fact of how increasingly important successful Data Management and eCommerce have become in terms of the value distribution a number of industrial areas. In general, the actual positive evolution of Knowledge Graphs is mostly based on the economic sector and not from the scientific community.

In a nutshell, Knowledge Graph is a trendy term to phrase and guide an important challenge that is crucial for the Digital Twin: current data (and service) integration problems.

IoT systems and IoT platforms are still in the phase of rapid advancement and development and there are still many open and challenging points about technology, for example, in [1], the paper offers a long list of technical challenges and this document consider two of them:

1. IoT is a very complicated heterogeneous network platform. This, in turn, improves the complexity between different types of devices through various communication technologies that show that the general behavior of the network is fraudulent, delayed and not standardized. The administration of connected objects by facilitating collaborative work between different things, for example, hardware components and software services, and their administration after providing addressing, identification and optimization at the protocol and architecture level is a serious investigation.
2. In addition, industries must look for the challenges of the coexistence of hardware software around IoT. The variety of devices combined with a variety of communication protocols via TCP/IP or advanced software stacks will surely manipulate the web services that will be implemented through various middleware solutions.

---

[1] A. Singhal: Introducing the Knowledge Graph, things, not strings. Blog post at http://googleblog.blogspot.co.uk/2012/05/introducing-knowledge-graph-things-not.html, 2012.

An architecture will be designed to take advantage of the facilitation of heterogeneous protocols.

A Digital Twin is digital representative of the real world can be named as and can be used, for example, for monitoring and controlling the physical entity and to compare the virtual digital twin with the reality. The Twin itself can be based on data from sensors or data from physical based simulations or on both. The name Digital Twin was first introduced already years ago by Grieves.

So, the Digital twin is, roughly speaking, a virtual copy of physical processes, systems, materials, products, assets and human individuals. It provides a (high-) fidelity representation and abstraction of their physical "twin" in the digital world. The Twin can be a part of the PLM system and can be focused on the development phase (BOL) Production Phase (MOL) or Product phase (EOL). Of cause these different domains can also be connected both in the real and virtual domain, leading to the research line 4 and 5.

For the past decades, the use of the (old-fashioned) Digital Twin has been crucial in modern engineering systems and it has taken various different forms. For instance, during the design/systems engineering phase, CAD/CAM and FE models are generally used for model-based design and virtual prototyping of high-tech systems, transfer function or state-space models are used for the control algorithm development, circuit models for the electronic analysis and realization of the final electronics using electronic design automation (EDA) software and finally various different computer-based formal models are used for monitoring and maintenance of the assets.

In the aforementioned examples, these models are typically based on fundamental physical and mathematical laws. Moreover, they are usually formulated as a priori, i.e., the models are developed and made available before the actual products/systems are realized. For such a scenario, interoperability between these different models is already identified as a key technical challenge in maintaining, reusing and exchanging information among them.

Complementary to the physical-model based digital twin, the ubiquity of IoT sensors and hyper-computing capabilities have enabled engineers to directly create a data-driven digital twin based solely on data collected from the realized processes/systems/products. This approach can thus be regarded as the a posteriori approach since they are only available after the underlying physical systems are realized and operational.

The models are typically used for monitoring, real-time process control and maintenance of the assets. Similar to the physical model-based approach, these different data-driven digital twins also face interoperability problems and do not allow the support of design cycles of non-existing products or processes. These data based Digital Twins from complex systems like Turbines are the most common ones at this moment.

4   A Methodology to Build a Digital Twin Based on IoT Data and Knowledge Graphs

In this section, we ponder on the methodology to build a Digital Twin based on IoT Data and Knowledge Graphs. We believe the steps are as follows:

1. Set Parameters: Since a DT is a virtual representation of a real-world system, we need to define first which parameters/properties of the system are we interested in measuring, analyzing and monitoring. We will call these parameters, Digital Twin Parameters (DTP). For example, those parameters could be: Time of Production of a Single Unit, Rate of Production of a Single Unit or Flow (Throughput) of Production of a Single Unit.
2. Set IIoT Sensors to capture DTP data, namely: the time to make a single unit could be measured by a time-sensing sensor, the rate of production with a light sensor that indicates the product is finished and it relationship with the others already produced, and so on.
3. Conceptualization: Relating DTP data captured through IIoT sensors would be useless if the relationships with the Knowledge Graph that represents the Knowledge base of the DT are not specified. Google started in 2012 to develop a so-called knowledge graph (see Footnote 1), which should contain significant aspects of human knowledge found semantically annotated on the web or in other data sources. Now, we consider a Knowledge Graph (KG) a semantically structured conceptualization. In this example, the KG would define an interrelate clearly the concepts of Time, Rate and Flow of Production of a Single Unit.
4. Algorithms: As it was pointed out in the previous section, the DT evaluates/analyzes de the DTP data, vary the DTP values and simulate the different features through a number of algorithms. Those algorithms could be diverse but they are usually found in the Artificial Intelligence (AI) area.
5. Impact Back on the System: Once the algorithms have found a number of optimizations in the system, based on the DTPs, these optimizations should be reflected back on to the real system. This implies that the methodology and the Digital Twin lifecycle would only be completed once the impact on the system has happened.

There are two major aspects to be considered regarding this methodology and steps:

1. The granularity of the DT depends on the level of detail in which it is being conceptualized, but also the perspective from which we are describing it. For example, a DT could be based on Time, Rate and Flow of Production of a Single Unit in we look at the operational perspective of the system. However, measuring Data Input/Output and Process Input/Output would yield a completely different DT.
2. The need for syntax and/or semantic transformations in the data modelling and access of the DT. According to Ehrlinger and Wöß [18] a very useful and concise survey on potential definitions of Knowledge Graphs illustrating their variations, would imply that KG use Ontologies and reasoners deriving new knowledge. That would include those semantic transformations. For example: if Time of Production of a Single Unit is called by other manufacturers or industrial applications, Lapse of Production of a Singleton, those concepts would be interlinked.

Finally, a number of issues for future work would be merging and managing different Digital Twins hosted by different eco-systems, use of HMI for operating DTs and, eventually, new business models based for operations and services.

5 Creating a Digital Twin for Industrial Optimization

In this section, we will describe a Digital Twin for Industrial Optimization. In this case, the Digital Twin is divided itself into two Digital Twins. We will elaborate on this in the following.

The first Digital Twin is based on operational efficiency and we codenamed it as OPTYFY. It focuses on operational efficiency, particularly on Time, Rate and Flow of production. According to the methodology described in Sect. 4, these would be the Digital Twin Parameters (DTP), namely, the variables that will be measured and populated through IIoT sensors. A first view of the OPTYFY visualization interface is shown in Fig. 2:

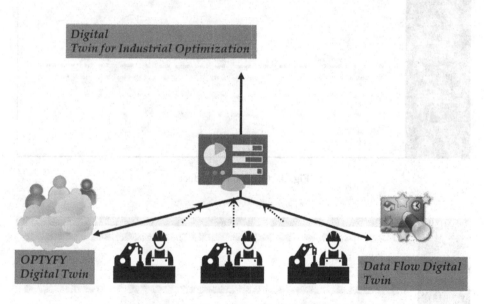

Fig. 2. Digital Twin for Industrial Optimization

Each Workstation represents an element of the production line (a human worker, a particular type of machine or a sensor). There are three different units: Kitting, Assembly and Testing Units, which encompass a set of Workstations.

The IIoT Sensors will provide the data for Time, Rate and Flow for each Workstation from an automatic manner. In this particular case, a Time sensor and a Light Sensor are providing those measures.

The next phase of our methodology would imply the use of a Knowledge Graph to conceptualize the production line. This would be a very simple Knowledge Graph with the concepts we mentioned, outlining the different relationships among them: Time, Rate and Flow.

Finally, the last step is applying a set of Algorithms that will be applied to the DTP data, once they are gathered by the IIoT sensors and conceptualized through the OPTYFY KG. In this case, we have chosen a set of basic algorithms that evaluate these data through different formulae based on thresholds (upper and lower) and standard deviation. For example, each time that if the Rate of a particular Workstation is lower than the lower threshold and its standard deviation versus the other Rates, an alarm is triggered. This implies that the Workstation is under-performing, and we signal this situation through a "red alarm". In case the Rate is among the thresholds, the "green alarm" implies that the Workstation is following the expected performance. The OPTYFY interface is shown in Figs. 3 and 4.

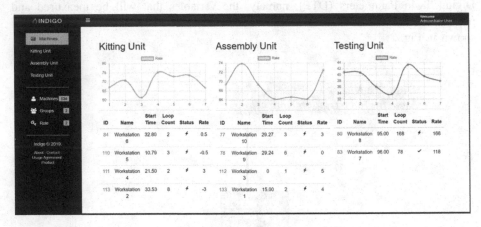

Fig. 3. OPTYFY interface

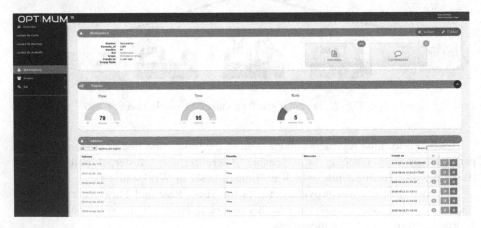

Fig. 4. OPTYFY interface for alarms

This latter example could be further extended through other type of algorithms, for example, lineal regressions or polynomial regressions that could check if the different DTPs are performing as expected.

As mentioned in the methodology, if and only if, these algorithms have detected potential optimizations and they are reflected back on the system, the whole Digital Twin lifecycle is completed.

The second Digital Twin is focused on the data flow perspective. In principle, we have considered a simple data format for the different Workstations in the industrial production line. Most industrial systems support the OPC-UA[2] protocol. This protocol supports two different type of communication paradigms: client/server as well as publish and subscribe, where the OCP-UA-Server is configured such that specific information is automatically delivered to OPC-UA-Clients that are interested in receiving certain information. Both solutions are also independent from the underlying Transport Layer and, depending on the application and performance that shall be realized, can be easily implemented over TCP, HTTP, HTTPs as well as UPD, AMQP and MQTT, by implementing different transport profiles.

The standard specifies mainly two different paradigms: OPC-UA for Services (client/server) and OPC-UA for Message Model (public and subscribe). As the name suggests, the first paradigm is specifically thought for the realization of (web) services, where information is exchanged in XML- or JSON-format. This particular encoding makes the exchanged data easy to read and to process, but it can be poorly performing for industrial application that have restricted available resources.

However, the OPC-UA Message Model presents very weak "semantics" in the sense that it builds on very simple data types, what could hamper a more refined or complex use of data. Since one of our steps of our methodology includes the use of Knowledge Graphs, it would be wise to solve with them a major bottleneck, which has appeared on trying to exploit the represented information and finding the specific piece of information we are looking for.

Knowledge Graphs were conceived with the purpose of solving the problem of the Web becoming a huge data repository in continuous growth and they aim at adding semantics to the data published so that machines are able to process these data in a similar way a human can do. For this, ontologies are the backbone technology. Ontologies are expected to be used to provide structured vocabularies that describe the relationships between different terms, allowing computers (and humans) to interpret their meaning flexibly yet unambiguously. The de facto KG standard ontology language is OWL (Web Ontology Language)[3]. A more lightweight ontology language is the Resource Description Framework (RDF)[4]. RDF is a family of specifications for a metadata model that is often implemented as an application of XML. The RDF family of specifications is maintained by the World Wide Web Consortium (W3C). The RDF metadata model is based upon the idea of making statements about resources in the form of a subject-predicate-object expression, called a triple in RDF terminology. The

---

[2] OPC-UA Protocol: https://opcfoundation.org/about/opc-technologies/opc-ua/.

[3] Web Ontology Language (OWL): https://www.w3.org/OWL/.

[4] Resource Description Framework (RDF): https://www.w3.org/RDF/.

subject is the resource, the "thing" being described. The predicate is a trait or aspect about that resource, and often expresses a relationship between the subject and the object. The object is the object of the relationship or value of that trait. The RDF simple data model and ability to model disparate, abstract concepts has also led to its increasing use in knowledge management applications unrelated to Knowledge Graph activity.

In our context, our second Digital Twin extracts the data from the different Workstations through OPC-UA, concretely through the OPC-UA Message Model, but stores, manages and deals with it using a Knowledge Graph. There are several alternatives such as the Semantic Observation Sample and Actuator (SOSA) [19] ontology or an ad-hoc domain dependent ontology, but this remains out of the scope of this work.

Those alternatives can use these languages to enhance the current capabilities of our data format in terms of the DTPs data. Since from an implementation perspective our data is sent and received in an XML syntax and both mentioned languages (OWL and RDF) do ground on such a syntax, it could be feasible to provide a suitable grounding for our data format.

Those two Digital Twins offer a different and complementary view of the whole system. DTs are envisioned to enable automatic discovery, simulation, evaluation and translation of data between different systems, providing a new and cutting-edge approach to industrial interoperability, modeling and management.

6 Conclusions and Future Work

In this paper, we have defined a Digital Twin from an industrial application perspective, proposed a methodology to build Digital Twins and shown a proof-of-concept of how two Digital Twins can be built from a "different semantic perspective", being based on Knowledge Graphs, namely: one based on three production-related Digital Twin Parameters (Time, Rate and Flow) and the other based on Data Flow-related issues.

Related to Data Flow, in a larger context on industrial applications, the above-mentioned problem of applying a Digital Twin in the industrial domain to integrate data may be multiplied by the complexity of thousands of data structures located in hundreds of incompatible databases and message formats. Actually, the problem is growing; the Industrial Internet of Things exponential growth, also empowered by the amount of user generated data from Smart Factories with applications which gather data constantly, reengineer intense and massive data techniques processes and integrate with more sources. Hence, we believe it is also an interesting future research line.

In addition, our future work research lines are fourfold. First and foremost, merging and managing Digital Twins hosted by different eco-systems. Syntax and semantic transformations in data modelling and functional elements with industrial applications could be then achieved through ontology alignment, since Knowledge Graphs are semantically structured data.

Secondly, functional upgrades, parameter changes and machine adaptation are currently based on shorter product lifecycles, increased variability in product types and rapid change in customer demands. DTs could help to reconfigure much faster and improve smart manufacturing processes.

On the other hand, new business models for DTs remain to be discovered and optimized. Digitalization is a strong trend in modern industrial economy, but the implementation of digitalization in manufacturing and industrial applications have been very modest, remaining a challenge to be addressed.

Finally, it would be interesting to include recommender system technologies based on ontologies such as the work presented in [20–22]. This kind of systems models the user profile in order to, through inference algorithms, identify the correlation between their preferences and existing products, services or contents [23].

Acknowledgment. This work is supported by the ITEA3 CITISIM project and ITEA3 SCRATCH project, all of them funded by the Centro Tecnológico de Desarrollo Industrial (CDTI) and the ITEA3 EU funding program.

References

1. Baheti, R., Gill, H.: Cyber-physical systems. Impact Control Technol. **12**(1), 161–166 (2011)
2. Uhlemann, T.H.J., Lehmann, C., Steinhilper, R.: The digital twin: realizing the cyber-physical production system for industry 4.0. Procedia Cirp **61**, 335–340 (2017)
3. Grieves, M.: Digital twin: manufacturing excellence through virtual factory replication. White paper, pp. 1–7 (2014)
4. Razzaque, M.A., Milojevic-Jevric, M., Palade, A., Clarke, S.: Middleware for internet of things: a survey. IEEE Internet Things J. **3**(1), 70–95 (2015)
5. Salas-Zárate, M.D.P., Valencia-García, R., Ruiz-Martínez, A., Colomo-Palacios, R.: Feature-based opinion mining in financial news: an ontology-driven approach. J. Inf. Sci. **43**(4), 458–479 (2017)
6. Rodríguez-González, A., García-Crespo, Á., Colomo-Palacios, R., Iglesias, F.G., Gómez-Berbís, J.M.: Cast using neural networks to improve trading systems based on technical analysis by means of the RSI financial indicator. Expert Syst. Appl. **38**(9), 11489–11500 (2011)
7. García-Crespo, A., Chamizo, J., Rivera, I., Mencke, M., Colomo-Palacios, R., Gómez-Berbís, J.M.: SPETA: social pervasive e-tourism advisor. Telematics Inform. **26**(3), 306–315 (2009)
8. Valencia-García, R., García-Sánchez, F., Castellanos-Nieves, D., et al.: Owlpath: an owl ontology-guided query editor. IEEE Trans. Syst. Man Cybern.-Part A Syst. Hum. **41**(1), 121–136 (2010)
9. Fuentes-Lorenzo, D., Morato, J., Gómez, J.M.: Knowledge management in biomedical libraries: a semantic web approach. Inf. Syst. Front. **11**(4), 471–480 (2009)
10. Rodríguez-González, A., Labra-Gayo, J.E., Colomo-Palacios, R., Mayer, M.A., Gómez-Berbís, J.M., García-Crespo, A.: SeDeLo: using semantics and description logics to support aided clinical diagnosis. J. Med. Syst. **36**(4), 2471–2481 (2012)
11. Paredes-Valverde, M.A., del Pilar Salas-Zárate, M., Colomo-Palacios, R., Gómez-Berbís, J. M., Valencia-García, R.: An ontology-based approach with which to assign human resources to software projects. Sci. Comput. Program. **156**, 90–103 (2018)

12. Colomo-Palacios, R., Gomez-Berbis, J.M., Garcia-Crespo, A., Puebla-Sanchez, I.: Social global repository: using semantics and social web in software projects. Int. J. Knowl. Learn. **4**(5), 452–464 (2008)
13. Lopez-Lorca, A.A., Beydoun, G., Valencia-Garcia, R., Martinez-Bejar, R.: Supporting agent oriented requirement analysis with ontologies. Int. J. Hum.-Comput. Stud. **87**, 20–37 (2016)
14. Ochoa, J.L., Valencia-García, R., Perez-Soltero, A., Barceló-Valenzuela, M.: A semantic role labelling-based framework for learning ontologies from spanish documents. Expert Syst. Appl. **40**(6), 2058–2068 (2013)
15. Paulheim, H.: Knowledge graph refinement: a survey of approaches and evaluation methods. Semant. Web **8**(3), 489–508 (2017)
16. Singh, D., Tripathi, G., Jara, A.J.: A survey of internet-of-things: future vision, architecture, challenges and services. In: 2014 IEEE World Forum on Internet of Things (WF-IoT), pp. 287–292. IEEE (2014)
17. Gubbi, J., Buyya, R., Marusic, S., Palaniswami, M.: Internet of things (IoT): a vision, architectural elements, and future directions. Future Gener. Comput. Syst. **29**(7), 1645–1660 (2013)
18. Ehrlinger, L., Wöß, W.: Towards a definition of knowledge graphs. In: SEMANTiCS (Posters, Demos, SuCCESS), vol. 48 (2016)
19. Janowicz, K., Haller, A., Cox, S.J., Le Phuoc, D., Lefrançois, M.: SOSA: a lightweight ontology for sensors, observations, samples, and actuators. J. Web Semant. **56**, 1–10 (2019)
20. Colombo-Mendoza, L.O., Valencia-García, R., Rodríguez-González, A., Colomo-Palacios, R., Alor-Hernández, G.: Towards a knowledge-based probabilistic and context-aware social recommender system. J. Inf. Sci. **44**(4), 464–490 (2018)
21. Colombo-Mendoza, L.O., Valencia-García, R., Rodríguez-González, A., Alor-Hernández, G., Samper-Zapater, J.J.: RecomMetz: a context-aware knowledge-based mobile recommender system for movie showtimes. Expert Syst. Appl. **42**(3), 1202–1222 (2015)
22. García-Crespo, A., Colomo-Palacios, R., Gómez-Berbís, J.M., García-Sánchez, F.: SOLAR: social link advanced recommendation system. Future Gener. Comput. Syst. **26**(3), 374–380 (2010)
23. Carrer-Neto, W., Hernández-Alcaraz, M.L., Valencia-García, R., García-Sánchez, F.: Social knowledge-based recommender system. Application to the movies domain. Expert Syst. Appl. **39**(12), 10990–11000 (2012)

Author Index

Printed in the United States
By Bookmasters